THE GULF WAR DID NOT HAPPEN

Popular Cultural Studies

Series editors: Justin O'Connor, Steve Redhead and Derek Wynne.

The Manchester Institute for Popular Culture was set up in order to promote theoretical and empirical research in the area of contemporary popular culture, both within the University and in conjunction with local, national and international agencies. The Institute is currently engaged in two major comparative research projects around aspects of consumption and popular culture in the City. The Institute also runs a numbers of post-graduate research programmes, with a particular emphasis on ethnographic work. The series intends to reflect all aspects of the Institute's activities. Current theoretical debates within the field of popular culture will be explored within an empirical context. Much of the research is undertaken by young researchers actively involved in their chosen fields of study, allowing an awareness of the issues and an attentiveness to actual developments often lacking in standard academic writings on the subject. The series will also reflect the working methods of the Institute, emphasising a collective research effort and the regular presentation of work-in-progress to the Institute's research seminars. The series hopes, therefore, both to push forward the debates around popular culture, urban regeneration and postmodern social theory whilst introducing an ethnographic and contextual basis for such debates.

Titles already published

Rave Off: Politics and Deviance in Contemporary Youth Culture

The Passion and the Fashion: Football Fandom in the New Europe

The Lads in Action: Social Process in an Urban Youth Subculture

Hosts and Champions: Soccer Cultures, National Identities and the USA World Cup

Game Without Frontiers: Football, Identity and Modernity

The Margins of the City: Gay Men's Urban Lives

(Cover photograph: Ian Katz)

The Gulf War Did Not Happen

Politics, culture and warfare post-Vietnam

edited by

Jeffrey Walsh

© Jeffrey Walsh 1995

All rights reserved. No part of this publication may be reproduced, stored in a retrieval system, or transmitted in any form or by any means, electronic, mechanical, photocopying or otherwise without the prior permission of the publisher.

Published by
Arena
Ashgate Publishing Limited
Gower House
Croft Road
Aldershot
Hants GU11 3HR
England

Ashgate Publishing Company
Old Post Road
Brookfield
Vermont 05036
USA

British Library Cataloguing in Publication Data

Gulf War Did Not Happen: Politics, Culture and Warfare Post-Vietnam – (Popular Cultural Studies; Vol. 7)
   I. Walsh, Jeffrey II. Series
   303.66
ISBN 1-85742-286-4 (pbk) 1-85742-292-9 (hbk)

Library of Congress Cataloging-in-Publication Data

The Gulf War did not happen: politics, culture, and warfare
   post-Vietnam / edited by Jeffrey Walsh
     p. cm. (Popular cultural studies: 7)
   Includes bibliographical references.
   ISBN 1-85742-292-9 (hbk): $59.95 (US: est.)
   ISBN 1-85742-286-4 (pbk): $29.95 (US: est.)
   1. Persian Gulf War, 1991 – miscellanea. 2. Persian
Gulf War, 1991 – Social aspects – Miscellanea.
   I. Walsh, Jeffrey. II. Series.
DS79.72.G843 1995   94-38271
956.704'42373–dc20   CIP

Printed and bound in Great Britain by
Hartnolls Limited, Bodmin, Cornwall

Contents

	Acknowledgements	vii
	Contributors	ix
1	Introduction: The Legacy of the Gulf War *Jeffrey Walsh*	1
2	Four Poems *W. D. Ehrhart*	21
3	Overcoming the Vietnam Syndrome: The Gulf War and Revisionism *Jon Roper*	27
4	The US Congress and the Gulf War *John Dumbrell*	49
5	Burial Party: The Gulf War as Epilogue to the 1980s *Phil Melling*	63

6	Vic Williams, Conscientious Objector and the Peace Movement *Jeffrey Walsh*	87
7	The Politics of Pop and the War in the Gulf *Deborah Johnson and John Storey*	101
8	War in the British Press *John Taylor*	119
9	The Media and the Military: An Historical Perspective on the Gulf War *Terrance Fox*	135
10	Pools, Minders, Unilaterals and Scud Studs: War Reporters in the News *Robert Hamilton*	159
11	*Ceasefire*: An Anti-war Comic for Women *David Huxley*	171
12	Monuments and Memorials *James Aulich*	189
13	Who's Responsible? Bobbie Ann Mason's *In Country*, Popular Culture and the Gulf War *W. D. Ehrhart*	207

Acknowledgements

The publishers and editor wish to thank the individuals and organisations who generously gave permission for the reproduction of copyright material. We particularly wish to thank the following: the Associated Press Limited; Ian Katz; Karal Ann Marling; Carol Bennett and Cath Tate of *Ceasefire* comic; the *Daily Star* newspaper; Adastra Press. The editor has tried to contact all copyright holders, but if proper acknowledgement has inadvertently not been made he will make suitable arrangements if contacted.

Sincere thanks to the staff of Dartmouth and, in particular, to John Irwin, Sonia Hubbard, Margaret O'Reilly, and Mary Starkey who have been especially supportive and patient in overseeing the book's progress towards publication.

This volume has been especially difficult to prepare, and has necessitated numerous revisions: such demanding work has called for varied administrative and computer skills. The editor has been fortunate to work with an excellent team, and warm thanks go to Helen Dawson, Hannah Nadim and to Maureen Williamson.

The editor wishes to thank all the following friends and colleagues who have supported the project: Colin Buckley, Stephen Kirby, Professor Diana Donald, Stephen Yates, the office staff in the Departments of English and History and History of Art and Design, the staff of the Manchester

Metropolitan University library and the Slide Library, in particular Nick Cass and Anthony Burns. Academic colleagues in the Department of English and History have also offered valuable support in covering for the editor while he was carrying out research for the book.

The title, *The Gulf War Did Not Happen*, refers to an essay by the French philosopher Jean Baudrillard which is discussed in the Introduction to this volume.

Acknowledgements would not be complete without mention of Jim Aulich whose perceptive advice, practical help and unfailing enthusiasm have remained constant over nearly a decade of co-operative work.

Because of its collective nature the volume does not have a single dedication, but those parts of the book written by Jeffrey Walsh are dedicated to Carole.

Contributors

James Aulich is senior lecturer in the Department of History of Art and Design at the Manchester Metropolitan University. He is editor of *Europe Without Walls: Posters and Revolution 1989-93; Framing the Falklands, Nationhood, Culture and Identity*, and is co-editor of *Vietnam Images: War and Representation*. He has also organised multi-media exhibitions on selected topics.

John Dumbrell is senior lecturer in American Politics at the University of Keele. He is the author of *The Making of US Foreign Policy* (Manchester University Press, 1990); *Vietnam* (British Association for American Studies pamphlet, 1992); and *The Carter Presidency: A Reevaluation* (Manchester University Press, 1993). He also edited *Vietnam and the Anti-War Movement* (Avebury, 1989).

W. D. Ehrhart, an ex-marine sergeant and Vietnam veteran, is author and editor of more than a dozen books of prose and poetry, and is the foremost poet to have expressed what is often called 'The Vietnam Experience'. He is a former Visiting Professor of War and Social Consequences at the William Joiner Center of the University of Massachusetts in Boston. His most recent books are the poetry volumes; *Just For Laughs* (Vietnam Generation, inc.) and *The Distance We Travel*

(Adastra Press), and the essay collection *In The Shadow of Vietnam* (McFarland and Co.). Bill Ehrhart is currently a Pew Fellow in the Arts for Poetry, and lives in Philadelphia with his wife, Anne, and daughter, Leela.

Terrance Fox, formerly assistant professor of Aeronautical Science at Embry Riddle Aeronautical University, has edited *The Palm Harbor Chronicle* from 1988 to 1990. He has also worked for US national newsmagazines. From 1991 to 1992 he was *Kiplinger Public Affairs Reporting Fellow* at Ohio State University. He is at present University Doctoral Fellow in Communication at Florida State University, Tallahassee.

Robert Hamilton is lecturer in the Department of History of Art and Design at the Manchester Metropolitan University. He has written widely on the subject of war and representation especially in the Vietnam era.

David Huxley is senior lecturer in the Department of History of Art and Design at the Manchester Metropolitan University. He completed a PhD on British Underground and Alternative Comics in 1991 and has written and lectured on comic books and comic strips in Britain and America.

Deborah Johnson is a freelance writer.

John Storey is senior lecturer in Cultural Studies at the University of Sunderland. His publications include *An Introductory Guide to Cultural Theory and Popular Culture* and *Cultural Theory and Popular Culture: A Reader*.

Phil Melling is senior lecturer in American Studies at the University of Wales, Swansea. His publications include *Vietnam in American Literature*, and edited texts such as *America, France and Vietnam: Cultural History and Ideas of Conflict*. He has published a biography of D. M. Davies and several articles on film and fiction in the 1930s, including ones on B. Traven and Mark Twain. He was awarded a Fulbright to Louisiana State University in the 1980s and has been visiting professor at the Universities of Wisconsin and North Carolina. He is the author of several plays which have appeared throughout Britain, one of which *Hotel Vietnam* was published in 1990.

Jon Roper is lecturer in American Studies at the University of Swansea, Wales. He is author of *Democracy and Its Critics* (1989) and co-editor of *America, France and Vietnam: Cultural History and Ideas of Conflict* (1991). He also co-edits *Borderlines: Studies in American Culture*, a new quarterly journal. He has been visiting professor at the Universities of Tennessee, Wisconsin and Ohio, USA.

John Taylor is senior lecturer in the History of Art and Design at Manchester Metropolitan University, and formerly lectured at the University of Wolverhampton. His most recent book is *War Photography - Realism in the British Press*, (Routledge, 1991). His forthcoming book, *Landscape with Colliding Figures - tourism and photography in England 1890-1990*, will be published by Manchester University Press in 1994.

Jeffrey Walsh is principal lecturer in English at Manchester Metropolitan University. He is the author of *American War Literature: 1914 to Vietnam* (Macmillan), and editor of *A Tribute to Wilfred Owen*. He has co-edited *Tell Me Lies About Vietnam* (Open University Press) and *Vietnam Images* (Macmillan). Recently he has published chapters in books on Ernest Hemingway; E. E. Cummings; The Falklands War in Film; Representations of Vietnamese Women; Radical Poetry in the United States; The Poetry of Robert Graves and Laura Riding. His two forthcoming books are *Analysing Television* and *Introduction to Contemporary Cinema*.

1 Introduction: The legacy of the Gulf War

Jeffrey Walsh

Whether or not the Gulf conflict of 1990-91 is judged to be successful depends upon the criteria used to evaluate it. If the war is assessed from the perspective of the United States and its closest allies, then its strategic objectives were triumphantly achieved: western supplies of Gulf oil were safeguarded, the Iraqi invasion of Kuwait reversed, and Saudi Arabia's stability consolidated. From the United States' point of view also the ghost of Vietnam was finally exorcized; acting as the leader of the morally coherent United Nations' coalition both its military forces and its ideology proved invincible. President Bush's rhetoric, which envisioned a new world order, did not seem entirely fanciful early in 1991; the former Cold War superpowers had cooperated to oppose aggression; states previously excluded as pariahs from international diplomacy, such as Syria, were persuaded to support the rule of law; and, most significantly, the United Nations demonstrated its resolve by urging decisive action against Iraq. Commentators often speculated at the time about the possibility of future concerted action being taken about other intractable global problems such as the Palestinian situation: and the latter issue is now nearer being resolved partly as a result of political and economic initiatives begun during the Gulf crisis.[1]

Other hopes of international co-operation outside the Middle East have, though, been less successful, most notably the failure of UN actions to prevent carnage in Bosnia where large numbers of people were until recently being genocidally killed every day, mainly Muslims. Somalia, too, showed signs of turning into a quagmire for the United States, as military operations frequently collapsed into chaos and political aims became increasingly confused. Even the former encouraging words of the United States about supporting opponents of Saddam in Iraq were shown to be worthless when Shias in the south and Kurds in the north were exterminated in the months following the United States' military withdrawal. Amnesty International has also condemned the continuing massacres carried out by Saddam Hussein against his own people during the second half of 1993. The Gulf war, therefore, examined in hindsight, far from being a moral beacon, looks to be politically compromised. It was portrayed as an idealistic crusade to liberate decent tiny Kuwait, and to defend benevolent Saudi Arabia against oppression, and yet the human rights record of both these countries is poor. Saudi Arabia has recently imposed severe constraints on opposition groups, while the ruling Al Sabah family of Kuwait, long known for its undemocratic ways, did little to restrain revenge killings of domiciled Palestinians after the war.

Rather than being appraised as a textbook war, fought to defend human rights and self determination, the Gulf war is now seen to be increasingly obsolete. Even its form and character are backward looking; it is unlikely that it will be the harbinger of future set piece battles against massively armed and entrenched ground forces. If it adumbrates any military pattern at all, it will probably be one in sharp contradistinction to itself. The future of United Nations' action will not depend upon large scale military engagements, but the reverse, low intensity, messy guerrilla wars on the Somalian or Bosnian model. What is implied by this is that the Gulf conflict symbolizes a dying order, its configuration representing what one commentator has called 'the last act of the Anglo-American imperium'.[2] Its public presentation as a war of integrity masked its real identity. Edward Said, among others, has interpreted the conflict along similar lines, believing it to be an embodiment of fading imperial power, the culmination of a deep American need to kick racially inferior 'ass'.[3] Such an evaluation of Desert Storm posits the conflict as a sublimation of the United States' Rambo tendency, which itself manifests a kind of tragic inevitability being the outcome of historical processes stretching back to Vietnam and beyond.

If Vietnam was, as Frederick Jameson suggested, a post modernist war, then the Gulf war of 1990-91 is a neorealist one characterized by peripeteia and multiple ironies. Its form is one of disparity between public myth and historical outcome. The signifiers of 1990-91, rather than breeding in endless random fashion, tend to cluster in patterns of reversal. The popular press has not been slow to catch on to this ludicrous sense of anti-climax. For example, President Bush, erstwhile Superman and decorated war hero, in the latter days of his presidency became Bart Simpson, a figure of fun; the grudge match between himself and the Iraqi dictator, Supersaddam turned out to be no contest.[4] This was focused symbolically, on the anniversary of Gulf war battles in 1993, when US aircraft supported by British Tornados attacked military targets to give Saddam a spanking. Several of the attacks were so bungled, resulting in the deaths of civilians, that Saddam won a propaganda victory, prompting *The Sunday Times* to speak of Operation Desert Storm degenerating into Operation Breaking Wind! Conforming to western stereotypes of cunning Arabs, Saddam's military tactics of Cheat and Retreat outwitted advanced weapons technology. Bush's game plan seemed at this time to be futile.

The war, then, appears more and more to be a last great flourish, its aims unfulfilled, leaving behind a riven Iraq in a region which grows daily more unstable. Some commentators have denigrated the war entirely by arguing that the case of South Africa proves that sanctions given time do work, and that the conflict was therefore unnecessary. The irony is at times consummate: for example in place of the bellicose Reagan or Bush sits the former draft dodger, Clinton, who supports the entry of homosexuals into the military and who seems to have little stomach for military adventures abroad. Bush's regional policy against Saddam is apparently now discredited not least because the air strikes carried out at the end of his presidency seriously alarmed such conservative states as Oman and Saudi Arabia; even the mainstays of the former coalition such as Egypt had second thoughts. In reality members of the former coalition against Saddam find more affinity now with the unwarlike Clinton, as the present Palestinian - Israeli pact demonstrates than with the strident Bush policy of giving Saddam a bloody nose every time he stepped out of line. Iran is now able to attack Mojahedin guerrilla bases in Iraq with impunity fearing a chaotic disintegration similar to that in Lebanon. The region thus shows continuing crisis as the stability that Bush's policy aimed for is a long way off.

It is inevitable that the Gulf conflict will greatly influence the rules governing the use of American military power in future policy. In a West Point speech on 5 January 1993 George Bush outlined key principles that should underlie the use of military force; for military intervention to succeed it should be pragmatic; there should be a 'clear and achievable mission, a realistic plan for accomplishing the mission and criteria no less realistic for withdrawing US forces once the mission is complete'.[5] This tenet of not putting American lives at risk has so far ruled out American involvement in Bosnia, a situation which signifies the Vietnam tragedy in its intractability.

From a strictly military viewpoint the Gulf war was in most respects predictable. The quality newspapers, for example, of August and September, 1990, forecast the relatively low number of Allied casualties, anticipated the awesome lethality of advanced weapon systems, and prophesied Saddam's crushing humiliation; remarkably, too, some of the less favourable outcomes of the conflict were prefigured. For example, *The Sunday Times* in September reported how Vietnam veterans in the Pentagon foresaw the deaths from Friendly Fire that tragically happened when they 'pointed out that even if the Iraqis did not manage to shoot down any American planes there were bound to be accidents - with American fighters hit by their own side, and helicopters strafing their own troops'.[6]

Although experts were unanimous in expecting a Coalition victory they were often incorrect about the battle toughness of the Iraqi forces. The large number of Iraqis surrendering and the widespread desertions that actually occurred were belied by media stereotypes of elite republican guards; and the prowess and efficiency of the world's 'fourth largest army', as it was always called, was also wildly exaggerated. The Iraqis turned out to be a poorly led force, understandably lacking in morale, and still suffering from the after effects of the long and arduous campaign against Iran; ill equipped conscripts and worn out regular soldiers, most of whom sensibly did not want to die for Saddam's futile cause, had no real chance against the combined professional armies and air forces of America, Britain, France and Saudi Arabia.

The strategy of Coalition military commanders was supremely vindicated in the swiftness and extreme savagery of the Air and Ground wars. No media pundit could fail to marvel at the sight of Tomahawk Cruise missiles turning right and left down Baghdad streets to hit their targets unerringly. The miraculous P.G.M.s (Precision Guided Missiles) were shown nightly on television penetrating underground bunkers and eliminating enemy nerve centres in clinically precise strikes; viewers were informed of Harm missiles that were guided by lasers to backtrack down enemy radar beams when Allied planes were illuminated (or painted). In the popular imagination Stealth fighter bombers, Patriot missiles knocking out dud scuds, electronic eyes in the sky, and Apache helicopters firing devastating Hellfire missiles, created an apocalyptic mythology of complex contradiction. The public were offered narratives of individual and collective heroism, but the war was also represented differently as a nintendo game, of video technology and orbiting satellite systems. On the one hand it seemed like Hollywood come true, starring

Seals, Delta Force commandos, Special Forces' operations and swashbuckling F-14 Tomcat pilots who watched *Top Gun* before embarking on the Basra Road 'turkey shoot'; on the other, the war was constructed futuristically as an icon of coming *fin-de-siècle* Star Wars, and was transformed into a sci-fi trip like The Empire Strikes Back. The western high tech crusaders were on a just mission against the Butcher of Baghdad.

Myths inevitably supplanted reality; and papers such as *The Sun* exulted in tales of Desert Rats, Battle of Britain type Tornado pilots, carrying on the tradition of the Dambusters in their low flying bravery, and of a bloodless battlefield where sterilized weapons in a kind of keyhole surgery 'took out' their targets, and so humanely avoided random civilian casualties. The truth of Allied military competence, of the finely executed air war, of the 'softening up' of the Iraqi army, and of the sophistication of western military technology, particularly during the tank battles of Desert Storm, cannot be denied. It was an overwhelming military success which demonstrated in classic form what is now textbook US military doctrine; in essence, avoidance of casualties at almost any cost; ruthless suppression of media; deployment of electronic intelligence systems and automated weapons; logistical capacity to override unfavourable terrain and weather; and, finally, propaganda-wise a subtle preference for not acting alone when America's interests can best be defended under the flag of the UN.

Myths, though, are more interesting than mundane economic and political facts, and continue to beguile the public consciousness: among them inevitably is the supposed brilliant strategic feint of Schwartzkopf before the ground war started, characterized as either a left hook that took Saddam utterly by surprise or more commonly as the famed Hail Mary manoeuvre of American football; De la Billière, the contrasting slim phlegmatic British toff, is also said to have borrowed a metaphor from American football when announcing with sophisticated irony in the Command and Control Centre before the ground war began, 'Iraq has won the toss and elected to receive'. Down at squaddie level there were stories of incredible heroism, of Lance Corporal Dewsnap, for example, who captured single handedly over one hundred Iraqis.

The mythical aura of the Gulf war lingers as the war itself recedes into history. Interestingly its most memorable images, of daring fliers in state of the art planes, were adumbrated in the revisionist film *Top Gun* (1986). In January 1993 an edition of the *Manchester Evening News*[7] borrowed the cadences of this fable of pristine American manhood nurtured upon the competitive ethic. Its report of an American airstrike is headlined, 'Top Guns' spot on blitz', and an F-14 Tomcat pilot from Iowa is quoted as saying 'It was a very nice light show'. Together with such disarming élan, guided bombs and pinpoint video accuracy are juxtaposed in the report, which described events that 'evoked images of the Desert Storm air war launched almost exactly two years ago'.[8] Thus the earlier exemplary war is copied in grotesque parody; air strikes executed without danger in a no fly zone are given a spurious heroism. Whenever Saddam violates the Gulf war ceasefire another simulacrum of the war is constructed. America ritually again tests its mettle and is energized by repeating its former success, this time on a surrogate and helpless target. In the frequent 'Cheat and Retreat' episodes of 1993 Saddam increased his stature as the only Islamic president to push America time and again to the brink, a defiance likely to be tolerated by fellow Muslims whenever Israel bombards surrounding states. The illusory narrative was extended further in the British press in snippets which related to Saddam's barbarism; his cruelty in keeping the UK hostages Paul Ride and Michael Wainwright, for example. Meanwhile, a US academic publishes a report about America's growing dependence on Middle Eastern oil[9] and Saddam's son, Uday, seems likely to consolidate his father's dynasty and perhaps give it a more acceptable face. President Clinton, bewildered by foreign crises, now occupies in Iraq demonology George Bush's place as the resident 'Dope-on-a-rope' when UN weapons inspectors are time and again made fools of.

The military campaign will continue to be subject to inquiry as more contradictory statistics and personal memoirs are published. Even the central issue of Iraqi deaths is now subject to revision and intense controversy. An American expert, John Hiedenrich, has recently argued that Iraqi casualties were miraculously low, perhaps as few as 1,500.[10] Hiedenrich's figures, supposedly based upon official Allied Statistics, mark him out as a maverick, yet all such reckonings by historians are qualified by uncertainty and lack of hard evidence. While political opponents of the war such as Tony Benn still speak of 200,000 Iraqi deaths, distinguished academic historians such as Laurence Freedman and Efraim Karsh suggest that the figure is probably nearer 35,000.[11] John Simpson's influential account of the conflict, *From the House of War*, tends to support the calculation of approximately 30,000 when he writes,

> The figure for the number of Iraqi soldiers who died is still unknown. Many people have put it at 100,000 or even twice that number. My own impression it that it too was much lower: maybe thirty thousand killed and fifty thousand wounded, though this can only be a guess.[12]

Such doubt about Iraqi deaths is typical of the obfuscation still surrounding the Gulf war where not a single photo of the ground war battle was ever released publicly. Fresh and disquieting reservations undermine narratives of Allied victory.

Profound questions thus remain for historians, many related to the conduct of the war. For example, did the Allies exceed their remit in systematically setting out to destroy Iraq's economy and infrastructure? Were some of the weapons used, such as cluster bombs or napalm, strictly necessary in a tactical sense? Was Mutla Ridge a barbarous revenge killing more like an execution or was it a restrained mopping up operation? Did the Allies stop too soon? Should they have pursued Saddam's forces into Baghdad? Were specific missions that resulted in civilian deaths, most notably the raid on the Amiriya shelter, simply misguided or were they intentional? These kind of questions sound naive, of course, especially when soldiers speak understandably of the suffering and chaos of warfare, yet in a highly automated war they ought not to be ignored. Sometimes the most direct questions are the ones that most need to be answered.

Apart from such ethical considerations there are other questions that arise from strategic planning and implementation. Grave doubts have been expressed, even within the US military, about the use of satellites for intelligence gathering. Clearly during the conflict Iraqi military capacity was consistently overestimated, for example. It is becoming increasingly apparent also that the 'space war' image of the campaign was grossly exaggerated, and that over half the unguided bombs missed their targets. Nowhere is this disparity between appearance and reality more apparent than in the tragic deaths from Friendly Fire.

What is most disturbing about the incidents of Friendly Fire during the Gulf conflict is that state of the art weaponry proved equally as vulnerable to human error as older, low tech equipment. An example of this is the way an American tank gunner was killed by a sabot round fired by another Abrams tank. The sabot, which is nicknamed the Silver Bullet and is a two foot steel dart tipped with depleted uranium, entered the tank and set it ablaze for two days. Of the gunner only a charred hipbone remained, perhaps signifying that the man's body was sucked by a vacuum through the three inch hole. Reporting the episode which took place during the Battle of Norfolk and resulted in a 'cover up', Patrick Sloyan reflects upon the fact that 53 per cent of battlefield deaths were caused by fratricide,

> The disaster has raised major questions about American armoured warfare tactics, the wizardry of night vision devices and the training of the men who shoot the Silver Bullet. When such icons

of the military industrial complex are at stake, it is easy to understand why emotions of... American families were callously brushed aside.[13]

Ironically it seems that the more sophisticated the weapons, the greater the risk there is of dying from Friendly Fire, given the constant of human proneness to accident. As this episode showed, the military is also likely to cover up its mistake, as in the nine Friendly Fire deaths when a British armoured personnel carrier was hit by a missile from a US A10 Thunderbolt aircraft. At the British coroner's court after the war the two US pilots involved were instructed not to attend, although an uncorroborated statement from them was read aloud to the jury. The families of the dead soldiers were doubly insulted and hurt by the clumsy attempts of both the American authorities and the British Ministry of Defence to conceal facts.

In the euphoria immediately following the end of the Gulf War it seemed that Saddam Hussein would be overthrown by Shia guerrillas in the south of Iraq and Kurdish *peshmerga* in the north who responded to George Bush's call for 'the Iraqi people to take matters into their own hands'. One quality British newspaper rejoiced at Saddam's 'last stand' implying that his demise was imminent.[14] As is now evident the American president gave verbal encouragement only, and clearly did not wish to negate the UN ceasefire terms nor to deploy American troops in support of Iraqi opposition groups; his attitude demonstrated the kind of duplicity frequently embodied in US foreign policy statements. Bush's swift reversion to the policy of non-interference is understandable politically in the context of growing concern felt by Iraq's neighbours about the likely disintegration of Iraq if Saddam fell. Some Arab countries are likely to have concluded also that the alternative to Saddam was more bloodshed, a devastating civil war between Sunnis and Shias and, as a result, further indirect western intervention in the region. Whatever the political equations, the population of Iraq has continued to suffer after the war, and the country itself still remains in a dangerous and unstable state. What had been one of the Middle East's most prosperous nations with a show case economy based upon oil exports is now seriously damaged.

Politically Saddam's Ba'ath party has retained its hegemony after successfully putting down the Kurdish and Shia uprisings. It is, however, in a perpetual situation of crisis, constantly threatened by the possibility of a bloody coup that continually drives it to exterminate paranoiacally those suspected of conspiring against it. Eyewitness accounts of Iraq in the three years since the war have reported the murderous deeds of

Saddam's *apparatchiks* while concurrently paying tribute to the dignity, resilience and cheerfulness of the Iraqi people in the face of adversity. Sustained by the richness of their tradition and culture, Iraqi citizens have rarely borne a grudge against those who bombed their cities and killed their relatives. Commentators have regularly observed Iraqis sending good wishes to the west while dissociating themselves from Saddam's brutal regime.

Resulting from the massive allied bombing campaign and the subsequent trade embargo, the country's infrastructure and social life have been gravely impaired. As well as the life threatening shortage of foodstuffs and medicines there have been extreme disruptions to institutions and to family life: crime has become more common in a society that was previously virtually crime free; the education of children and students has been wrecked owing to lack of resources; there have also been unforeseen social changes which have led to professional people losing their standard of living, and unscrupulous black marketeers profiting from the economic blockade though sanctions busting and illicit activities. Psychologically it seems that the Iraqi people, after having endured eight years of war against Iran together with a million dead, find it inconceivable that the countries of the civilized west could have attacked them directly, and thus betrayed them in what has turned out to be a botched crusade against Saddam. Many Iraqis are convinced, too, that the war was essentially a staged confrontation to guarantee Arabic oil supplies to the US after Saddam proved an untrustworthy ally to America.

Most tragic perhaps of any of the consequences of the war fought to free Kuwait was the fate of the Kurdish people who, in the immediate aftermath of the conflict, seized what they thought was their historic opportunity to overthrow Saddam and liberate their nation. Their success was shortlived, although it gave momentary catharsis to long repressed hopes and ideals and allowed thousands of Kurds to make a pilgrimage to Halabja, the town where 5,000 people died in the poison gas attack in March 1988. A brave people, martyred, tortured and driven from their villages by Saddam, the Kurds were no match for the Iraqi troops ordered to quell their transitory revolution; nor did they receive the western backing they expected. Saddam's retaliation was ruthless as his army harried and killed the fleeing Kurds, thousands of whom became refugees in Turkey and Iran. Almost out of a guilty conscience it seemed, the west, through Operation Provide Comfort, finally came to the rescue of those Kurds who fled to the mountains and settled in the extreme northern regions of Iraq. Currently the situation of the Kurds, despite their national assembly and aspiration to be a separate Kurdish nation, remains perilous as they are totally dependent on air cover from Turkish bases to ward off Saddam's harassment. Surrounded by the antagonistic states of Turkey and Iran, living in a hostile environment, and beset by internal political rivalries and western donor fatigue, the future of the Kurds looks unredeemably bleak.

Equally serious, and perhaps more so, is the appalling suffering of those Shias in the south who took part in the uprising against Saddam in February and March 1991. This post war rebellion was suppressed with ruthless efficiency, and Saddam's forces were not deterred by the Allied no-fly zone from repressing dissidents and eliminating all traces of the 1991 revolt. Because world opinion did not support the Shias as it did the Kurds those people in the south of Iraq who defied the regime received almost no humanitarian aid, and justifiably feel that they have been abandoned by the west. Their worsening situation has been exacerbated by the deliberate attempts by Saddam's forces to wreak revenge; those seeking refuge in the southern marshlands, for example, have been subject to purges, to the poisoning of water supplies by chemicals and to systematic destruction by drainage of their land. Occasionally newspaper reports are published bearing witness to this deteriorating situation[15], but the Shias, who comprise 55 per cent of Iraq's population and who fought loyally for Saddam against Iran, are stealthily being subjugated. The tragic fate of these Shias is one of the war's gravest legacies, and should be a source of shame to Coalition leaders.

The Gulf War and Anglo-American culture

The impact of the Gulf war upon Anglo-American culture is not likely to be as pervasive or long-lasting as that of Vietnam. The war, though, did generate an urgent ethical debate among intellectuals and artists. Central to such controversies were two issues: whether the war was morally justified in the context of 'just war' theories, and whether its prosecution was aided by a subservient and corrupt media. Philosophers such as Michael Walzer and J. Brian Hehir, while dismissing the dubious morality of fighting to gain access to cheap oil, suggested that the old Augustinian doctrines of fighting for the human rights (of Kuwait's population) were largely relevant.[16] If the war were limited and fought with restraint then the ideals of collective security, regional stability and defending the helpless could be adduced as principles worth upholding. Within such disputations there was initially an evaluation of the likely outcome of further sanctions as a means of avoiding the use of force.

Most of the leading intellectuals of the left, in the US Noam Chomsky and Edward Said, in Germany Gunter Grass, in the UK Terry Eagleton,

John Berger and John Pilger, as well as such academics as Philip M. Taylor and David Morrison, focused upon the perfidious role of the media in shaping the outcome of the war.[17] Generally these critics accused the media, and in particular television, of whorish subservience to military and political elites. Such criticism echoed Gramscian and other dominant ideology theses which posited the masses as willingly submitting to the propaganda of the ruling classes and thereby ensuring the latter's hegemony.

A more sophisticated theoretical critique of the Gulf war is found in Christopher Norris's *Uncritical Theory* which castigates Jean Baudrillard and other postmodernist intellectuals for arguing that the conflict was unreal and essentially fictive.[18] In two articles, one printed in *The Guardian* in January 1991 and in a follow-up piece after the ceasefire in March, Baudrillard suggests that the Gulf war is illusory, a non-event or 'gigantic simulator'. Before the land war started he detected a phenomenon that was different from the older type of 'pure' war which was clearly marked by a declaration of hostilities;

> The United Nations has given the green light to a diluted kind of war - the right to war. It is a green light for all kinds of precautions and concessions, making it a kind of extended contraceptive against the act of war. First safe sex, now safe war. A Gulf War would not even register two or three on the richter scale this way. It is unreal, war without the symptoms of war, a form of war which means never needing to face up to war, which enables war to be 'perceived' from deep within a darkroom.[19]

Christopher Norris, with wit and discrimination, deconstructs such an extreme point of view and refutes Baudrillard's contention that events in the Gulf were 'virtual' (not real).

Norris's measured academic intelligence frames telling arguments, yet he lacks the partisan passion of both John Pilger and Edward Said in their eloquent polemics against the conduct of the war. In *Culture and Imperialism* Said establishes a tragic context for the war, incorporating it within the inevitable march of a Manifest Destiny. America, in this hypothesis, acts out its creed, its mission to intervene in trouble spots in order to 'supervise' the rule of international law.[20] This imperialist dynamic portrays Arabs as sleazy and unreliable through a slavish media which readily manufactures consent for their elimination like unwanted cockroaches.

John Pilger's standpoint has much in common with that of Edward Said. Pilger in *Distant Voices*, 1992, in a section entitled 'Myth Makers of the Gulf War', launches an impassioned critique of Coalition attitudes and actions.[21] His sense of outrage marks him out as a powerful journalist when exposing the hypocrisy and disinformation of political leaders and senior military figures. His chapter on Mutla Ridge, entitled 'a Bloodfest', typifies the fine, controversial writing that is found throughout his Gulf war pieces: in this commentary he accuses the Allies of callously shooting retreating troops in the back.

Pilger, Said, Chomsky and other heavyweight opponents of the war have frequently commented on the debasement of language frequently occasioned by the conflict. In an interesting article Brian Appleyard has also examined some of the characteristics displayed in such usage. Noting that war inevitably *is* language, he hypothesizes that America's involvement with its allies in the Gulf demanded a brand new linguistic register, sharply different from that used in Vietnam, to express the unique character of the war. Appleyard contended that this innovatory discourse necessitated a public relations ambience: it should resonate, on the one hand, ethical correctness, cleanliness and scientific efficiency, and, on the other, glamour, machismo and derring do. Such a discourse would provide a suitable 'antidote to the blood and dirt of Vietnam'.[22] A millennial war called for millennial metaphors.

Top Gun, the movie, perhaps more than any other popular narrative, supplied the sexy high tech overtones that the military needed to halo itself. Appleyard notes the juvenile, comic book cadences of the film and its Hollywood simplification, a blend of attitudes later displayed by Gulf pilots when their rhetoric of efficiency explained how they were 'just doing their job'. For ideological slanting the use of distancing language was vital to conceal unpalatable facts about deaths and injuries; perhaps the most famous example of such utterance is the term 'collateral damage' which means something very sinister, 'destruction exceeding the expected level'.

Any analysis of the downmarket newspaper and television coverage of the war will observe such dehumanisation of expression, whether it be the febrile inanities of military jargon or the advertising gloss put on events by some politicians. Military commanders substituted 'to stealth' as a synonym for 'to kill' and deployed the word 'hellacious' as a missile to take out meaning while politicians occupied the high ground of vocabulary and syntax when they contrasted the benign new world order of George Bush and his Coalition partners with the cancerous, malign aberration that Saddam represents.[23]

Soldiers, too, in their everyday speech offer singular insights into the military mind. A guide to Warspeak, for example, originally published in *The Sunday Times* reveals many of the deeper meanings of the war that are usually hidden from civilians.[24] Squaddies' slang is above all humorous and folksy, for example, referring to Yanks as septic tanks, Saddam as Stan or officers as Ruperts, yet it also articulates deeply held sexist and racist attitudes; British soldiers called a Saudi woman a BMO or black moving object, for example. Most remarkably the argot of the troops borrows the shiny spuriousness of what Appleyard has called the 'slick, hawkish, hardware' of state of the art weapons.[25] Such locutions place a premium upon rendering hostile actions so remote as to remove responsibility for their committal. The innocuous abbreviation MCB, for example, translates into awesomely lethal 'multiple cratering bomblets' and LANTIRN signifies 'low altitude navigation and targeting infrared system: carried on aircraft for use at night'. Embedded among such cliches, too, is the kind of jingoistic vocabulary favoured by panels of retired experts, ex-generals and air vice-marshals. Here the television screen becomes its own 'kill box' where truth is blown up before the viewer's eyes, like a target exploding on an aircraft's radar screen. Among such repellent cliches is one central metaphor dredged up unmercifully to sustain the nightly discourse of nationhood on UK television, the patriotic lie that the Gulf war equates with 'our finest hour', paralleling the fight against Hitler when the nation eschewed appeasement and endured blood, sweat and tears to confront fascism. Clearly the overkill and massively one sided action in the Gulf were nothing at all like the battles of the Second World War, yet pundits sought to legitimate Tornado sorties and tank incursions with the nomenclature of the Battle of Britain or of the famed Desert Rats who defeated Rommel.

In discussions of the degradation of language in wartime, poetry is often elevated as the only linguistic form capable of resisting propaganda and forging counter truths. Brian Appleyard, for example, has suggested 'the language of war has been effectively denied to poets since the Somme',[26] while the poet Douglas Dunn has speculated that poetic language remains 'indignant' and 'undented' by martial events.[27] Both of these opinions are valid: that war excludes poetry, and, conversely, survives it. There has been no outpouring of poems nourished by the public diction of 'proportionality', but there have been outspoken poems that counter the chauvinistic bias of public statements in favour of the war.

Most ambitious of such work are the Gulf war poems by Tony Harrison, one of Britain's two or three finest living poets, which were published at the time of the conflict, and later were collected in *The Gaze of the Gorgon*, 1992.[28] In this volume the pieces reflecting on the barbarities of 1990-91 are integrated into a historical discourse that looks back to previous wars and to earlier battlefields, both real and imaginary. Although the long title poem, 'The Gaze of the Gorgon', alludes to the

Gulf, two more memorable of Harrison's poems representing the fighting in Iraq are 'Initial Illumination' and 'A Cold Coming'. The former poem, 'Initial Illumination', based loosely on Anglo-Saxon alliterative verse, contrasts the illuminated manuscripts portraying the scriptures produced by Eadfrith and Billfrith, the anchorite scribes , with the Pentagon warspeak of George Bush which has 'conscripted' the word of God for bellicose purposes. Harrison's poem is admonitory in tone as he writes,

> Now with noonday headlights in Kuwait
> and the burial of the blackened in Baghdad
> let them remember, all those who celebrate,
> that their good news is someone else's bad
> or the light will never dawn on poor Mankind.

This poem's subdued anger is less apparent than the overt bitterness expressed by the Iraqi soldier's ghost in 'A Cold Coming', which was based upon the most famous photograph of the war, Kenneth Jarecke's newsphoto of the charred head of an Iraqi[29] soldier who was incinerated as he sat in the cab of a lorry during the retreat from Kuwait City. 'A Cold Coming', written in rhymed tetrameter, purports to be the after death soliloquy of the dead soldier, perhaps alluding to Wilfred Owen's *Strange Meeting*. Sardonic as Harrison's disciplined couplets are, 'A Cold Coming' lacks the visionary intensity of Owen's poem: its rhyme scheme lacks flexibility, and its integral imagery of reproduction and fertility sounds forced and over colloquial. The poem, though, as expected from a poet of Harrison's stature, contains some impressive passages, notably when, in a surprise reversal of attitudes, the dead Iraqi admits his own complicity in events,

> Lie and pretend that I excuse
> my bombing by B52's,
>
> pretend I pardon and forgive
> that they still do as I don't live,
>
> pretend they have the burnt man's blessing
> and then, maybe, I'm spared confessing,
>
> that only fire burnt out the shame
> of things I'd done in Saddam's name,
>
> the deaths, the torture and the plunder

the black clouds all of us are under.[30]

'A Cold Coming', despite its raw power, lacks the assurance of Harrison's more accomplished work. Its surreal ambition tends to debar it from the more candid and unaffected intimacy that marks out those individual poems which have commented most profoundly upon the war such as W. D. Ehrhart's 'The Gun' or Edwin Morgan's 'An Iraqi Student'.[31]

The long standing dispute about the relative merits of autonomous art of transcendent merit as against occasional work which displays contemporary urgency is relevant to cultural productions about the war. It is clearly evident that some popular works, while demonstrating topicality, are imaginatively limited and are rather narrow or dated in responding to the moral and political issues raised by events. In such a category are some of the thrilling memoirs narrating the experience of participants in dangerous actions such as the POW's account by John Peters and John Nichols, *Tornado Down*, 1992, or Andy McNab's pseudonymic description of an SAS mission to destroy Scud missiles, *Bravo Two Zero*, 1993. Similar reservations occur in reading popular fiction such as the action novels, David Mason's *Shadow Over Babylon*, 1993, or Jeffrey Archer's best seller *Honour Among Thieves*, 1993; both of these works draw upon the historical reality of the war as an integral part of their narratives.

In more complex artefacts explorations of the morality of warfare find more serious expression, and provide the ethical mainspring of writing. Trevor Griffiths's *The Gulf Between Us* which was written in 1991 and produced at the West Yorkshire playhouse in Leeds is a lyrical, experimental drama that represents the war's insane destruction of Iraqi life and culture: it is unambiguous in condemning Allied attacks, and conforms to its author's long held radical convictions. A similar point may be made about Sam Shepard's *States of Shock*, 1991, a pacifist play that critics have savaged as a sixties agit-prop piece. Shepard's plot centres upon how a grieving father who has lost his son in war tries to activate the dulled American conscience; its appearance during US celebrations of the victory over Iraq strengthens its dissenting overtones. Interestingly neither Shepard's nor Griffiths's anti-war plays received the critical approval that was accorded to earlier works by their authors. One may speculate cynically that it may take a proposed film about the deaths of British servicemen from Friendly Fire, and which is likely to star Tom Cruise, Kiefer Sutherland and Jack Nicholson as Saddam to transform the Gulf war into a charismatic subject for popular cultural consumption. For war to become marketable entertainment it needs bolstering by the star system. The sober and censorious dramas of Shepard and Griffiths lack sufficient glamour and mystique for a blockbuster movie.

A feature film directed, say, by Oliver Stone is unlikely to offer insights into the Gulf tragedy as profound as those found in Werner Herzog's austere film essay, *Lessons of Darkness*, shown on BBC television in 1992. This bleak and elegiac work largely comprises a loosely-linked collage of scenes, each one surveying the ravages of war upon a sterile landscape. Filmed mainly from the air the Kuwait desert is shown devoid of life like a pitted lunar wasteland. Although in two of its sequences *Lessons of Darkness* includes interviews with the innocent victims of torture, some of whom are struck dumb by Iraqi brutality, Herzog's requiem is essentially an abstract ensemble of images of destruction. The panorama it scrutinizes is a void where decaying machinery and apocalyptic fire scar everything in sight. Herzog's film counterpoints its photographs of abandoned vehicles, rubble and twisted metal with laconic quotations from Jewish sacred texts; its soundtrack is similarly judgemental comprising a sublime score drawn form Verdi, Wagner, Prokofiev and Grieg. Ultimately, though, the work leaves the impression of silent awe at the prospect of destruction. Herzog's postmodernist images of unrelated things inhere in the contemplation of fragments.

Such an aloof vision of modern war as typified by Herzog's epic of dehumanisation is discussed in an essay by Mark Holborn which considers the way war photography has changed.[32] Holborn argues that the old-style war photographers such as McCullin, who sent back news photos from the immediate battlefront in Vietnam have now been largely superseded. It is logical that in modern conflicts the photojournalist will be strictly excluded from proximity to the front. Thus a new iconography of war has emerged which constructs a symbolism from rubble and shattered machinery. Holborn perceptively describes this new aesthetics as demonstrated by Sophie Ristelhueber's more abstract and fractional images: she concentrates on the forensic traces of combat, the geometrical patterns left behind by troop movements and the operations of military hardware.[33] Older conventions of photojournalism, which traditionally emphasized closeness to traumatic events, have yielded to a remote, wide-angled lens. Ristelhueber's aerial photographs of the Kuwait desert in the aftermath of Gulf hostilities connote this new role; as Holborn suggests, 'The photographer is left the residual evidence: fragments, melted metal and blasted remains'. After the censor, steps forward the photographer who seeks to uncover from war's remains its buried reality.

Holborn's argument about the critic compelled to operate from imaginative distance is reinforced by many of the non-realist and satirical representations throughout visual culture. Abstract photomontage is one mode that functioned in this way as in the work of Peter Kennard.[34] In addition some of the most memorable cartoons drawn during the war and collected in *Dispatches from the Gulf War*, edited by Brian MacArthur in 1991, depend for their effects upon a similar vein of intellectual sophistication; notably such wit is commonly found in work by Steve Bell, Garland, Doonesbury, Gerald Scarfe and Heath.[35] In the field of comic book art, too, as discussed later in this collection[36], Carol Bennett the initiator of *Ceasefire*, an anti-war comic for women, similarly subverts documentary realism through parody, pastiche and feminist humour.[37] If, as now seems evident, it is much harder to make anti-war arguments directly by shocking the audience with live pictures of dying civilians, then such arguments must be made as forcefully as possible through lampoon and ridicule or other forms of resistance.

An overworked headline used to refer to the Gulf war is one which exploits the eponymous metaphor of separation: 'the Gulf between us', 'the Gulf in our midst' and 'the Reality Gulf' have all functioned in this way as figures implying a chasm in understanding which manifests a cultural gap between ourselves in the west and the Arab 'other'. Such a crevasse is not easy to bridge, yet need not deepen into an abyss. One way in which the split can be repaired is to listen to Arab voices, as John Berger has eloquently argued and thus break the habit of a deafness which originates from solipsism.[38] Another means of atonement is to try to uncover facts about the war that have so far been concealed. The Scott inquiry, which is investigating Britain's 'Iraqgate', shows how difficult this is. The habit of being 'economical with the truth' is deeply ingrained in British foreign policy.

The Gulf war's repercussions, both political and cultural, have continued to reverberate throughout 1994. In October Saddam's armies again threatened the Kuwaiti borders, occasioning a prompt and massive response by the US: President Clinton gave assurances that America would guarantee, on the UN's behalf, Kuwait's right to independence based upon existing frontiers. Both Russia and France, sensitive to the terrible suffering still endured by Iraq's population, have urged that consideration be given to dropping the international arms embargo. The United States, though, has continued to insist, taking a tough stance, that all UN conditions are met before the sanctions are lifted.

As Vietnam inevitably recedes, its impact blurred by history, the Gulf war has taken its place as the most recent and memorable conflict. A number of literary works link both wars, their subject matter the illogical military processes leading from the Indochina war up to the events of 1990-91. Naomi Wallace's play, *In the Heart of America*, performed in London during 1994, makes this connection, pointing to a developing moral and military crisis; and an anthology of poetry, published in 1993, edited by H. Palmer Hall and including poems by Vietnam veterans, together with Gulf veterans, is arranged in such a way as to connect both wars, thereby foregrounding the developing sense of ethical confusion and political barbarism. Such a perspective, of disorientation and cruel suffering, is found also in Michael Kelly's 1993 journalistic memoir, *Martyr's Day*, the most intelligent and well-written prose account of the Gulf war yet published. Operation Desert Storm and its ramifications have thus proved that they have the potential to inspire work in a variety of literary genres: from the docu-drama, *Half the Picture*, written by Richard Norton-Taylor and John McGrath in 1994 satirising the British arms scandal and the Scott Inquiry, to Frederick Forsyth's 1994 action thriller, *The Fist of God*.

Notes

1. 'The peacejam breaks', (1993) *The Sunday Times*, Opinion p. 3, 5 September.
2. Walker, Martin (1993), 'America is coming home', *The Guardian*, p. 20, 25 May.
3. Said, Edward, 'Empire of Sand', *Weekend Guardian*, p. 5, 12-13 January.
4. Adams, James (1993), 'U.S. tells Iraq: no more "cheat and retreat"', *The Sunday Times*, World News, p. 17, 10 January.
5. *Atlantic Outlook*, (1993), p. 3, 8 January.
6. Adams, James (1990), 'Apaches that strike by night', *The Sunday Times*, The Gulf Crisis: Week 8, p. 16, 23 September.
7. Palmer, Randall (1993), 'Top guns' spot-on blitz', *Manchester Evening News*, p. 3, 14 January.
8. *Ibid.*
9. *Atlantic Outlook*, (1993), p. 2, 8 January.
10. Bellamy, Christopher (1993), 'Gulf war body count drops to 1,500 Iraqis', *The Independent*, p. 1, 11 March.
11. Freedman, Lawrence and Karsh, Efraim (1993), *The Gulf Conflict, 1990-1*, Faber and Faber, London, p. 408-9.
12. Simpson, John (1991), *From the House of War; John Simpson in the Gulf*, Arrow Books, London, p. xv.
13. Sloyan, Patrick (1992), 'The Silver Bullet in Desert Storm', *The Guardian*, p. 23, 16 May.
14. Glover James, Ian (1991), 'Saddam under siege, prepares for last stand', *The Sunday Times*, p. 1, 24 March.
15. For example, Bhatia, Shyam (1993), 'Murder in the Marshes', *Observer Review*, p. 49, 28 February.
16. Woodward, Kenneth L. (1991), 'Ancient Theory and Modern War', *Newsweek*, p. 47, 11 February.
17. See especially Morrison, David E. (1992), *Television and the Gulf war*, Academia Research Monograph 7, John Libby, London and Taylor, Philip M. (1992), *War and the Media: Propaganda and Persuasion in the Gulf War*, Manchester University Press, Manchester.
18. Norris, Christopher (1992), *Uncritical Theory: Postmodernism, Intellectuals and the Gulf War*, Lawrence and Wishart, London.
19. Baudrillard, Jean (1991), 'The Reality Gulf', *The Guardian*, Europe, p. 25, 11 January.
20. Said, Edward W. (1993), *Culture and Imperialism*, Chatto and Windus, London.

21. Pilger, John (1993), *Distant Voices*, Vintage, London.
22. Appleyard, Brian (1991), 'Shell-shocked by war's words',*The Sunday Times*, War in the Gulf, p. 16, 27 January.
23. Harris, Robert (1990), 'This is not our finest hour and Saddam's not Hitler', *The Sunday Times*, Opinion, p. 16, 23 September.
24. 'A to Z of warspeak',(1991) *The Sunday Times*, News Review, p. 18, 3 February.
25. Appleyard, Brian *Op.Cit*
26. Appleyard, Brian *Op.Cit*
27. Dunn, Douglas (1991), 'Sound of thunder fades', *Weekend Guardian*, p. 10, 2-3 March.
28. Harrison, Tony (1992), *The Gaze of the Gorgon*, Bloodaxe Books, Newcastle upon Tyne.
29. Jarecke, Kenneth (1991), 'The charred head of an Iraqi soldier leans through the windscreen on his burned-out vehicle, February 28. He died when a convoy of Iraqi vehicles retreating from Kuwait City was attacked by Allied forces', *The Observer*, 10 March.
30. Harrison, Tony *Op.Cit*, p. 53.
31. Ehrhart, W. D. (1991), 'The Gun' is printed in this book, and Morgan, Edward (1991), 'An Iraqi Student' is included in *You (One World)*, Keith Murray Publishing, p. 2.
32. Holborn, Mark (1993), 'Leaving Scarred Earth', *The Independent on Sunday Magazine*, p. 10-12, 21 February.
33. Ristelhueber, Sophie (1993), *Aftermath*, Thames and Hudson. An exhibition of her photographs was shown at the Imperial War Museum, in March-April.
34. Kennard, Peter (1991), 'Beyond Words', photo-montage, with images and text, *Weekend Guardian*, p. 24-5, 2-3 March.
35. McArthur, Brian (1991), *Despatches from the Gulf War*, Bloomsbury, London.
36. See Huxley, David, essay for a full discussion of *Ceasefire*.
37. See also Corbett, Jan (1991), 'Writing off the Superhero', *The Guardian*, p. 36, 12 September.
38. Berger, John (1991), 'In the land of the deaf', *The Guardian*, p. 23, 2 March. (One way of listening to Arab voices is to read some of the Arab world's most perceptive writers, for example, the Egyptian novelist, Naguib Mahfouz or the Saudi Arabian exiled historian, Abdel Rahman Munif).

2 Four poems

W.D. Ehrhart

Guns

Again we pass that field
green artillery piece squatting
by the Legion Post on Chelten Avenue,
its ugly little pointed snout
ranged against my daughter's school.

"Did you ever use a gun
like that?" my daughter asks,
and I say "No, but others did.
I used a smaller gun. A rifle."
She knows I've been to war.

"That's dumb," she says,
and I say, "Yes," and nod
because it was, and nod again
because she doesn't know.
How do you tell a four-year-old

what steel can do to flesh?
How vivid do you dare to get?
How explain a world where men
kill other men deliberately
and call it love of country?

Just eighteen, I killed
a ten-year-old. I didn't know.
He spins across the marketplace
all shattered chest, all eyes and arms.
Do I tell her that? Not yet,

though one day I will have
no choice except to tell her
or to send her into the world
wide-eyed and ignorant.
The boy spins across the years

till he lands in a heap
in another war in another place
where yet another generation
is rudely about to discover
what their fathers never told them.

After the Latest Victory

I call the sea. The wind calls back.
No seagulls' cries, no sailors' ghosts,
not mermaids, God, nor any human voice
disturbs the silence closing hard behind
the last reverberations of that solitary cry.

Does sound just die? Or does the universe
reverberate with cries from Planet Earth?
Novenas, speeches, shouts, whole supplications
striking Jupiter, careening off the stars
like frozen screams or unsaid thoughts?

Only the wind, and the waves' dull roar,
the dune grass dancing for the moon.
Behind me lies a continent asleep,
drunk with martial glory and an empire's pride,
though each is transient as sand.

This continent was called the New Jerusalem.
So much hope and expectation carried
in the hearts of men and women brave
enough to hazard all in search of this.
Look what we have made of it.

In Fairmount Park, a girl is raped.
Her father is a soldier in the Middle East.
Her brother cannot read or write.
The rapist wants a pair of sneakers
like the ones he's seen in Reebok ads.

The moon's wide river rides the swells
from breakers to the dark horizon.
Above me, like a dignified procession,
the stars turn slowly through the night,
indifferent to our helplessness.

The Cradle of Civilisation

Where the Tigris and Euphrates meet,
human beings planted seeds and stayed
long enough to harvest them
on common ground.
This is where the world we know began.

How very far we've come
that we should come to such a place
not with gratitude and wonder

but with bombs and guns,
that we should not find this odd,
that we should so believe our otherness
that we would rather kill and die
than search for common ground.

Why the Kurds Die in the Mountains

Twenty years was long enough.
We were tired of being abused.

We said: it's time to win one
for the Gipper, for John Winthrop,
General Jacob Smith, the twilight's
last gleaming, and that gleaming
black wall of fallen heroes.

Think of all that shame,
those 58,000 dead in vain
because we did not have the stomach
for a fight.

Never again.

Never.

From *The Distance We Travel*, Adastra Press, Easthampton, Massachusetts, USA, 1993. All four poems are reprinted with kind permission of the publisher and author.

3 Overcoming the Vietnam syndrome: The Gulf War and revisionism

Jon Roper

> It is said, however, that each one of us behaves in some respects like the paranoiac, substituting a wish-fulfilment for some aspect of the world which is unbearable to him, and carrying this delusion through into reality. When a large number of people make this attempt together and try to obtain assurance of happiness and protection from suffering by a delusional transformation of reality it acquires special significance. ...Needless to say, no one who shares a delusion recognizes it as such.
>
> Sigmund Freud, *Civilization and its Discontents*

> North Vietnam cannot defeat or humiliate the United States. Only Americans can do that.
>
> Richard Nixon in a speech, November 3, 1969

The failure of United States foreign policy in South-East Asia, and the experience of defeat in Vietnam, has had a traumatic, resonating and continuing impact upon American political life and culture. In his inaugural address in 1989, George Bush argued that the Vietnam War: 'cleaves us still. But, friends, that war began in earnest a quarter of a century ago; and surely the statute of limitations has been reached. This is a fact: the final lesson of Vietnam is that no great nation can long afford to be sundered by a memory'. The new President was inviting the nation to forget the domestic political divisions and self-doubt caused by its greatest international embarrassment.

Yet Bush did not take his own words seriously. Three years later, in his faltering re-election campaign, he attempted to exploit rather than paper over the fault lines in American political discourse that were caused by Vietnam. He accused Bill Clinton of a lack of patriotism for his involvement in anti-war demonstrations while he was a student overseas. Such youthful protest, it appeared, was not to be excused by Bush's initial desire to move beyond recollections of the divisive impact of the Vietnam War upon American society. It rendered his opponent unfit to occupy the White House.

In between the inaugural and the battle for re-election it was the Gulf War that dramatised the legacy of Vietnam. As George Herring put it: 'such was the lingering impact of the Vietnam War that the Persian Gulf conflict appeared at times as much a struggle with its ghosts as with Saddam Hussein's Iraq'[1]. In the immediate aftermath of 'Desert Storm' the Bush administration argued that success in the Gulf had exorcized defeat in Vietnam. Had it? Was the Gulf War the concluding episode in a process of political and military revisionism, begun in the 1980s, and aimed at transforming America's involvement in Vietnam into Ronald Reagan's 'noble cause', a failure that might reasonably be excused? Or is that view an example of Reaganite wish-fulfilment that encouraged a continuing national capacity for self-delusion? In the Gulf, did America beat not only Iraq, but also, as George Bush claimed, overcome the Vietnam syndrome once and for all?'[2]

It had made its debut in American political debate soon after the last US troops were withdrawn from South-East Asia, and South Vietnam had succumbed to invasion from the north. At that stage, the 'Vietnam syndrome' was, as Michael Klare points out, a simple idea which referred to 'the American public's disinclination to engage in further military interventions in internal Third World conflicts'[3]. It was that sentiment which characterised President Carter's administration, although there was still some rhetorical sabre-rattling. The 'Carter Doctrine' in January 1980, could have been designed with 'Desert Storm' in mind. 'An attempt by any outside force to gain control of the Persian Gulf region will be regarded as an assault on the vital interests of the United States'. As such, it would 'be repelled with any means necessary, including military force'[4]. Throughout the decade, the Reagan and then the Bush administrations endorsed that strategic view.

It was during Carter's presidency, however, that the limitations implied by the self-denying ordinance of the 'Vietnam syndrome' became apparent. The consequence of a reluctance to sanction a military commitment both to support a continuing policy of containment, and to preserve American influence overseas, was thought to be international impotence. Events in the Middle-East seemed to confirm America's malaise. The nation itself was taken hostage along with the imprisoned staff of its embassy in Iran. That crisis effectively ejected Carter from the White House. The pure, non-interventionist formulation of the 'Vietnam syndrome' hence became regarded, by advocates of renewed activism at least, not as a useful reminder of the limits of an over-zealous foreign policy, but as a serious inhibition on the nation's capacity to preserve and pursue its interests overseas.

By 1980, therefore, and particularly among conservative analysts, the 'Vietnam syndrome' had been co-opted and had been invested with a new significance. Rather than a self-imposed caution against the pursuit of an expansionist foreign policy, now it was a barrier to business as usual; to 'empire as a way of life'[5]. No longer a restraint, instead it became a constraint: an obstacle that had to be confronted if popular support was to be re-engaged for the projection of American military power abroad. Apparently traumatised by its experience in Vietnam, the fact of failure and the idea of defeat challenged America's sense of purpose. National self-confidence might be restored only if the 'syndrome' could be overcome.

Reagan's election itself exploited and symbolised the frustration felt with the Carter years. America had become 'an ordinary country', no longer able nor willing successfully to exercise its influence overseas. The new President rejected the agonising of his predecessor over the complexities of international relations and America's place in them. Instead he retreated to the simple formula of Cold War rhetoric, characterising once more the role of the United States as the opponent of communist expansionism. To carry conviction, however, the message had to take account of the nation's defeat in its previous self-assigned mission of containment in South-East Asia.

So 'explaining why America lost the Vietnam War (but need not lose the next time around)' became 'central to the revisionist project'. And 'with his uncanny sense of the lowest common denominator in the popular culture', Reagan realised the necessity of providing a simple account of America's failure which could be used as a spring-board for regenerating national self-confidence[6]. The idea that America had been defeated in Vietnam began to be rationalised and amended through a process of historical revisionism.

A political explanation for the failures of the immediate past was offered. 'Never again', suggested Ronald Reagan in 1981, would the US 'send an active fighting force to a country to fight unless it is for a cause that we are prepared to win'[7]. The implication was that America had faltered in Vietnam merely because of the lack of political resolve. In the same year, the military added its own analysis to Reagan's sentiment. Colonel Harry Summers' book, *On Strategy: the Vietnam War in Context*, which has been described as 'the semi-official US Army view of the war', argued that had the military been able to fight a war free from political constraints and uncontaminated by theories of counter-insurgency, the outcome would have been different[8]. So if America's failure was America's fault, then Vietnam became a problem of political attitude and a question of military strategy, rather than a reversal of fortune at the hands of a resolute and defiant enemy.

Such an interpretation of the nation's experience in Vietnam invited Americans to confront their failure rather than their defeat. Intellectuals, whose tradition is, as Noam Chomsky argues, 'one of servility to power' seemed willing to collude with new orthodoxies[9]. Liberals had found an earlier apologia in Arthur Schlesinger's conclusion that Vietnam had been a 'tragedy without villains'[10]. Now Reagan's nostrum, Vietnam as a 'noble cause' which had been imperfectly executed, became a convenient platitude for conservatives. The sentiment re-echoed in Hollywood's Vietnam, from Rambo's plaintive 'do we get to win this time', as he prepared for yet another mission to South-East Asia, to the hero of Oliver Stone's *Platoon* discovering that the enemy in Vietnam 'was ourselves'.

So revisionism in the Reagan years focussed first on practical matters: political will and military tactics. Speaking to Bobby Muller, a founder of the Vietnam Veterans of America Foundation, the President summed up his version of America's involvement in South-East Asia: 'Bob, the trouble with Vietnam was that we never let you guys fight the war you could have done, so we denied you the victory all the other veterans enjoyed. It won't happen like that again, Bob...'[11]. The mood had shifted. Vietnam veterans were no longer scapegoats. As Muller commented elsewhere: 'it's a changing dynamic ...That's what revisionism is all about'[12].

The political and military explanations of America's failure allowed the war in Vietnam to be discussed, but the fact of the Vietnamese victory to be dismissed. The revisionist interpretation of America's experience in South-East Asia was accompanied by a refusal to accept that the opposition had won. That act of denial meant that the re-establishment of national self-confidence rested on the belief that 'next time' American power would prevail. Revisionism demanded historical amnesia: to ignore the Vietnamese role in America's defeat was a step towards escaping past embarrassment. There was no need to admit that the Cold War certainties believed by Graham Greene's generation of *Quiet Americans*, and now once more in fashion, had been perhaps mistaken.

In the aftermath of his failed summit meeting with Khruschev in Vienna in 1961, President Kennedy observed that the US was faced with the problem of making its power seem credible, and that Vietnam 'looked like the place' where it might do this. Defeat in South-East Asia meant that America once again faced Kennedy's problem, not just internationally, but internally as well. Domestic doubts remained about the nation's capacity to remain committed to the projection of American power abroad. Revisionism was based upon the idea that failure in South-East Asia had been due America's own shortcomings. But even if these were remedied, would future adventures work?

The 'Vietnam syndrome' in the 1980s thus proved to be not just about a popular reluctance to endorse military intervention abroad, and the creation of a framework within which such involvement could be supported by some and tolerated by most Americans. It had still to do with the way in which the Vietnam experience permeated the national consciousness and the political culture of the United States itself. As a Vietnamese refugee, now assimilated as an American, pointed out: 'But Vietnam - well, Vietnam is special. What Henry Kissinger described as a "fourth-rate power" has cracked our ivory tower and plagued the American psyche; that hell in a small place devastated the bright and shiny citadel. For the first time in American history, we are caught in the past, haunted by unanswerable questions, confronted with a tragic ending'[13]. Revisionist arguments about the mechanics of failure also needed to be able to address such feelings, which were not accommodated by simple pragmatic assessments of the inadequacies in America's approach to the Vietnam War.

After Vietnam the successful projection of American power abroad was no longer a foregone conclusion. Indeed, as long as the 'Vietnam syndrome' remained as an obstacle to be cleared every time involvement abroad was suggested, it implied that for many, the revisionist message was not completely convincing. The 'syndrome' was invested with a psychological dimension. And for those anxious to promote a more activist foreign policy, it took on its medical meaning. It became an illness to be cured. This would involve dealing with a problem in the American psyche; the collective post-traumatic stress of a nation that, in the Reagan years, was being persuaded to re-invent its experience in Vietnam.

To carry conviction the revisionist argument had to demonstrate that America could confront the psychology of the 'syndrome'. Mary Kaldor, criticising America's bombing raid upon Libya in 1986, argued that military power 'if it is to remain popular domestically, ...has to stay at the level of psychological spectacle ...But so long as military power remains in the psychological realm, its effectiveness depends on its psychological success'[14]. Vietnam too had shown that. Beating the 'Vietnam syndrome' would thus mean rehabilitating America's sense of its military superiority over others. And yet the 'syndrome' was still presented as a barrier to the effective use of military power, to the extent that it implied that overseas commitments would be domestically popular only in clearly defined circumstances.

During the 1980s the Reagan and then the Bush administrations acted on the assumption that to successfully combat the 'Vietnam syndrome', certain pre-conditions were necessary. First, intervention overseas should be accompanied by sustained political resolve. Second, the military should be allowed to perform its task free from political constraint. These arguments flowed naturally from revisionist analysis. A third factor was also thrown into the calculation. Vietnam had become an open-ended commitment. Future overseas adventures should be swift. Whereas the conflict in South-East Asia was characterised as the 10,000 day war, General Norman Schwarzkopf tells of the decision to time the cease-fire announcement in the Gulf so as to make it a 100 hour war. 'I had to hand it to them; they really knew how to package a historic event'[15]. Finally, to confront the psychological trauma still affecting a nation which needed to convince itself that its mistakes in Vietnam were self-inflicted, future overseas adventures had to promise -and deliver - military success.

No political intervention for 'unclear goals'; no political limits on the military's freedom of action; no protracted commitment overseas; and no military intervention unless victory could be 'guaranteed'. If any one of these guiding principles was threatened, then the self-imposed constraints implied by the 'Vietnam syndrome' might continue to obstruct an activist American foreign policy. America would thus fight only a proxy war in Nicaragua, since a full-scale commitment of military force implied a long-term involvement with no surety of success. This was despite President Reagan's protestations that here was a clear-cut ideological battle of containment that must be joined. He also withdrew forces from the Lebanon when faced with the alternative of likely further military losses. On the other hand, Reagan's military intervention in Grenada and the air-strike upon Libya both boosted his domestic political popularity, and violated none of the principles implied by the modified formulation that condoned overseas adventurism within the agreed constraints. Similarly, George Bush's invasion of Panama followed the pattern established during Reagan's administration.

Throughout the 1980s, then, fear of further failure confronted a wish to redress defeat. Reluctance to assert power was accompanied by a psychological desire to demonstrate that American military force could be used successfully abroad. This was why some Americans were unwilling to become involved in Nicaragua - 'another Vietnam' - or the Lebanon, but others were enthusiastic in their support for the invasion of Grenada and their desire, reflected in some mid-1980s university campus graffiti, to 'Nuke Gaddafi', as the Libyan leader became a symbol of international terrorism.

In so far as it inhibited complete freedom of foreign policy action, however, the 'syndrome' still could be described in the language of psychological disturbance as easily as it could be expressed in the rhetoric of political commitment and in the analysis of military mistakes. General William Westmoreland, the former commander of American forces in Vietnam, considered the phenomenon in these terms. 'Vietnam was a war that continues to have an impact on politics. I fear that one of the big losses, in fact, probably the most serious loss of that war, is what I refer to as the Vietnam psychosis. Any time anybody brings up the thought that military forces might be needed, you hear the old hue and cry "another Vietnam, another Vietnam". That can be a real liability to us as we look to the future'[16]. In Westmoreland's world, the 'syndrome' was a synonym for a national mental derangement which needed to be treated.

Westmoreland's remarks encapsulate the dilemma of revisionism. The idea of the 'Vietnam syndrome' as a constraint upon an activist foreign policy, as something that had to be overcome if life was to return to normal, was the imaginative creation of the Reagan years. Revisionists might argue that Vietnam should be seen as a unique experience: America's frustration had been its fault. And failure could be fixed. That case would be proven by the evidence of future military success: overcoming the 'syndrome'. But at a practical level doubts remained. If the commitment of manpower - or even resources - to an open-ended interventionist adventure seemed likely, the Reagan administration still confronted the reality of public opinion. Westmoreland's 'psychosis' reached beyond the blandishments of revisionist persuasion. The limitations placed upon an interventionist foreign policy resulted in the pursuit of aims by other means. And the outcome was the Iran-Contra scandal.

The Vietnam War had encouraged President Nixon to embark upon the covert policies which escalated into the crimes and misdemeanours of Watergate. Fear of the 'Vietnam syndrome' similarly persuaded the

Reagan administration to privatise American foreign policy, as it became apparent that revisionism could not build the democratic consensus necessary to achieve some of its purposes. The consequences unravelled in the revelations of Irangate. When Congress, sensitive to public opinion, prevented the executive from implementing its explicit policy of containing communism in Nicaragua, the encouragement was given to Oliver North's 'neat idea': trading arms for hostages with Iran, and using the proceeds to fund the Contras in Central America.

In 1987, Immanuel Wallerstein made the point that 'if Reagan has not been able to invade Nicaragua, the reason seems clear enough. The US public seems ready to tolerate maximally the loss of a handful of lives in an action over three days (Grenada), but not the loss of 200 lives in a situation of indefinite further loss (Beirut), and surely not the prospective loss of tens of thousands of lives in a far-off warfare zone (Nicaragua). Call it the Vietnam syndrome, or what you will, but the fact is that it has become a political reality so clear that *even* Reagan has not dared go against it directly. This is the simplest explanation of the inefficacious convolutions of the Iran-Contra fiasco'[17]. Reagan had been frustrated by a different form of containment: America's desire to contain itself. Despite revisionist rhetoric, public opinion still raised the spectre of 'another Vietnam' as a self-imposed restraint.

That political reality also suggests a reason for George Bush's call in his inaugural address for a 'statute of limitations' on the divisions caused by Vietnam. A member of the administration that had been caught out in the Iran-Contra scandal, Bush could not risk another foreign policy adventure that went beyond the bounds of constitutional propriety. He had succeeded to the presidency with first-hand experience of the way in which the revisionist assessment of the 'Vietnam syndrome' as an obstacle to activism had corrupted Reagan's foreign policy: limiting options to the point where conspiratorial choices appeared preferable to legal actions. So Bush was right to identify Vietnam as an enduring influence in American political life. And the crisis in the Gulf would be his opportunity to stage what he imagined was a final confrontation with the legacy he had inherited from America's failure in South-East Asia.

By the end of the 1980s, then, America seemed caught between the desire for a decisive military victory overseas to purge the revisionist feeling that its own failings had led it to lose the Vietnam War, and the nagging fear that a wholehearted commitment to another adventure, on the scale of that undertaken in South-East Asia, might lead once again to defeat. In these terms, Grenada, Libya and even Panama were sideshows: sparring matches before the main event. The Gulf crisis provided the prospect for the completion of the process which aimed to transform defeat in the Vietnam War in the nation's historical memory into at least an honourable failure of well-intentioned policy. If the war against Iraq was a success, the 'Vietnam syndrome' might not only be overcome, it could also be cured. After a decade of revisionism, was George Bush, and were many of those who sought to influence political opinion in the US, indeed spoiling for this fight?

In a controversial article published in the *Nation* in March 1991, America's involvement in the Gulf War was seen as the product of a collective psychosis. Lloyd De Mause, a psycho-historian, addressed the possibility that 'the homicidal and suicidal acts of entire nations - wars - might ...stem from mental disorders'. In this analysis, American media images of Saddam Hussein as a 'terrifying parent' figure, conspired with feelings of depression and guilt among those suffering in the aftermath of the 'success binge' of the 1980s, to create an atmosphere in which support for war could be nurtured. So '...right after Iraq invaded Kuwait, grateful comments appeared in the media'. Even liberal publications were not immune. '*The New Republic*, for example, said, "Saddam Hussein did the world a favor by invading Kuwait", and Ben Wattenberg headlined his column, "Thanks, Saddam, We Needed that"'[18]. In diagnosing this national psychological disorder, moreover, De Mause argued that it was reminiscent of a condition made familiar by the Vietnam War.

'If a patient were to walk into a psychiatric clinic suffering from intrusive images of terrifying figures torturing children, severe depression unrelated to current life events, and suicidal wishes, a post-traumatic stress disorder (P.T.S.D.) would likely be suspected'. This, then, was 'the diagnostic category' which most closely coincided with 'the popular mood in America during the months leading up to the gulf crisis'[19]. In his attribution of such feelings to the post-traumatic stress of infancy, De Mause calls to mind Michael Herr's observation in *Dispatches*: 'I think that Vietnam was what we had instead of happy childhoods'[20]. Had a 'revisionist psychosis' emerged as a counterpoint to Westmoreland's refrain: the 'syndrome' as a continuing psychological impediment on America's capacity to go to war?

If America was influenced by a collective predisposition that encouraged a war mentality at the beginning of the 1990s, then another important question is raised. How far did the United States collude, consciously or unconsciously, in the creation of the crisis in the Gulf? There is no doubt that its policy in the region, which, during the 1980s, had 'tilted' towards Iraq in the hope of thereby containing Iran, was in retrospect optimistic if not opportunistic. Mark Hosenball, writing in *The New Republic* in June 1992 argued that 'in hindsight, the extent to which the Bush and Reagan administrations collaborated in Saddam's ruinous military delusion is appalling'. Furthermore, 'President Bush points to his conduct of Operation Desert Storm as proof of his mastery of international affairs, yet his files demonstrate how he helped to create his own nemesis'[21]. The way to remedy bad policy may be to fight a war, but at the same time, the desire for a conclusive military victory to purge the feeling of failure in Vietnam had influenced foreign policy for the previous decade.

Iraq's take-over of Kuwait was an accident that happened without too long a wait. According to John Pilger, for example, 'there is other evidence that Saddam Hussein was deliberately squeezed or "entrapped" into invading Kuwait. As a US client, he had become too powerful, too cocky and so - rather like Noriega - he had to go'[22]. A week before Iraq invaded Kuwait, the American ambassador in Baghdad told Hussein that the President had instructed her that the US was agnostic about the border disputes between the two countries. When Ross Perot, the maverick Texan candidate for the presidency, repeated this charge in the third presidential debate of 1992, George Bush was immediately defensive and vociferously denied the allegation that Iraq had thereby been encouraged to occupy a neighbouring state.

In the event, the Gulf War presented the President with an opportunity to deal with what revisionists thought to be the pervasive psychological influence of the 'Vietnam syndrome' upon popular attitudes. He could confront too the popular reservations about his own capacity as 'commander in chief', which had emerged as he succeeded Ronald Reagan in the White House. In the immediate aftermath of the conflict, then, 'not only did Bush earn kudos for deftly orchestrating the allied success in driving the Iraqis from Kuwait, but he definitively quashed the "wimp factor" that dogged and annoyed him throughout his 1988 campaign'[23]. The Gulf War thus promised to resolve the dilemma of post-Vietnam foreign policy and would become the defining event of Bush's presidency. If the 'syndrome' could be overcome, America itself would no longer be a 'wimp': self-confidence would replace self-doubt.

'Desert Storm' was fought with Vietnam specifically in mind. When war broke out, Bush was adamant that it would not be 'another Vietnam'. The US would not fight 'with one hand tied behind our backs'. As Pilger points out, at a basic humanitarian level such a comment is disingenuous. 'If seven-and-a-half million tons of bombs dropped on a peasant land and two-and-a-half million people killed is the result of such constraint, the prospect of both hands free ought to bring pause to those who believe the end justifies the means'[24]. But Bush was expressing what had become the revisionist orthodoxy: lack of political conviction had inhibited the military's freedom of action and had led to failure in Vietnam.

Lawrence Freedman and Efraim Karsh have summarised the way in which strategy in the Gulf applied the 'lessons' of Vietnam. 'Key actors in the American political process were determined not to repeat the mistakes of the 1960s: the administration was resolved not to get trapped in an unwinnable war; the military would not allow civilians to impose artificial restrictions that would deny them the possibility of decisive victory; Congress refused to be railroaded into giving the executive *carte blanche* to wage war; and the diplomats did not wish to find themselves supporting a military campaign in isolation from natural allies'[25]. Here all of the assumptions are based upon revisionist arguments. America had been 'trapped' in Vietnam in a doomed enterprise. The military, due to 'artificial restrictions' had been prevented from achieving - presumably - a 'natural' victory. The Vietnam War was the unilateral responsibility of the 'imperial presidency' that had manipulated the democratically elected Congress. And the foreign service had been unable to persuade other countries - Australia was overlooked as one example - from assisting as America confronted its challenge alone.

The Gulf War was thus fought mindful of such revisionist 'errors'. The pre-conditions for the successful projection of power abroad finally had been met. The confrontation presented Bush with his opportunity. It would not be 'another Vietnam'. For, as Stephen Vlastos points out, revisionists believed that in their analysis of America's mistakes in South-East Asia, they had found some answers. 'In the final analysis, the cause of failure is easily remedied: to win the next one, send packing the unmanly Washington bureaucrats and politicians who chose the path of gradual escalation; put real men in charge who will go in big, hard and fast'[26]. Was that what had happened by the time that 'Desert Shield' became 'Desert Storm'?

The Gulf crisis tested this post-Vietnam relationship between politicians and their generals. On the eve of the land war, Norman Schwarzkopf revealed how revisionist views had influenced administration attitudes, and the extent to which Colonel Summers' strategic analysis had permeated the American military mind. President Bush had called him. 'As I hung up the phone, I was struck by what the president had chosen *not* to say: he'd given me no orders and hadn't second-guessed the decisions I'd made. His confidence in the military's ability to do its job was so unlike what we'd seen in Vietnam that the conversation meant the world to me'[27]. The result was the quick fix of a high-technology campaign, with few American casualties. For Iraq, however, it was a different story.

Noam Chomsky has referred to the Gulf War as an example of a 'constructive bloodbath', an adventure undertaken 'for a power purpose'. He also points out that 'the Gulf War was particularly pleasurable to elite groups because there was a guarantee that they (Iraq's forces) weren't going to shoot back. There was no war. A war is something where two sides shoot at each other. This is just a slaughter ...And it achieved power ends'[28]. America's action in the Gulf has been described in similar vein as 'the professional military's therapeutic revenge for the political restraints imposed during the Vietnam war'[29]. It was, indeed, a 'turkey shoot'.

In the immediate aftermath of 'Desert Storm', writing in the *Nation*, Michael Klare argued that 'President Bush was never really worried about Iraqi military capabilities: his every move was dictated by his fear of the "Vietnam Syndrome". This can be seen in his decision to act quickly and with overwhelming force, and in the muzzling and manipulation of the mass media'[30]. And yet there is evidence to suggest that some of the media were also mindful of America's experience in Vietnam, and appreciated Bush's opportunity in the Gulf. In a survey of 66,000 news stories that appeared between 1 August 1990 and 28 February 1991, the word 'Vietnam' was used over 7,000 times, almost three times more often than the next most frequent phrase, 'human shields'[31]. So 'the lost Vietnam War was also in the minds of many US citizens, including the reporters and the people they interviewed - politicians, military spokesmen, soldiers and their relatives or the general public. Even if the moral justification for the war was linked to UN resolutions, the finding suggests that an element of "holy war" to restore US honour was also involved'[32].

During the 'uncensored' Vietnam War, the media had become increasingly critical of the political and military conduct of the conflict. The Tet offensive of 1968 stands out as a turning point because what the American military would claim later as a tactical victory was reported at the time as a psychological defeat. Such reportage determined the future course of American involvement in Vietnam. Contrast the Gulf. One correspondent from the *Christian Science Monitor* commented on the televised press conferences where 'the military had direct access to the people - and at the same time was able to undermine the credibility of journalistic interpretations. It was a stunning reversal of roles from Vietnam, where the press called military credibility into question'. A Swedish journalist 'thought it remarkable to see how the US journalists took part in a show arranged by the military, how they walked around the passages at the press centre dressed in combat uniforms thinking they were covering the war'[33].

The administration's domestic political agenda in the Gulf War was broadly supported by the American media. It included, as Adrian Hamilton wrote in *The Observer*, the objective of winning 'a decisive victory that would erase the memory of Vietnam, with the lowest possible Allied casualties'[34]. In the moment of victory, the President announced that the 'Vietnam syndrome' had been beaten: later in a speech on July 4th 1991, he welcomed home not only the veterans of the Gulf, but also, belatedly, the Vietnam veterans as well. The Americans who had been both victims and initially victimised as a result of the popular perceptions of defeat in South-East Asia were now to be rehabilitated as they were swept up in the euphoria of success in the Gulf. Yet the rhetoric of victory confronted political reality. In the post-Gulf period, doubts soon surfaced over the nature of the President's proclaimed triumph.

Strobe Talbott, one of Bill Clinton's principal foreign policy advisers, wrote an article in *Foreign Affairs* early in 1992, entitled 'Post-Victory Blues'. In effect, he aimed to undercut Bush's ability to use the political capital of 'Desert Storm' during the election year. He had an easy target. Talbott argued that 'when Americans fight, they want to see not just victory but virtue ...In mobilizing his fellow citizens to go to war against Saddam Hussein, Bush had suggested that what was at stake were standards, championed by the United States but applicable to all humanity, about how governments should govern. But in the way he ended the war, he repudiated that principle'[35]. Having ejected Iraq from Kuwait, therefore, the American led coalition forces did not pursue the war against Saddam. George Bush's demonized adversary, in the moment of military defeat, retained power through crushing the political opposition of the substantial Kurdish minority within Iraq.

Moreover, the liberation of Kuwait hardly represented a triumph for American values. Reservations were expressed about the nature of the regime that had been re-installed. As Thomas Omestad points out: 'Bush had appealed to Americans' idealism to win support for the war; afterward, he neglected the most basic ideal: democracy. Regaining power, thanks to American soldiers, was the autocratic emir of Kuwait, a man whose idea of pluralism was to take a new wife on Thursdays'. Sentiments such as these suggested that the triumph was transitory. So 'the glory of Bush's shining moment, the victory over Iraq, faded like a desert mirage. In its aftermath came serious doubts about his judgment and his credibility. And for that, the president had mostly himself to blame'[36]. Bush was facing, and shirking, some important political truths.

While asserting that the 'Vietnam syndrome' had been finally buried, Bush in effect demonstrated its continuing relevance to the conduct of American foreign policy. As Talbott pointed out, 'curing the "Vietnam Syndrome" was seen as an important benefit of Desert Storm, not to be jeopardized by over-reaching in the flush of victory'. The simple restraint remained. The President was unwilling to risk his military success by committing forces to an open-ended conflict against Iraq. In so doing, he called into question the principle upon which he insisted that the Gulf War had been fought. During 1991, 'administration spokesmen from the president down had cited the Gulf War as proof of the relevance and efficacy of American power'[37]. But Saddam Hussein's continuing survival exposed Bush's 'credibility gap'. The 'Vietnam syndrome' still existed as a constraint that counselled caution.

What, then, had America achieved? If the Gulf conflict was fought in part to redeem the failure of the nation's self-assigned mission in South-East Asia, then the 'post-victory blues' suggested that the initial boast that the United States had overcome the 'Vietnam syndrome' might become more muted as time went by. As George Herring observed: '...it seems doubtful that military victory over a nation with a population less than one-third of Vietnam in a conflict fought under the most favorable circumstances could expunge deeply encrusted and still painful memories of an earlier and very different kind of war'[38]. The attempt at historical revisionism embarked upon in the 1980s, far from being sealed by success in the Gulf, was exposed by it.

The message of the 1980s had been that America could understand its failure in Vietnam if the depth of self-examination did not go beyond consideration of what it believed were its own political and military mistakes in South-East Asia. Indeed, the identification of the 'Vietnam syndrome' itself effectively removed the need for foreign policy planners to analyse the reasons as to why and how the Vietnamese had successfully resisted the strategy of containment. Instead a domestic psychological block was thought to represent an obstacle to the further projection of military power abroad. If that 'syndrome' could be 'beaten', the coruscating impact of the Vietnam experience upon American society would end.

The Gulf War promised revisionists such a cure. In military terms it could be represented, according to Paddy Ashdown, as a chapter in 'the story of the United States Army: in poor shape and badly led after Korea; demoralised and unpopular after Vietnam; restored by the experience of success against Iraq'[39]. For American foreign policy-makers it might be, as Martin Indyk suggests, a turning point as '...the Bush administration found itself in the unprecedented position of being able to set the postwar Middle East agenda'[40]. And yet domestically, less than two years after America's victory, the President who orchestrated it was defeated at the polls.

The political omens seemed initially so promising. In March 1991, the

President had an 89 per cent approval rating. The *Congressional Quarterly* wrote that 'Bush's successful gamble in the gulf has given him a level of stature and popularity that presidents rarely achieve. In the war's afterglow, the immediate question is not whether he might be beaten in 1992 but whether he could establish a record-high winning percentage in a presidential election, surpassing the 61.1% rolled up by Lyndon B. Johnson in 1964'[41]. Leading Democrats were reluctant to confront an incumbent who appeared destined for a second term. What went wrong?

Johnson's presidency was destroyed by the war in Vietnam. George Bush eventually confronted a candidate from the same constituency that had repudiated LBJ in 1968, only for it to see Richard Nixon elected and the war continue for a further five years. In these terms, what was the nature of Clinton's challenge to Bush in 1992? For E.L. Doctorow it had a symbolic significance that stemmed from America's experience in South-East Asia.

> Mr. Clinton's dissenting actions during the Vietnam War place him at the head of the dark and threatening coalition of faux Americans. He is, finally, the treacherous son who dares oppose the father. As far as Mr. Bush and his backers are concerned, when the young people of this country rejected the war in Vietnam, they gave up their generational right of succession to primacy and power. They could no longer be trusted[42].

So might the election campaign of 1992 be seen in this sense as another referendum on the Vietnam War?

On May 1 1970, Richard Nixon, having authorised military operations in Cambodia, made some impromptu remarks at the Pentagon. Anti-war protestors were: 'these bums ...blowing up campuses. Listen, the boys that are on the college campuses today are the luckiest people in the world, going to the greatest universities, and here they are burning up the books, I mean storming around about this issue...' On the other hand, in Vietnam, 'we've got kids who are just doing their duty ...when it really comes down to it, they stand up and, boy, you have to talk up to those men'[43]. In that same year George Bush was running for election to the Senate from his adopted state of Texas. Nixon would campaign for him, and, after his protege's defeat, would appoint him ambassador to the United Nations. Bill Clinton was then a Rhodes scholar at Oxford, and had become involved in demonstrations against the Vietnam War.

In Nixon's demonology, the 1992 presidential election pitted a 'kid' against a 'bum'. Bush had done his duty as the youngest American naval pilot in the second world war. He would have been on the side of

Nixon's angels in 1970. But Clinton had committed the generational heresy: he had doubted America's mission. In 1992, Bush disinterred those memories of conflict, not simply between generations but within 'the Vietnam generation' of which Clinton was a member. He tried to make personal conduct during the conflict in South-East Asia a litmus test of presidential 'character'. If 'Desert Storm' truly had completed the revisionist process in reconstructing popular perceptions of the Vietnam War as a 'noble cause', he might have made the charge stick. But the lingering doubts about the nature of Bush's victory in the Gulf, and the superficiality of his analysis of anti-war feeling during America's involvement in Vietnam combined to undercut the political force of his accusation.

When George Bush seized upon the rhetoric of revisionism to attack Clinton's patriotism, his argument, like his earlier claim that the 'Vietnam syndrome' had been finally overcome by military success in the Gulf, was tested and found wanting. Already beset by domestic troubles during the re-election campaign, the President's attempt to re-invent the memories of the war that had sundered the nation seemed to be almost a final act of political despair. Clinton's conduct during the Vietnam War recalled the dilemmas faced by many of his generation, for whom the political and moral ambiguities of America's involvement in South-East Asia were indeed divisive issues that subsequent revisionist arguments might not easily resolve. Bush's simplistic accusations made little impact on popular opinion.

E.L. Doctorow argues that 'all the Presidents since Vietnam, from Nixon to Bush, have been of the same World War II generation. They will not be moved. The thrust of their government has been, punitively, to teach us the error of our ways, to put things back to the time when people stayed in their place and owed their souls to the company store'[44]. In 1992, this revisionist message no longer worked. Clinton managed to pre-empt the domestic political agenda - it was indeed 'the economy, stupid' which proved to be at issue. But Bush's electoral defeat also represented a transfer of power to one of the 'Vietnam generation'. It was a watershed not only for the liberal interventionist architects of Cold War American foreign policy, but also for the conservative revisionists who had sought to excuse defeat in the aftermath of Vietnam.

Their Cold War was already officially over. At the beginning of that era of sublime international tension, the Department of War had been renamed the Department of Defense. Such an alteration of title did not imply necessarily a change in purpose. But the use of different language does have an implication for the ways in which reality is perceived and expressed. During the 1960s and 1970s, that same Department of

Defense prosecuted a war in South-East Asia. What was the nature of that conflict? According to Noam Chomsky it continues to be hidden. 'No journalist, no intellectual, no writer can simply express the truth that the United States attacked South Vietnam. That's inexpressable'[45].

In similar fashion, the history of America's defeat in that war was manipulated by the language of revisionism. The need to overcome the 'Vietnam syndrome' was the expression of an agreement urged upon Americans in the 1980s that their failure had been their fault. The chance to confront that version of the past was presented to the nation after Iraq's invasion of Kuwait. Yet the Gulf War, in its own aftermath, revealed the contradiction between self-congratulatory rhetoric and political fact. Swift success brought ephemeral gains, as long as Saddam Hussein remained in power.

In 1991, therefore, George Bush made a claim for his victory over Iraq which, in the afterglow of 'Desert Storm', his policy effectively undermined. He would not commit America to an open-ended war against Hussein, much less involve the nation in Iraq's internal civil conflict. The metaphor of Vietnam, the country as 'quagmire', might have been re-invented in Iraq if America had become involved in a desert 'quicksand'. But the message would have remained the same. The 'syndrome' still counselled against prolonged overseas adventurism. While he was telling Americans that success in the Gulf atoned for America's failure in Vietnam, Bush's inaction was creating his 'credibility gap'. The following year, during his re-election campaign, he offered such a strained interpretation of American attitudes towards Vietnam in the 1960s that he failed to convince many with his argument that opposition to the war then had been an unpatriotic cause. Revisionist ideas must remain plausible. Taken too far, they can exhaust belief.

The extent to which revisionism thus embodied an inability to admit reality suggests why it was unable to cure its own creation: the complex psychological obstacle of the 'Vietnam syndrome'. Instead the earlier and more simple formulation of restraint, Vietnam as a reminder of the possible outcome of involvement overseas, remained as a political refrain. As George Herring observes, 'Vietnam should stand as an enduring testament to the pitfalls of interventionism and the limits of power, something to keep in mind after the deceptively easy military victory in the Persian Gulf'[46]. The revisionism of the Reagan and Bush years confronted a tortuous and complicated version of the 'Vietnam syndrome'. And yet, in his conduct after the conflict in the Middle-East, and in his comments on Clinton's 'character' during the 1992 campaign, it was Bush himself who finally gave the lie to the idea that the Gulf War had in some way erased fears of 'another Vietnam', and had transformed memories of American involvement in South-East Asia.

George Bush might be excused his mistakes. For during the 1980s, revisionist political and military explanations of America's failure in South-East Asia had retained a certain popular political resonance. Such ideas indulged the nation's capacity for self-delusion. And for many in America, wish-fulfilment was a comfortable psychological tactic for interpreting the nation's past. As the first member of the 'Vietnam generation' occupies the White House, the alternative is more challenging. To move beyond revisionism, to understand the legacy of the Vietnam War, rather than simply to try and overcome its surrogate 'syndrome', would be to accept the need for more strategic confrontations with history, reality and truth.

Notes

1. Herring, G. (1991), 'America and Vietnam: The Unending War', *Foreign Affairs*, vol. 70, no. 5, pp. 104-19, p. 104.
2. Bush's speech of 1 March 1991 where he claimed America had 'kicked the Vietnam syndrome' has been widely cited. See *Congressional Quarterly Weekly Report*, (1991), vol. 49, no. 9, p. 549, 2 March.
3. Klare, M. (1981), *Beyond the Vietnam Syndrome*, Institute for Policy Studies, Washington D.C., p. 1.
4. Quoted ibid. p. 23.
5. See Williams, W.A. (1980), *Empire as a Way of Life*, Oxford University Press, Oxford.
6. Vlastos, S. (1991), 'America's "Enemy": the Absent Presence in Revisionist Vietnam War History' in Rowe, J.C. and Berg, R. (eds.), *The Vietnam War and American Culture*, Columbia University Press, New York pps. 67 & 69.
7. Quoted in Klare, *Beyond the Vietnam Syndrome*, p. 13.
8. Summers, H. (1981), *On Strategy: The Vietnam War in Context*, US Army War College, Pennsylvania. The description is from Knockton, Jack (1991), 'Vietnamese Social Conflict and the Vietnam War', in Melling, P. and Roper, J. (eds.), *America, France and Vietnam: Cultural History and Ideas of Conflict*, Avebury, Aldershot, p. 109.
9. Chomsky, Noam (1992), interviewed by John Pilger on BBC2, *Late Show*, November.
10. Schlesinger jr., Arthur (1969), *The Bitter Heritage: Vietnam and American Diplomacy 1941-68*, Houghton Mifflin, Boston, p. 48.
11. Pilger, J. (1992), 'New Age Imperialism' in *Distant Voices*, Vintage, London, p. 107.
12. Muller, R., quoted in MacPherson, M. (1985), *Long Time Passing: Vietnam and the Haunted Generation*, Signet, New York, p. 725.
13. Lam, A. (1990), 'My Vietnam, My America', *Nation*, p. 724, 10 December.
14. Kaldor, M. (1986), 'Introduction' in Thompson, E.P., Kaldor, M. et al., *Mad Dogs: The US Raids on Libya*, Pluto Press, London, p. 10.
15. Schwarzkopf, H. N. (1992), *It Doesn't Take a Hero*, Bantam Press extract in *The Sunday Times*, 11 October, 1992.
16. Westmoreland, William, in Hearden, P.J. (ed.) (1990), *Vietnam: Four American Perspectives*, Purdue University Press, Indiana p. 45.

17. Wallerstein, I. (1987), 'The Reagan Non-Revolution, or the Limited Choices of the US', *Millenium: Journal of International Studies*, vol. 16, no. 3, pp. 467-72, p. 472, Winter.
18. De Mause, L. (1991), 'The Gulf War as Mental Disorder', *Nation*, 11 March.
19. Ibid. p. 304.
20. Herr, M. (1987), *Dispatches*, Picador, London, p. 195.
21. Hosenball, M. (1992), 'The Odd Couple', *New Republic*, p. 27 & p. 35, 1 June.
22. Pilger, 'Sins of Omission', in *Distant Voices*, p. 89.
23. Omestad, T. (1992-3), 'Why Bush Lost', *Foreign Policy*, no. 89, pp. 70-81, p. 71, Winter.
24. Pilger, 'Turkey Shoots', in *Distant Voices*, p. 105.
25. Freedman, L. & Karsh, E. (1991), 'How Kuwait Was Won: Strategy in the Gulf War', *International Security*, vol. 16, no. 2, pp. 5-41, pp. 15-16, Fall.
26. Vlastos, 'America's Enemy', p. 69.
27. Schwarzkopf, (1992), *It Doesn't Take a Hero*, extract in *The Sunday Times*, 4 October.
28. Chomsky interview, BBC2 *Late Show*.
29. Berman, L. & Jentleson, B. (1991), 'Bush and the Post-Cold-War World: New Challenges for American Leadership', in Campbell, C. & Rockman, B. (eds.), *The Bush Presidency: First Appraisals*, Chatham House, New Jersey, p. 116.
30. Klare, M. (1991), 'The Peace Movement's Next Steps', *Nation*, p. 361, 25 March.
31. Cited in Ottosen, R. (1992), 'The Media and the Gulf War Reporting: Advertising for the Arms Industry?', *Bulletin of Peace Proposals*, vol. 23, no.1, pp. 71-83, p. 77, March.
32. Ibid. pp. 77-8.
33. Mary Mander of the *Christian Science Monitor*, and Stig Nohrstedt quoted ibid. p. 78.
34. Quoted by Pilger, 'Liberal Triumphalism', in *Distant Voices*, pp. 117-18.
35. Talbott, S. (1992), 'Post-Victory Blues', *Foreign Affairs*, vol. 71, no. 1, pp. 53-69, p. 69.
36. Olmestad, 'Why Bush Lost', pp. 71-72.
37. Talbott, 'Post-Victory Blues', pp. 59 & 55.
38. Herring, 'America and Vietnam: The Unending War', p. 104.
39. Ashdown, P. (1992), review of Schwarzkopf, *It Doesn't Take a Hero*, *The Sunday Times*, 25 October.
40. Indyk, M. (1992), 'Watershed in the Middle East'. *Foreign Affairs*,

vol. 71, no. 1, pp. 70-93, p. 85.
41. *Congressional Quarterly Weekly Report*, (1991), vol. 49. no. 10. p. 584, 9 March.
42. Doctorow, E.L. (1992), 'The Character of Presidents', *Nation*, p. 535, 9 November.
43. Quoted in Ambrose, S. (1989), *Nixon: The Triumph of a Politician*, Simon & Schuster, New York, p. 348.
44. Doctorow, 'The Character of Presidents', p. 535.
45. Chomsky interview, BBC2 *Late Show*.
46. Herring, 'America and Vietnam: The Unending War', p. 119.

4 The US Congress and the Gulf War

John Dumbrell

Although the US Congress alone has the constitutional authority (under Article I, Section 8) to declare war, only five wars in American history have actually formally been declared. The 1991 Gulf War was no exception. Modern deference to executive crisis management and the Congressional fear of appearing unpatriotic have mitigated against effective use of the legislative war power. With regard to the Korean War (1950-1953), President Truman declined to ask for a Congressional resolution authorising force, even after the event. In Vietnam, the legislature in effect abdicated its authority in the 1964 Gulf of Tonkin resolution. The War Powers Resolution and Act (1973 and 1974) attempted to redress the balance and prevent a replay of Vietnam. Yet it failed to restrain the executive in episodes such as the 1975 *Mayaguez* incident, Jimmy Carter's 1980 Iranian hostage rescue mission, the 1983 Grenada and 1989 Panama invasions.[1] To some degree the ineffectiveness of the War Powers Act is traceable to the inherent ambiguities of some of its clauses - the problem, for example, of how to define 'hostilities'. More crucial, however, has been the lack of institutional will on Capitol Hill. As Senator Jacob Javits described his own position during the *Mayaguez* crisis : 'The overwhelming temptation is to wait and see..., to let the President take the lead, postponing criticism and opposition until the dust has settled.'[2]

In some respects, legislative attitudes towards the Gulf conflict evidenced greater awareness of the responsibility of Congress to provide a democratic check on executive war-making powers than at any time since World War II. After all, the January 1991, Capitol Hill debate on President Bush's use of force authorization represented the first direct legislative consideration of such a request since Pearl Harbour. Some commentators concluded that the ending of the Cold War had opened new democratic opportunities. Writing for *Congressional Quarterly*, Pamela Fessler considered the debate 'an almost idealized image of how Congress should work'. William C. Olson described a level of debate that was 'extraordinary in its insight, knowledge, conviction and sincerity'.[3] The January debate indeed was an extraordinary Congressional occasion, with a wide and sophisticated array of opinions on public display. Yet closer examination of the legislative role in the Gulf crisis and combat reveals not a newly revived democratic control of foreign policy, but rather the ascendancy of the war-making executive in the new, post-Cold War environment.

Before the invasion

America's 'tilt' towards Iraq, itself engaged between 1980 and 1988 in the First Gulf War against Iran, commenced in the early Reagan years. (It has even been alleged, though denied by National Security Adviser Zbigniew Brzezinski, that in September 1980, in the last months of the Carter Administration, the US encouraged Iraq to invade its Eastern neighbour). In 1982, Iraq was removed from an official State Department list of nations furthering state terrorism. In November 1984, full diplomatic relations - broken off in 1967 - were restored with Iraq.[4]

Many members of Congress shared the Reagan Administration's desire to see Iran, viewed as the standard bearer for anti-Western Islamic fundamentalism, defeated. However, the tilt towards Iraq did offend two significant factions on Capitol Hill: the pro-Israeli and human rights lobbies. The former lobby has long been recognised as one of the best organised of all foreign policy legislative pressure groups, while human rights organisations - though no longer enjoying the strength which accrued to them in the immediate post-Vietnam era - still commanded attention in Congress.[5] Representative Jonathan Bingham (Democrat from New York) protested the Administration's 1982 dropping of export controls to Iraq, Syria and South Yemen in the following terms:

> I think it's a shocking example of the hypocrisy involved in their

claim that they're really putting terrorism as a matter of top priority. In this case, they're putting profits for business first.[6]

Four Senators (Democrats Paul Tsongas and Edward Kennedy, and Republicans Rudy Boschwitz and Larry Pressler) introduced legislation designed to restore Iraq to the list of terroristic states. Yet trade expanded. Farm sales were supported by loans made through the US Commodity Credit Corporation and, by 1989, reached the level of approximately one billion dollars. Overall US trade with Iraq (including high technology transfers) amounted to 3.6 billion dollars by 1989.[7]

By the late 1980s some Members were seeking to subject these burgeoning trade networks to closer scrutiny. Congressional unease was intensified by at least four related developments: President Reagan's 1987 decision to allow Kuwaiti oil tankers in the Persian Gulf to sail under the American flag; the use by Iraq of chemical weapons against Kurdish separatists in 1988; 1989 investigations about loans made to Iraq by the Atlanta branch of an Italian bank; and growing legislative suspicions that the US was actually supplying military aid and equipment to Iraq.

During 1987, both houses of Congress voted to delay the re-flagging policy. (Kuwait was allied with Iraq in the First Gulf War, with re-flagging being intended to deter Iranian attacks.) Reagan's action in the Gulf also provoked a lawsuit, brought by 110 members of the House and designed to trigger the war powers legislation. (Under the War Powers Act, the President must withdraw military personnel within 60 - or, in special circumstances, 90 - days in the absence of specific Congressional authorization of their deployment.) Such challenges lapsed, however, in the face of arguments for executive discretion. During the 1987 Gulf debate Senator John McCain, Republican from Arizona, identified the central mistake of the War Powers Act as 'the idea that Congress should have control over tactical military decisions'.[8] The Congressional challenge to the Administration's alliance of convenience with Baghdad shifted to issues regarding Iraqi use of chemical weapons. In September 1988, following Saddam Hussein's chemical weapons assault on Kurdish insurgents, the Senate voted to cut off all US aid to Iraq, including loan credits. Administration pressure on the House was successful in derailing this initiative. However, between January 1989 and July 1990 Congress and White House engaged in a prolonged conflict over sanctions towards Iraq. The Bush Administration succeeded in deflecting calls for mandatory sanctions, though credit to Iraq was temporarily suspended in November 1989 following investigations into the activities of the Atlanta branch of Banca Internationale del Lavoro. Further credit restrictions were passed by both houses in July 1990, immediately prior to Iraq's invasion of Kuwait. The sanctions debate witnessed a mobilisation of members representing US farming interests. An amendment offered by Congressman Doug Bereuter succeeded in allowing the Secretary of Agriculture to ignore the credit restrictions if they were seen to have 'a negative impact greater upon American farmers' than upon the country violating human rights. A similar motion was defeated in the Senate, which passed a wide-ranging sanctions bill.[9]

The pre-invasion sanctions soon became inoperative, with stronger measures being adopted after the August 2 Iraqi incursion into Kuwait. As President Bush moved towards his new Gulf policy, however, he faced a legacy of Congressional suspicion in this area. In the July 1990 debate, for example, Republican Senator William Cohen of Maine requested:

> When are we going to start exercising some moral leadership in this country, saying that we are not going to support nations like Iraq that engage in acts of terrorism, that engage in the use of chemical weapons, that engage in the attempt to intimidate their neighbors who supported them during the war against Iran?[10]

Major Congressional investigations - for example those conducted by the House Banking Committee chaired by Henry Gonzalez - into Administration involvement in arms transfers to Iraq in the 1980s were actually begun prior to the August 1990 invasion.

Desert Shield

President Bush's post-invasion sanctions won immediate support on Capitol Hill, though some legislators persisted with complaints about what Senator Alfonse D'Amato of New York described as the longstanding State Department 'mollycoddling' of Saddam. Mass US troop commitment to the Gulf took place with Congress in recess. Bush's formal notification of the deployment studiously avoided the implication that American forces were in 'imminent' danger under the terms of the war powers legislation.[11]

Both the fact that Congress was in recess at the outset of Desert Shield, and the imminence of the 1990 Congressional midterm elections, worked to strengthen the Presidential hand. Defence Secretary Richard Cheney openly acknowledged to *The Washington Post* that it was 'an advantage that Congress was out of town'. An August 28 briefing for 150 Members provoked some worries that the Administration was acting too much on its own, but clearly illustrated that Congressional leaders were prepared to accept the White House lead. Similarly, when Secretary of State James Baker eventually appeared before the House Foreign Affairs and Senate Foreign Relations Committees in early September, he presented Desert Shield as a *fait accompli* and received only mild criticism for not keeping Congress better informed. Members were aware of criticism being turned against them in the upcoming election races. (In Oregon, for example, Republican Congressman Denny Smith berated his opponent for warning against military action. A radio advertisement featured the voice of Adolf Hitler, with Smith intoning that 'appeasement is wrong'.)[12]

Nevertheless, important rifts and differences in emphasis between the executive and legislative branches did become obvious in the later months of 1990. Questions continued to be raised about US - Iraqi relations before the invasion. Senator Bob Kerrey of Nebraska pointed, for example, to supposed encouragement given to Saddam by US Ambassador April Glaspie: 'a clear message that...it might be OK if he took a little bit of Kuwait...'[13] Members consistently voiced apprehensions about the safety of American citizens in Iraq, about the need for greater allied burden sharing and about the probable shallowness of the public's commitment to Dessert Shield. In November, for example, Senator Cohen, invoked Mark Twain's remark that a man might fight to defend his home, but not a boardinghouse:

> Right now, the American people are not persuaded that Kuwait is in fact our home, or Saudi Arabia's our home, but rather the equivalent of the boardinghouse...Why are we willing to die for the Kuwaitis at this moment?[14]

Many legislators urged that Bush ensure that Arab nations be included in the anti-Saddam alliance. However, the plan to cancel 6.7 billion dollars in Egyptian debt, though eventually approved, provoked severe criticism. Pro-Israeli forces urged that Israel's 4.6 billion debt also be forgiven, while many Members questioned the wisdom of supplying arms to Saudi Arabia. It was pointed out that such arms might one day be turned against Israel; unsuccessful efforts were made to excise advanced weapons (such as multiple launch rocket systems) from the Saudi military package. Attention was drawn to the poor human rights record of America's Syrian ally. On December 6, Democratic Congressman Sam Gejdenson told Baker that his description of Saddam as a new Hitler could 'with the exception of one or two small details...easily be laid at the feet of...President Assad' of Syria. Even more ominously for the Administration, indications soon began to emerge of an alliance between doubters on the liberal and conservative wings of Congress. Republican

Congressman R.K.Dornan of California declared:

> Americans don't die for princes, sultans and emirs. It will only be a matter of time before Republicans ask why American boys are fighting to defend one monarchy and restore another.[15]

(The Vietnam years had also seem signs of an unholy convergence between rightist-isolationist and leftist/anti-imperialist critiques of the war.)[16]

Underpinning Congressional anxieties were two central concerns: firstly, the debate about whether Desert Shield was an operation designed to secure access to oil, rather than to pursue international justice and a new world order; and secondly, the fear that Congress was, as in Vietnam, in the process of abdicating its constitutional responsibilities. Bush's invocations of the new world order and concern to operate under the auspices of the United Nations gained wide support on Capitol Hill. However, legislative voices were also insistent that the real issue - for good or ill - was oil. John McCain begged America to 'have no illusions'. In 'another part of the world, we would not see this response'.[17]

The Gulf now began to replace the annual budget battle as the main source of executive-legislative tension. From September 1990, the issue of whether and how Congress should move to pass an enabling resolution dominated the Desert Shield debate. The executive managers themselves differed markedly over the advisability of seeking such a resolution. (Secretary Cheney swiftly concluded that the White House should proceed with a minimum of Congressional interference. Colin Powell, chairman of the Joint Chiefs of Staff (JCS), tended to favour the security of a legislative resolution.)[18] Non-binding resolutions were passed by both House (380-29) and Senate (96-3) in early October. Hovering over these debates were the spectre of Vietnam, notably of the 1964 Gulf of Tonkin resolution, and the desire to proceed without contravening the war powers legislation. In effect, the resolutions omitted references to the War Powers Act and embodied a general approval of Desert Shield, while also emphasising the need to avoid excessive reliance on purely military solutions. House and Senate leaders emphasised that the resolutions did not constitute a 'blank check' on the Gulf of Tonkin model.

As Congress moved towards its election recess, the war powers issue loomed ever larger. Senate Majority leader George Mitchell held that only Congress could declare war, and that the President must convene a special legislative session if conflict appeared 'imminent' under the War Powers Act. James Baker consistently held that the Administration could not be bound by requirements of prior Congressional approval for going to war. Newly insistent legislative protest followed Bush's November 8 announcement - two days after election day - of a doubling of the number of American troops in the Gulf. Previously supportive elements in Congress began to claim that the sanctions option had now, in effect, been abandoned without any consultation with lawmakers. A group of Democratic Congressmen filed a lawsuit under the War Powers Act to prevent Bush pursuing the war option without legislative approval. (On December 13, US District Judge H.H. Greene declared the suit premature.) Intensive White House lobbying emphasised the degree to which Baghdad was enjoying these Congressional dissensions. Both George Mitchell and House Speaker Thomas Foley were personally persuaded by Bush to the view that the Administration had not become irrevocably committed to war.[19]

At this juncture, with even the previously supportive House Armed Services Committee chairman Les Aspin voicing disquiet, attention turned to hearings held under the auspices of Senator Sam Nunn's Senate Armed Services Committee. Nunn promised a full-scale review of policy. Memories were kindled of Senator Fulbright's various hearings on Vietnam in the 1960s. A succession of witnesses testified to the costliness and unpredictable outcome of war. Former JCS chairman William Crowe testified that the issue was 'not whether an embargo will work', but rather 'whether we have the patience to let it take effect'. Nunn chided Cheney to the effect that, if there were a war, no-one would ever know if sanctions would have worked.[20] Aspin's committee held similar hearings in mid-December. The House Armed Services Committee chairman accused Cheney of having, at the time of the November troop buildup been, 'committed to the notion of bringing this thing to a head early on'.[21] By December 4, the House Democratic caucus resolved that, unless American lives were directly threatened, the President must seek Congressional approval before launching an attack.

The war debate of January 1991

The very early days of 1991 saw vigorous Congressional assertion of its constitutional prerogatives. House Majority Leader Richard Gephardt spoke of the possibility of Congress cutting off funds for an undeclared war. In the face of such assertions, President Bush submitted a formal request on January 8 for Congressional authority to use force. His letter - the first such request since 1964 - carefully avoided any suggestions that such authority was constitutionally or legally necessary. Its purpose was rather, according to the President and the GOP leadership in Congress, to send the strongest possible signal to the Iraqi leadership. As the United Nations deadline for withdrawal of January 15 approached, Senate Minority Leader Bob Dole argued that the 'best hope of peace' lay in a strengthening of the President's hand.[22]

In essence, Dole's argument carried the day. Most Congressional Democrats supported alternative resolutions, calling for further persistence with sanctions. However, enough Democrats supported the President's request - formally submitted in the form of a resolution on the second day of the debate, when the weight of legislative opinion had become clear - for it to be carried: 52-47 in the Senate and 250-183 in the House.

Supporters of President Bush in the Senate argued that in a crisis such as this the legislature must be seen to support the White House. Senator Al Gore, the only prospective candidate for the Democratic nomination in 1992 to back Bush, criticised the President's unilateral raising of troop levels in November but argued that the executive should now be given authority to use force. The debate about Congressional war powers was, according to Gore, best postponed 'for another day'. The President needed to be supported here and now against an Iraqi leader who 'has more troops than Hitler did in the early days of World War II'. Gore argued that this was no replay of the 1964 Gulf of Tonkin resolution, where there had been clear deception on the executive's part. To Republican Senator Malcolm Wallop, Congress was not fit to make Gulf policy in any case:

> Regrettably Congress, the modern Congress, is designed to evade its responsibilities...Is there any wonder that the executive branch refuses to relinquish its powers to such a body?

Several pro-Bush Senators spoke of the allied action against Iraq as an exemplar for the new world order. Democrat Joseph Lieberman of Connecticut considered it 'a moment of extraordinary opportunity for the United Nations and the rule of law in the world'. Republican Warren Rudman of New Hampshire identified the 'stakes involved here' as 'nothing less than the creation of a new international security framework'. The failures of the League of Nations to halt international aggression must not be repeated. Senator McCain admitted that the US was bearing the major share of the burden in the Gulf, but looked forward to a better future:

> ...We are in a time of transition to a new world order ...Hopefully, when the next crisis arises, and unfortunately there will be one, we can expect a greater participation on the part of our allies.

Other Senators pointed more directly to the threat posed by Saddam to the world's oil supplies - a threat magnified by his closeness to acquiring nuclear capability. Senator Coates (Republican: Indiana) noted:

> If Iraq were to gain permanent control of Kuwait's oil supply, Saddam Hussein would control 22 percent of the worldwide proven oil reserves and he would be a neighbor to an additional 49 percent in Saudi Arabia and other Gulf countries.

Republican D'Amato of New York considered Iraq capable of developing 'a crude nuclear device within a few months'.[23]

Senate supporters of persisting with sanctions tended to dwell on the horrific costs of war and on the need for Congress to avoid abdicating its authority. According to Senator Boren (Democrat: Oklahoma), sanctions *were* working -though the US might also consider 'taking out by air strikes certain key facilities...' Boren opposed the force authorization resolution primarily on the grounds - echoed by many other Senators - that war would create uncontrollable 'power vacuums...in the Middle East'. Joseph Biden of Delaware offered a rigorous rebuttal of pro-war arguments. War would be likely to interrupt further rather than guarantee, the flow of oil. War would lead to anarchy in the Middle East, with appalling environmental and security implications. As for the new world order, Biden argued that it was a case of America leading, with Europe and Japan being 'content to hold our coats':

> Let us stop to consider the effect on the American people of a perception that the 'new world order' will be one wherein we are the world's policeman, shedding our blood and treasure to stop aggression around the globe.

Senator Nunn spoke eloquently of the uncertainties of war and the failure of the Administration to consider the effects of war on international terrorism and anti-Western Islamic fundamentalism. Memories of Vietnam were continually invoked, with Senator Kerrey, a veteran of the earlier conflict, warning against precipitate action. Edward Kennedy forecast far more casualties - perhaps 3,000 a week - than in Vietnam. He continued:

> Not a single drop of American blood should be spilled because American automobiles burn too many drops of oil a mile.

Democratic Senator Ernest Hollings of South Carolina pointed to the putative hypocrisy underpinning the American position:

> The President likes to ride us all up about the wild man Saddam Hussein, saying that Saddam has attacked two of his neighbors in

the last 10 years. But that is exactly what the US has been condemned for in the United Nations in 1983, not by 12 votes as in the case of Resolution 678, but by 109 members of the United Nations condemning the United States for an act of aggression in Grenada, and by 75 votes...for an act of aggression in Panama.

Hollings pointed out that in Lithuania a 'parliamentary government' had recently been 'assaulted by naked aggression':

> Are we going to intervene to rescue Lithuania? Not a chance. Oh, Lithuania does not have oil.[24]

In the House debate, the force authorization resolution was co-sponsored by liberal Democrat Stephen Solarz. Arguing that the resolution represented a proper application of the constitutional responsibilities of Congress, Solarz represented a potentially powerful influence upon those Democrats who broadly supported the President but were anxious not to give up the legislature's prerogative. In one of the most poignant speeches in the debate, Speaker Foley, addressing the chamber from the well of the House, argued that a vote for the Solarz-Michel resolution was a vote for a Presidential war. Points familiar from the Senate debate were made. Republican Congressman Packard of California declared that the debate came 'down to one simple fact': the Iraqi leader 'will withdraw his troops...faster with a loaded and cocked gun' at his head. Congressman Thomas of Georgia held:

> ...this is not a war over oil...But the wealth that would flow from oil for years to come is what would transform Saddam Hussein from being just another petty tyrant into the unchecked commander of a nuclear arsenal.[25]

On the anti-Bush side, members concerned themselves with the war powers issue and with the apparent invidiousness of the President's new world order. Lee Hamilton, chairman of the House Foreign Affairs Committee, announced that the 'President's resolution means Congress gives up the right to decide'. Mary Oakar (Democrat:Ohio) argued, that irrespective 'of what the U.N. resolution says' it was 'the American people who are picking up the tab'. She forecast that a world war could result from the authorization of force in the Gulf. Democrat Gerald Klecza of Wisconsin described Solarz-Michel as 'a backdoor declaration of war'. Japan and Germany received the bulk of their oil from the Gulf, but 'none of their sons and daughters are at risk'. William Roth (Republican: Delaware) felt the only difference between the new and old world orders to be that 'American troops will die enforcing U.N.

resolutions' instead of 'enforcing our own unilateral policies'. Suspicion of multilateralist internationalism underlay the contribution to the debate from Democrat Gene Taylor, representing in South Mississippi one of the most conservative areas in the nation. Taylor excoriated those Members who 'travelled thousands of miles to investigate the wrongdoings in the Middle East' but would not 'raise a hand' in opposition to organised crime in the US. Anthony Beilenson (Democrat: California) argued that domestic education and health care reform were far more important to most Americans than affairs in the Gulf. Democrat Esteban Torres of California starkly enquired:

> Why should American men and women die in Kuwait and Iraq so that the multinational oil corporations continue to reap huge profits for Kuwaits (sic) who have not supplied soldiers in their own defense, while Americans may die to perpetuate a monarchy that has no commitment to democratic values?[26]

Bush was able to win the authorization of force votes largely because of the unwillingness of significant numbers of Democrats to oppose the Commander-in-Chief in such circumstances. Yet Democrats were severely divided. House Democrats were significantly more hawkish than their Senate colleagues. A widely noticed Democratic division was that among Jewish Members. (The six Jewish members of the California delegation, for example, split evenly on the votes). Congressman Henry Waxman, who opposed the use of force, said that he feared 'the political instability that could lead to even less U.S. leverage with Arab nations'.[27] As we have seen, opposition to the use of force was also not restricted to liberal Democrats. Key dissenters included Democrats with conservative roots, like Senator Hollings[28], as well as the anti-war Republican Senator Hatfield. The January votes did give President Bush the practical equivalent to a declaration of war. They did not guarantee him open-ended Congressional support in a protracted conflict.

Desert Storm

The conflict, of course, was not protracted and, between January 16 and Bush's triumphant March 6 appearance on Capitol Hill, Congress was firmly relegated to the sidelines. On January 17, the Senate passed a resolution of approval by 98-0; the House followed the next day, 399-6. During the conflict individual members did continue to raise the constitutional war powers issue, and also to urge the President against a precipitate ground war. Representative Ronald Dellums (Democrat:

California) consistently accused Bush of irresponsibility. Indeed, the most concerted opposition to the war came from the Congressional Black Caucus, of which Dellums was a leading member. (Of the twelve representatives who voted either 'present' or 'no' on January 18, ten were Black Caucus members.) African-American groups generally complained about the inevitability of black service personnel making up a high percentage of the war's casualties. Some women's groups also opposed action to defend Saudi Arabia, with its long history of restricting female rights.[29]

Nevertheless, at least before the liberation of Kuwait and the start of a new debate about what Bush should do next, Congress essentially backed the president. Resolutions were passed congratulating Israel for its forbearance and protesting Saddam's treatment of American prisoners-of-war. Senator Bob Kerrey, an early opponent of the use of force, took soundings about Saddam in his home state and concluded: 'People in Nebraska want this guy dead'.[30] It may nonetheless be surmised that the potentially fragile nature of Congressional support was an important factor behind Bush's decision to pull out quickly after the Kuwaiti liberation. (Senator Robert Byrd of West Virginia, for example, warned Bush against the US becoming the permanent 'Middle East riot squad').[31]

Congress did have important effects on Desert Shield and Desert Storm. Bush's December 1991 decision to send James Baker to Baghdad, for example, was certainly - at least at one level - an attempt to divert attention from the Nunn hearings.[32] At least during Desert Shield, Congress provided the focus for a sophisticated debate about war aims. Yet war was not formally declared and the War Powers Act remained under wraps. Executive domination of war-making in the post-Cold War era was intensified rather than challenged.

Notes

1. See e.g, Rystad, G. (1989), 'Who Makes War?', in Adams D. K. (ed.) *Studies in US Politics*, Manchester University Press, Manchester, pp. 49-77; Rubner, M. (1985-6), 'The Reagan Administration, the 1973 War Powers Resolution and the Invasion of Grenada', *Political Science Quarterly*, 100, pp. 627-47.
2. Javits, J. K. (1985), 'War Powers Reconsidered', *Foreign Affairs*, 64, pp. 130-40, 138; Koh, H. H. (1990), *The National Security Constitution*, Yale University Press, New Haven, pp. 123-33.
3. *Congressional Quarterly* (CQ) *Weekly Report*, (1991), p. 67, 12 January; Olson, W.C. (1991), 'The US Congress : An Independent Force in World Politics?', *International Affairs*, 67, pp. 547-63.
4. See Sick, G. (1991), *October Surprise*, I.B. Tauris, London, p. 106; *CQ Almanac* (1990), p. 722.
5. See, e.g., Tivnan, E. (1987), *The Lobby*, Simon and Schuster, New York; Forsythe, D. P. (1989), *Human Rights and U.S. Foreign Policy*, University of Florida Press, Gainsville.
6. *CQ Weekly Report*, (1982), p. 563, 13 March.
7. *CQ Almanac* (1990), p. 722.
8. *Congressional Digest*, (1987), 66, 'The War Powers Act and the Persian Gulf', p. 229.
9. *CQ Almanac* (1989), p. 501; (1990), p. 724.
10. *CQ Almanac* (1990), p. 724, see also Hiro, Dilip (1992), *Desert Shield to Desert Storm*, Paladin, London, p. 200; Timmerman, Kenneth (1992), *The Death Lobby -How The West Armed Iraq*, Fourth Estate, London.
11. *CQ Almanac* (1990), pp. 726-7.
12. *ibid.*, p. 736; Cohen, R. E. (1990), 'Back from Vacation, Joining the Choir', *National Journal*, p. 2150, 8 September.
13. *Congressional Record (CR)*, (1990), S14045, 27 September.
14. Cited in Woodward, Bob (1991), *The Commanders*, Simon and Schuster, New York, p. 339.
15. *CQ Almanac* (1990), pp. 728, 734, 740.
16. See, e.g., Holsti, O. R. (1974), 'The Study of International Politics Makes Strange Bedfellows', *American Political Science Review*, 68, pp. 217-42.
17. *CQ Almanac* (1990), p. 728.
18. See Woodward, *The Commanders*, pp. 355-6.
19. *CQ Almanac* (1990), p. 738.
20. *CR*, (1991), S340, (extracts from Nunn hearings), 12 January.
21. Hearings transcript, (1990) p. 2, 14 December.

22. *CR*, (1991), S366, 12 January.
23. *Ibid.*, S335; (1991), S272, 11 January; (1991), S377, 12 January; *ibid.*, S325; (1991), S232, 11 January; (1991), S363, 12 January; *ibid.*, S385.
24. *CR*, (1991), S332, 12 January; *ibid.*, S336; *ibid.*, S365; *ibid.*, S374; *ibid.*, S370; *ibid.*, S328.
25. *CR*, (1991), H444, 12 January; *ibid.*, H441; *ibid.*, H416; *ibid.*, H464.
26. *CR*, (1991), H406, 12 January; *ibid.*, H463; (1991), H243, 11 January; (1991), H161, 10 January; (1991), H340, 11 January; (1991), H439, 12 January; *ibid.*, H431.
27. Cited in Cohen, R.E. (1991), 'Another Gulf that Divided Democrats', *National Journal*, p. 176, 19 January.
28. Despite conservative roots in South Carolina, Hollings had cast votes against President Nixon in Vietnam and for President Carter over the Panama Canal.
29. See *CQ Almanac* (1991), p. 443; *CQ Weekly Report*, (1991), p. 17, 5 January.
30. *CQ Almanac* (1991), p. 447.
31. *Ibid.*, p. 450.
32. See Hiro, *Desert Shield to Desert Storm*, p. 267.

5 Burial party: The Gulf War as epilogue to the 1980s

Phil Melling

Iraq's real offence in the Gulf was that at a crucial moment in the decline and fall of the Soviet empire 'a small, non-white country', as Edward Said puts it, presented itself as a centre of influence in the Middle East and a source of resistance to Americanisation.[1] When Iraq took the lead in arguing the case for Palestinian autonomy and Arabic nationalism it threatened to steal the thunder of the United States at a time when, as George Bush put it, 'America's leadership was instrumental' in securing 'the triumph of democratic ideas' from Eastern Europe to Latin America. Iraq's invasion of Kuwait questioned the role of the United States as a moral and spiritual leader of the planet, (a role which the US had claimed as its own since colonial times) and its ability to fulfil, by way of errand, a divine appointment to rid the world of its sin, savagery and 'lawless aggression'.[2] Iraq disputed America's right to bear, what Herman Melville describes in *White Jacket*, as 'the ark of the liberties of the world'. Its action disturbed and 'rankled a suddenly energized super-nation imbued with fervour' and seeking to fulfil a compelling commission from God.[3]

Saddam Hussein had misunderstood the historical plot: the moral leadership of the planet was not up for grabs nor were divine errands of the West transferable to the Middle East. If Baathist imperialism was seeking to outdo the Islamic fundamentalism of Khomeni's Iran or Gaddhafi's Libya it ought never to believe it could seriously challenge the 'pre-eminent' position of the United States as the 'undisputed' champion of democratic values. The US was the guardian of new world belief, the one country all nations could 'trust', as President Bush put it, 'to be on the side of decency'.[4] For this reason the alliance that underpinned Operation Desert Storm was 'a community of conscience', a multinational task force designated to restore democracy and the rule of law to a country that had been the victim of 'aggressive totalitarianism'.[5]

The errand to 'assemble the forces of peace' was, of course, a pretext for restoring the credibility of the Protestant imperial mission, the errand in the wilderness that the war in Vietnam had done much to undermine.[6] As Edward Said tells us in his analysis of American journalistic and political debate on the eve of war, the Puritan legacy of errand and adventure remained a compelling memory for political and military supporters of intervention. When we read *Moby Dick*, says Said, we find it 'irresistible' not to 'extrapolate from the novel to the real world', and therein discover a version of American behaviour in which 'the American empire' prepares itself, like Ahab, 'to take after an imputed evil', and to embark upon some 'unexamined moral mission'. Since the mission in the wilderness is a Protestant expression of duty, those who resist the United States in the execution of that duty are bound to incur 'the wrath of a stern White Man, a kind of Puritan super-ego whose errand into the wilderness knows few boundaries and will go to very great lengths indeed to make his point'.[7] For this reason, a righteous egotism underlines many of Bush's pronouncements, especially his State of the Union Address of January 30, 1991, in which he remarked that 'The triumph of democratic ideas in Eastern Europe and Latin America - and the continuing struggle for freedom elsewhere around the world - all confirm the wisdom of our nation's founders'. Throughout his term of office George Bush frequently defined his intentions in a rhetoric, as Said puts it, of 'moralistic' piety and 'grandiose self-endowment'. Conscious of the fact that the original Puritan errand to civilize the wilderness had been grounded in metaphors of the visual and visionary Bush explained the need for military action in the Gulf by asking the American people to commit themselves to a 'purpose' 'higher than themselves', to fulfil the promise of 'renewal' that God's moral law and its enforcement makes possible.[8]

The biblical language that Bush used, with its emphasis on the celestial, invested the American act of intervention with the luminous purpose of the westerner as visionary. The Christian ideal was thus fulfilled for, as Charles L. Sanford tells us, in the journey patterns of scripture as well as the language of medieval church symbolism, the spiritual quest is traditionally known as a 'journey toward light'. According to this interpretation, if the bower of life is Paradise or the Celestial City, the original source of the bright beam is God, symbolized by the life-giving sun. The sun in medieval popular thought represents God's truth and righteousness, illuminating the dark corners of sin with His saving radiance in its solar cycle from East to West. The antithesis of perfection through illumination represents spiritual denial and the ignorance of those who live in darkness and perpetual sin.[9]

Satanic Centres: East and West

Throughout the 1980s successive Republican administrations defined the enemies of freedom as lovers of darkness. They did so in order to sustain a climate conducive to intervention. Presidents Reagan and Bush, for example, were able to justify their overt and covert support for the Contras of Nicaragua and the Salvadorian military by employing a number of 'rhetorical gambits', a sign language, says Harold Pinter, which inverted the 'structures of language and reality' through a medieval format.[10] When Reagan described the Contras - a gang of murderous abductors - as 'the moral equivalent of our Founding Fathers' and the Sandanistas Nicaragua as a 'Marxist-Leninist totalitarian dungeon' he hung a label of medieval repression around a government whose only crime was to assert its economic independence from the United States and to resist, by nationalistic and democratic means, the incursions of foreign capital and US based corporate investment. By creating the illusion that Nicaragua was a gothic wasteland in which innocent people and moral principles simply disappeared without trace, Reagan established a chain of causation in which Nicaragua was akin to those Third World countries - Iran, Lebanon, Vietnam and Eastern Europe - where things went missing every day of the week. Reagan fostered the belief, as did Bush, that the light of truth was always extinguished by the enemies of freedom. What he co-opted was a medieval principle which made the United States a 'shining' example of divine faith and reason, a land of visible promise which enabled those who lived in it to claim for themselves the status of most favoured nation in His celestial plan. To refuse the righteous an opportunity to illuminate the dark corners of sin was contrary to America's rendezvous with destiny and beyond her powers of spiritual tolerance. Those who extinguished the light of truth and professed themselves the enemies of America threatened to destroy that visionary gift bequeathed by God to the visible saints in Puritan New England. To obstruct that gift of vision was to deny the West its role in history, a role defined by Governor John Winthrop in 1630 on board the

Arbella as the construction of a New World city, a righteous metropolis whose appearance would glow henceforth with a 'shining purpose'.[11]

Throughout their Presidencies both Reagan and Bush sought to unearth, if not to invent, an array of enemies who appeared to resist the illuminating mission of the American state. In their dealings with Vietnam both Presidents projected themselves as tough but humane politicians who refused to establish diplomatic and commercial relations with the government of Hanoi until all political prisoners were freed from the re-education camps and outstanding questions about P.O.W.s and M.I.A.s were answered satisfactorily (until Vietnam was prepared, as *Newsweek* put it, to 'shed light' on the problem).[12] The subterfuge was effective. The publicity surrounding the P.O.W. and M.I.A. issue obscured the problems faced by the Vietnamese people in the aftermath of war and successfully undermined the legacy of Vietnam's military and ideological achievement. Vietnam was not only discredited by its inability to placate US public opinion, it was strategically undermined by the imposition of a trade embargo and its repeated exclusion from the I.M.F. and World Bank.

In his State of the Union address of January 29, 1992, President Bush congratulated the US on its willingness to seek out and expose the enemies of civilization, whether it be 'imperial communism' or Baathist nationalism. The task, said Bush, had been a divine duty unequivocally accepted by a country which had proved itself, by the end of Operation Desert Storm, 'the undisputed leader of the age'. America had confronted her adversaries, each of whom had identified themselves, said Bush, as the master practitioners of hostage taking. From Korea to Vietnam American soldiers had disappeared in pursuit of freedom. The liberation of Kuwait and the return of the 'last American hostages' to the United States had retrieved the memory of those lost in battle and had 'vindicated' the 'policies' that underwrote the act of sacrifice. With Hussein routed and the Cold War won the US had proved itself the dominant power in an age when 'changes' had occurred of 'almost biblical proportions'. Only the steadfastness of the nation's moral vision to defend freedom and democracy throughout the world - in Vietnam, Grenada, Libya, and Kuwait - had secured the eventual peace and upheld the 'idea of America' as the last best hope for mankind, the ultimate expression of human aspiration.[13]

Disremembering: from amnesia to revisionism

In the Bush and Reagan Presidencies the fate of the disappeared remained at the forefront of public attention. What was often kept secret, however, was the way in which the tactic of vanishing the enemy was co-opted both by the political and military establishment, and by large sections of the media. In the popular and political culture, media censorship, economic embargo and the use of violence were commonly used to overcome the nation's perceived opponents. The need to eliminate the memory of the 'other' (under the pretext that if you don't bury him he will bury you) became a central feature of the cultural politics of revisionism. Methods of disappearance included the use of cordon sanitaires, disinformation, as well as random displays of amnesia and deafness. An early example of what Toni Morrison calls 'disremembering' occurred when President Jimmy Carter informed the American people in the late 1970s that the payment of cultural reparations to the Vietnamese - the need, that is, to make amends for the death of three million people and the wounding of five - was wholly unnecessary. As he put it: 'we went to Vietnam without any desire to impose American will...I don't feel that we ought to apologize or to castigate ourselves...I don't feel that we owe a debt'.[14] Carter's remark psychologically prepared the American people for the language of deniability that characterised much of the 1980s and the idea, as Noam Chomsky puts it, that it's better, 'to avert our eyes' from the suffering for which 'we all share responsibility'. In the words of a senior associate of the Carnegie Foundation for International Peace the cause of reconciliation ought to be pursued by putting aside 'the agony of the Vietnam Experience' and 'the injuries of the past' and by striving to recover those American soldiers 'missing in action' in Vietnam's re-education camps. As Chomsky suggests: 'The slaughter of millions of Indochinese and the destruction of their countries' was 'far too slight a matter' to consider when compared with 'the domestic problems' that the M.I.A. issue still gave rise to in the United States.[15]

With the election of Ronald Reagan to the Presidency the ritualistic washing of hands and emptying of minds was formally adopted as a political requirement. Strategies of burial were integrated with strategies of renewal while the ethos of Puritan adventurism and errand, from Grenada to the Gulf, reappeared in the form of regeneration through violence. In the 1980s the desire to remove the legacy of failure overseas and to rehabilitate the status of the American errand reached psychotic proportions. Behind the bravado of the victorious Puritan George Bush there lay, in the aftermath of the Gulf, the insistent desperation of a committed amnesiac striving to wipe clean the memory of loss. 'This is a proud day for America', declared Bush immediately following the allied coalition's successful military conclusion to the Gulf War in 1991. 'By

God, we've kicked the Vietnam Syndrome once and for all'. The remark was 'greeted with ecstatic applause', says Philip Taylor.[16] The Gulf was a vindication not just of Vietnam, but of an entire Cold War thesis, a confirmation that history could be rewritten, wars refought and failures overturned through rapid demonstrations of military authority.

In spite of de Tocqueville's observation that when 'the past' ceases 'to throw light upon the future, the mind of man wanders in obscurity', the task of disinvesting the past took the form of a national obsession in the 1980s. 'We are the nation that believes in the future', said Bush. 'We are the nation that can shape the future'.[17] The trauma of recent history, it was believed, could best be avoided not by seeking reconciliation with Indo-China but by inventing wars that the US military could find enjoyable. In this way the aberrant tendencies of history could be overridden and the old verities and values reasserted with renewed vigour. Throughout his Presidency, says John Pilger, Ronald Reagan deepened the state of 'historical amnesia' within America, accelerated 'the obsolescence of truth' and the rate at which 'state propaganda' was 'transmuted into history'. The Gulf War, continues Pilger, was 'promoted as a "noble cause"', allowing thereby a reworking of history and the justification of 'other Gulfs' (revisionist policies in Latin America) as 'the basis for the "new world order"'.[18]

If, as one commentator has recently argued, 'Vietnam is a ghost not yet exorcized from America's political house', then it hasn't been for the want of trying. Republican administrations in the 1980s were determined, says Robert J. Mckeever, 'to revise the history of America's involvement in Vietnam'. Foreign policy was 'underpinned, not merely by the belief that the Vietnam War was both honourable and winnable', but that it was part of an ongoing global conflict that had yet to be concluded. Reagan and Bush presided 'over nothing less than an attempt to revive in even stronger form the very myths that were exposed as disastrous during the Vietnam War', says McKeever. They did so through a policy of military intervention and political adventurism in countries with populations smaller than five million: Grenada, Libya, Nicaragua and Panama, where the risk of failure and protracted involvement was minimal. In Central America Reagan and Bush played to the Cold War gallery. The struggle, said Patrick Buchanan, Reagan's Director of Communications was a 'simple one'. It came down to 'who wants Central America more - the East or the Warsaw Pact?'.

Central America was the symbolic centre piece of Reagan's foreign policy, 'the litmus test of the Reagan Doctrine', and a place where failure could be remedied and history reversed in 'a traditional sphere of influence'.[19] By winning a war 'without having to pay any price' the

United States, says Jonathan Schell, conducted a 'political pollster's dream'. The invasions of Panama and Grenada allowed 'a providential White House' to claim it had 'triumphed' over the forces of the antichrist, an 'objective that had eluded the policy-makers for more than a decade in Vietnam'.[20] By the end of the 80s, says Noam Chomsky, 'the sickly inhibition against the use of military force' appeared to have been dispelled by the use of what Reagan called his 'rescue mission'. The 'mood of jingoism' that finally came of age in the Gulf fulfilled the prediction made by Robert Tucker in 1980, that a 'resurgent America' would find expression in a more active and authoritarian foreign policy.[21]

Missing In Action

Outside as well as inside Central America the desire to plot the downfall of a Marxist or revolutionary antichrist remained a thing of enduring fascination in the political and popular culture of the United States. If revisionist historians like Norman Podhoretz, Timothy Lomperis and Gunter Lewy argued that the Vietnam War might well have been won, revisionist film makers tended to suggest that military victory might still be achieved on an issue of remaining mutual dispute. The missing-in-action of American solders in Vietnam provided rich material in the furtherance of that dispute and allowed the American public to return to Vietnam and wage war on its enemy as a legitimate pursuit. By exploiting the M.I.A. issue Hollywood could remove from public attention the tens of thousands of Vietnamese civilians who had disappeared as a result of US bombing raids. By identifying Vietnam as a country in which the use of enforced captivity and imprisonment without trial was a commonplace the M.I.A. film reawakened memories of the notorious detention centres like the Hanoi Hilton prison camp in which captured American airmen were imprisoned and held in solitary confinement during the war. The allegation that American soldiers were still alive in North Vietnam and held in obscure and degrading conditions gave the impression that Vietnam was a country where humanist principles had been disregarded and the articles of the Geneva Convention did not apply. In so doing it dramatically revived the mythology of Puritan New England and the cultural fantasies of the captivity narrative (the first expression of popular entertainment in colonial America) in which innocent settlers were abducted and imprisoned in godless villages and godfearing American families were split apart by the agents of Satan.

If the M.I.A. film cleverly exploited the Puritan fear of the black man in the forest it also showed the way in which the memory of his menace as an agent of disguise might best be overcome. In the person of Rambo the American warrior played the devil at his own game. Rambo's rescue mission was successful because he confronted the enemy with the skills the enemy did not expect: the American as Native American, the Green Beret as Navaho Indian, the soldier whose 'journey toward light' was proven, as Adi Wimmer puts it, by an 'almost messianic ability to endure pain'. Rambo was the 'praying Indian' and converted heathen redeemed by civilizing influences but who still possessed the hunting instincts of an alternative culture. In the figure of Rambo the hunter as proto-fascist, the American vigilante overcame his fear of the unreconstructed forest and stole 'if not, the magic of (his) enemy, at least his signs'.[22]

By usurping 'contemporary historiography' in films such as *Rambo*, *Uncommon Valor* and *Missing in Action I and II*, the US film industry, says John Pilger, removed attention from the memory of US genocide and laid the blame for the disappearance of innocent Americans squarely at the door of the Vietnamese. By projecting onto the Vietnamese the sin of international terrorism Hollywood offered the film-going public a convenient scapegoat for the problems of the age. Thus, at the very moment Jimmy Carter was wrestling with the hostage crisis in Iran, Hollywood was issuing *The Deer Hunter* (1978), a film that emphasises the Third World's obsession with hostage taking and reaches its climax 'during orgiastic scenes in which the American heroes (are) forced to play Russian roulette with their Vietnamese captors'.[23] *The Deer Hunter* gave the impression that the taking of hostages was a feature of those countries whose ideologies were politically opposed to that of the United States. This made sense in a world in which the problem of 'the disappeared' (Yossarian's phrase in *Catch 22*) had long haunted the twentieth century imagination. By the late 1970s hostage taking and political abduction as well as the random elimination of suspected political opponents had become a familiar feature of military dictatorships, neo-fascist regimes and nationalist movements from Chile to Entebbe, from Northern Ireland to Iran, from Beirut to Buenos Aires. In a political culture in which, as Jeff Walsh puts it, 'virtually all the world's peoples inhabit a terrorist culture either as producers or consumers of terrorism' Vietnam was portrayed as a centre of infamy and a source of inspiration for international opponents of cultural protestantism - from the Ayatollah to Hezbollah, from the hostage takers of the Middle East to the Marxist guerillas of Latin America.[24]

No one was more supportive of the need to exploit the M.I.A. issue than Ronald Reagan. Reagan raised the hopes of the families of missing veterans and repeatedly ignored his own Defence Intelligence Agency reports that suggested it was highly unlikely any Americans were left in Vietnam. When an American passenger aircraft was hijacked to Beirut in July 1985, Reagan announced: 'After seeing Rambo again last night I know what to do next time this happens'. A few months after giving the film his seal of approval Reagan was sending American aircraft to force down an Egyptian plane carrying Palestinian hijackers. American newspapers immediately began to refer to Reagan as 'Ronbo'.[25]

In the 1980s war was box-office, a homoerotic dream of the military in which risk-free sex was always possible through a rapid penetration of the enemy's defences. A character like Rambo did for America what America could not always do for itself. At the time that new hostages like Allen Steen, Terry Anderson and Joseph Cicipio were being captured in the Middle East, the idea of an America impotent to react was vigorously refuted by the film industry. Stallone's Rambo was the authentic Reaganite. He fought a low-intensity, low-risk conflict - swift, conclusive and highly symbolic. He endorsed the interventionist politics of the 1980s and served as an inspiration for US military activity in political troublespots like the Middle East. Not surprisingly the attack on Libya in 1986 by British-based American F-III's demonstrated a willingness on the part of the military to imitate Rambo's spontaneous aggression; to demonstrate, as Salman Rushdie puts it, 'the sexuality of the American male'.[26]

Capitalism and the last man

A need for dominance is reflected in what Susan Jeffords describes as the cultural remasculinisation of the United States in the 1980s. There is a strong correlation, for example, between the interventionism of the M.I.A. film in which opposition networks are easily penetrated by homoerotic western strength and the work of revisionist academics and journalists in which the collapse of ideological territory is attributed directly to the influence of a virile and penetrative capitalism. Capitalist promotion exercises formed the cornerstone of Republican orthodoxy in the 1980s. The Foreign Affairs Section of the 1991 Bush administration budget took as one of its central priorities the promotion of peace through 'a world system based on democratic government and market-oriented economies'. For Bush, the emergence of the free-market economy signalled the end of historical conflict as defined by the clash of rival ideologies. The resolution of history was confirmed by the progress of the United States and the history of what Francis Fukayama calls 'the last man'. A new world order beckoned, one governed by the processes of American modernism: industrialisation, the growth of cities, technological advance and the emergence of new cultural frontiers which appeared to free individuals from their old dependencies and bound them to new ones, such as a borderless, tariff-free, marketplace economy. The belief that modernisation came out of the logic of American conditions and also out of the logic of the American mind, the conviction that the United States represented the apex of cultural growth in modern civilization, that it had 'done the hard work of freedom' and led the world 'in facing down a threat to decency and humanity', these ideas received considerable support from the academic and journalistic professions.[27]

For the historian Francis Fukayama it is not so much the 'sexuality of the American male' but the sexuality of American capitalism that has spawned a new beginning in global history. If what we are living in, says Fukayama, is a world beyond history then the absence of ideology is also concurrent with the absence of prejudice and the release of a new consumer community. This is the age of redemption through capitalism, says Fukayama, an age in which the twentieth century has fulfilled itself as the American century, a century in which we have all been granted the Adamic opportunity to begin our lives all over again and seek out the freedom to trade. The link which Fukayama proposes between 'industrialisation', 'liberal democracy' and the power of increased consumption firmly establishes the American experiment in liberal democracy as 'the only legitimate ideology left in the world'. What the American model of historical progress holds out to Third World nations, says Fukayama, is a morality of enlightened rationalism infused with the dynamic of free-market economics. Democratic capitalism, he says, now represents the only effective 'ideology left in the world'. This ideology has been successfully exported by the US, especially to Southeast Asia and Latin America where the need for economic reconstruction has been heavily reliant on free market capital. East Asia and Latin America, says Fukayama, 'demonstrate that latecomers to the process of economic development are in no way disadvantaged, and in fact can achieve the highest levels of technology and consumption, provided they remain connected to world markets and permit free competition at home'.

In our post-historical landscape, says Fukayama, it has become abundantly clear that market forces and free competition will determine 'the strength of a nation's domestic base, and its ability to create decent and prosperous lives for its citizens'. What we are increasingly seeing, he argues, is not a world bifurcated 'along East-West lines, but...a post-historical and an historical part. Each part will play by a completely different set of rules: economics will dominate the former while military power will reign in the latter'.[28] In the democratic desire to appreciate the benefits of mass culture, says Fukayama, Marxism has suffered a terminal decline. The products of the marketplace and the benefits of mass culture offer the consumer, in the words of C.W.E. Bigsby, 'a model not merely of balance and completion but also of confident assurance - an assurance contained in the product itself and therefore projected on to those exposed to it'.[29] Richard Gott puts it more vigorously: it is, he says, the 'headlong rush towards capitalism' that has toppled and transformed most of the hard-line socialist regimes throughout the world.[30]

The idea of being born again as a consumer in the redemptive fire of American capitalism accords well with the idea that modernity is a thing of American definition. And if by modernity we mean, more specifically, the rationalisation of culture through commodity - a process for imposing hegemonic control through corporate management - then the market economy has become, in effect, a convenient way of re-articulating a 'born-again' myth. A myth, that is, of advanced capitalism rather than advanced Christianity, yet one, nevertheless, which owes its origins to the business metaphor that Winthrop employed on board the Arbella when he exhorted his colonists to build and exhibit a shining metropolis.

Moreover, if the world has recently been born again through its secular rather than spiritual convictions, the process of redemption has still been accompanied by a physical journey (what the Puritans referred to as an 'ocean crossing'). In East Germany the act of self transformation that accompanied the journey from one economic and ideological state to another involved a tearing down of walls, a symbolic act of physical passage from East to West through the Brandenberg gate. In this respect, says George Steiner, the lure of American consumer capitalism is the ultimate arbiter of democratic desire.

> American standards of dress, nourishment, locomotion, entertainment, housing are today the concrete utopia in revolutions. Video-cassettes, porno-cassettes, American-style cosmetics and fast foods, not editions of Mill, DeTocqueville or Solzhenitsyn, were the prizes snatched from every West Berlin shelf by the liberated. The new temples to liberty (the 1789 dream) will be McDonalds and Kentucky Fried chicken.[31]

The ideal of revolution for Steiner, is no longer an expression of political will - an event determined by ideological arousal - but a yearning for inertia, political impotence, social apathy, anti-intellectualism. As a bourgeois process, history becomes a thing of 'surface and superficiality', an event which surrenders its ideals and allegiances to the products of the marketplace, to a world where, as Karl

Jaspers has predicted, there is 'no continuity only past time'.

In the context of the late 1980s Fukayama's thesis is seductive. In the context of the 90s it is totally redundant. It encourages us to believe that 'the imagination is summoned by possibilities larger than any that have dominated creative life in the postwar world'. Freed from the confrontational debates of the past and the nightmare of imminent nuclear conflict memory, it says, is no longer necessary as a mechanism of protection in an adversarial world. This argument doesn't get us very far when considering an issue like Bosnia. In a world overrun with provincial conflict Fukayama's thesis looks in fact, distinctly specious. We still live, as Malcolm Bradbury puts it, 'in a time of rising uncertainties...developing hopes and estranging features, above all in a world that will not stay still'. A change of ideology or institutional practice has not brought with it a loss of memory or a discrediting of tradition. Memory has the wit to submerge itself, to lie dormant only to re-surface generations later in unexpected ways. As Iraq's invasion of Kuwait and the present Balkan conflict illustrates the free market economy has proved ineffective as a way of liberating Third World people from the ethnic and tribal tensions of history. 'Frontiers' are 'mysterious', says Bradbury, while 'borders fracture and re-form'. If we have been losing our parochialism, becoming more European and more global, we find that we do not know where the edges of our new Europe will lie, or what the coming shape of the larger globe will be. This tempts new philosophies, and it 'encourages new fundamentalisms'.[32]

The other central weakness of Fukayama's thesis is its willingness to over-promote the evolutionary potential of liberal capitalism and the extent of its indifference to economic imperialism. History does not happen of its own accord. Even where it does appear to have decided in favour of America we can not deny the legacy of the past or exonerate America from the sin of interventionism. The fact remains that in the 1970s and 1980s the United States deliberately set about recreating the world in its own image. During that period capitalism was both punitive and coercive. 'The role of the Third World within the Grand Area structure', says Chomsky, was 'to serve the needs of industrial sources', while the 'protection' of US corporate 'resources' was considered 'a major concern'. Throughout the period such was the degree of 'consensus' within 'the business community' that US economic policy toward the Third World was not interrupted or 'deterred' in any way by the military setback of Vietnam. On the contrary, the pre-requisites of American business interests still demanded that 'nationalistic regimes' be aggressively resisted in order to protect American assets and to maintain 'a climate conducive to private investment'. Alternative questions of principle - the moral right of a sovereign country to determine its economic future - 'rarely' arose, says Chomsky, and if they did they were pushed to one side, in order 'to protect and promote American investment and trade'. Just as America intervened in the Gulf on the basis of the Reagan doctrine to protect the supply of oil to the west, so, under the Monroe Doctrine, 'a right of intervention' was claimed in Central America against those governments which lacked 'elites responsive to US interests' and which proved themselves unwilling to regulate nationalistic movements by 'military' and oligarchic means.[33]

The glamourisation of sex and money and men with money - as well as the liaison between purchasing power, masculinity and the military ethic - was one of the principal mechanisms through which the United States attempted to overcome the debilitating effects of the Vietnam war, a war incidentally in which money, masculinity and military muscle had conspicuously failed to subdue what was often regarded in the United States as a poverty-stricken race of ideologues who lived on rice, looked like androgynes and wore black pyjamas. The power of money and the assertiveness of American products - together with the use of right-wing, virile spokesmen who worked alongside them - Stallone, Cruise, Connors, Schwarzenegger - were the promotional symbols of capitalist masculinity, key players in the psychic recovery of America in the eighties. The idea of a thrusting centralised authority - or an agent of authority - dispensing justice and legislating against pre-modern sources of resistance - always underwrote the imperial mood of the Reagan presidency.

Journalism and the political consensus

The virtuous penetration of socialist society and the sexual potency of American capitalism in Third World markets appealed to journalists across the political spectrum in the 1980s. Those who returned to Vietnam to examine the achievements of the Hanoi government frequently downplayed the element of coercion and the role that embargoes had played in bringing Vietnam economically to its knees. Instead they emphasised a failure of faith in Vietnam brought about, they claimed, under the burgeoning pressure of urban consumerism. In their articles the sins of US intervention tended to disappear in a fog of amnesia. The past was an 'aberration'. American military failure was irrelevant. What the future promised was the dominant march of evolutionary capitalism.[34]

The idea that Vietnam has 'caved in' to capitalism has been a constant theme in American journalism since 1985, the tenth anniversary of the fall of Saigon. For a *Time* correspondent of the mid 1980s capitalism has staged a remarkable comeback on the streets of Saigon. Vietnam is a 'pinched and hermetic land' and has suffered a disastrous collapse of confidence in the achievements of the Revolution. Market economics are on the march. So too is entrepreneurial ambition fuelled by the power of American popular culture:

> North and South, Coca-Cola is for sale, but the black market stalls of Ho Chi Minh City are packed with foreign goods: Spam and Tang, Zest and Lux, A & W root beer and Del Monte prunes, Remy Martin Cognac, Wilson tennis racquets and balls, Japanese TVs and calculators. Vietnamese are allowed to receive up to four packages each year from friends or kin abroad. Some families subsist exclusively from the sale of such foreign goods. 'One country, two systems', is the rueful, sloganized explanation for the North-South differences. Yet some of the cultural Westernism has filtered north. Cassette tapes of US pop music are played all over. More striking still, the rare US visitor is everywhere treated with respect and, frequently, spontaneous displays of affection.[35]

In exposing what he sees as the fallacy of ideological unification in 1990, the journalist Michael Fathers points to a collapse of national identity and a failure of political will and revolutionary belief in Vietnam.

> Don't laugh, but 1990 is The Year of the Tourist in Vietnam. Bang-bangs are over, Rambo is dead, re-education camps are being handed over to private enterprise, the tarts are back. The massage parlour is installed in government hotels, a floating five-star tin can has arrived from the Great Barrier Reef and is moored in the Saigon river; the disco is thriving.

The revival of capitalist practice, says Fathers, indicates that America was right in its attempt to liberate the business ambitions of the Vietnamese people from the repressive influence of communist collectivism. The military failure of the United States in the war against nationalism has shown itself to be irrelevant. Where military power proved of little use in subduing the Vietnamese, cultural consumerism and the commercial triumph of western values has become irresistible. He concludes:

> Communism is a meaningless ideology in Vietnam nowadays. Since 1986, doi moi, or renovation, is the philosophy of government. Translated into real terms that means making money, and the whole country is taking to it with the dedication of a

drunk who has fallen off the wagon after decades of enforced abstinence.[36]

Journalists in the 80s preferred to bury the opponents of interventionism rather than evaluate the problem of maintaining a culture of resistance. The press abandoned its adversarial role, uncritically accepted the norms and values of mainstream society and operated within a 'sphere of consensus' rather than one of 'deviance' or 'controversy'. The media in the 80s, as Daniel Hallin puts it, played the classic role of defending hegemonic interests, while 'exposing, condemning or excluding from the public agenda those who violate or challenge the political consensus. It (marked) out and (defended) the limits of acceptable political conflict'. Interventionism was once again regarded as a valid activity as journalists chose to endorse the idea that a revitalised capitalist and military crusade in Third World regions was a legitimate way for the United States to display its authority.[37]

In *Deterring Democracy* and *Necessary Illusions* Noam Chomsky has listed the various foreign policy initiatives undertaken by Presidents Reagan and Bush that the nation's newspapers unequivocally supported throughout the eighties. 'Media obedience' is the term he uses to describe 'the overwhelming tendency' in the American press during this period 'to jump up and down and bark in concert whenever the White House "snapped" its fingers'. This is particularly evident in Central America where, says Chomsky, the media was beset by the question of how to restore 'Nicaragua' to the Central American fold and how best to impose the 'standards' required of other 'client states' such as 'the death squad democracies next door'. The media reaction to President Bush's decision to send military aid to Columbia, says Chomsky, was one of 'immediate support' even though the policy was blatantly interventionist and designed to distract attention from more sinister activities in the region, especially, what he calls, the 'international terrorist project in Nicaragua'. If 'hostility' toward the Sandinistas, says Chomsky, was 'virtually uniform in media commentary and other elite circles' the invasion of Panama was supported by a media spearheaded by the *New York Times, The Washington Post, Los Angeles Times, Miami Herald* and all of the major T.V. networks. With some notable exceptions such as *The Nation*, the media 'launched a campaign to convert' Noriega from the ally he had been 'into the most nefarious demon since Attila the Hun', a replay, says Chomsky, 'of the Gaddafi project a few years earlier'. Except for a radical fringe 'the media rallied around the flag with due piety and enthusiasm, funnelling the most absurd White House tales to the public', invoking Noriega's drug connections in Panama as the pretext for intervention but not investigating the extent of civilian casualties in the invasion of Panama or Noriega's support for the Contadora peace process in Central America, to which the US was strongly opposed. On the question of atrocities committed by US allies in the 1980s, especially the human rights violations of the Iraqi government against the Kurds, 'the media generally were not interested', until Iraq's invasion of Kuwait justified 'the search for new enemies' under a policy guided by economic self-interest.[38]

Orientalism

Edward Said offers support for Chomsky's thesis, especially in his discussion of the prevalence of 'Orientalism' in the American media. 'No major cultural group', he says, 'is as little known' as the Arab Islamic people. American journalists display no 'particular knowledge of them' in spite of the fact that 'Western media coverage' of Arab-Islamic conflicts is unprecedented. 'Historically', he says, 'the American and perhaps generally the Western media have been sensory extensions of the main cultural context. Arabs are only an attenuated recent example of Others', and so are condemned to a position of caricature: to the role of camel lovers and khebab eaters. During the Reagan and Bush presidencies, he argues, the western media failed miserably in its attempt to question the assumption and exercise of American power in key regions for American Foreign Policy. At the time of the Gulf War, says Said, there were few discussions of substance in the western - and especially the American - media which challenged the philosophy and legitimacy of imperial errand, nor was there a fundamental examination of America's right to a compelling moral commission in His extending Israel, a wide debate on Palestinian legitimacy or the effect of intervention on Arabic identity. Key issues were buried from view as was any clearly defined picture of Iraq as the adversary. The media and T.V. networks refused to investigate the historical relationship of the United States with the Arab people nor did they seek to associate themselves with the Arab cause, as if offering the Arabs a platform for their views was tantamount to trading philosophically with the enemy. If dialogue was harmful then ignorance was bliss, since the voice of the unregenerate might easily contaminate the minds of the righteous. Instead of debate what the American people were subjected to was 'an ominous strain of unmistakably racist, anti-Arab sentiment' which 'consistently emanated from the column of William Saffire and A.M.

Rosenthal of the *New York Times*; along with other muscular moralists these media authorities...routinely urged the elimination of Iraq as a modern nation'. The idea of sheltering a righteous citizenry from difficult conceptual arguments and the danger of exposing them to unreconstructed cultural knowledge suggests that the media tended to view their task within the 'sphere of consensus journalism'. By refusing to acquaint an ill-informed public with new and adversarial forms of knowledge they confirmed a number of hoary, old maxims: firstly, that 'God's American Israel' has a continuing mission to act as 'trustee under God of the civilisation of the world'; and secondly, that Americans, in general, ought not to debate the principle of errand for they live in a world where God has decreed that they, by definition, are the embodiment of errand, a race whose God-given task is to exercise control over those people who oppose their moral superiority.[39]

On the eve of the Gulf War, says Said, critical analysis of each of these premises was rigorously avoided. 'I cannot recall a single mainstream television guest or programme that raised the issue of what right "we had" to get Iraq out of Kuwait', he says. 'Nor were programmes that dealt with the enormous human, social and economic costs to the Arabs of an American strike'. The American media, he continues, 'sheepishly followed the government policy - model and mobilised for war right from the start'. It wheeled in a variety of supposedly well-informed Arab experts who, 'with few exceptions...were pro Israeli and, in their disquisitions in print or on the air about the Arab mind, (were) ludicrously and tendentiously reductive'. The 'disheartening thing about the media', says Said, was that 'This was not only tolerated...it was sought'. The enormity of what got left out of these discussions, says Said, 'was enormous. Little was done to report company profits, or how the surge in petrol prices had little to do with supply, which remained overproduced'. And so on. 'The central media failing' Said continues,

> 'was an unquestioning acceptance of American power: its right to ignore dozens of UN resolutions on Palestine...to invade Panama, Grenada, Libya, and also to proclaim the absolute morality of its Gulf position sanctimoniously. Rarely did the media speak to power, or let others do so'.

Not only were the events of history stage managed, says Said, the voice of the 'other' was misrepresented or blatantly ignored. 'All roads lead to the bazaar; Arabs only understand force; brutality and violence are part of Arab civilization; Islam is an intolerant, segregationist, "medieval", fanatic, cruel, anti-woman religion'. There was only one available conclusion to be reached. 'There seemed considerable (but to me inexplicable) enjoyment to be had in the prospect that at last "the Arabs" as represented by Saddam were going to get their comeuppance'.[39]

Technology, hygiene and burial parties

And get it they did in much the same way that the people of North Vietnam had got theirs some twenty years earlier. As if to vindicate that earlier use of smart, technological weaponry the media endorsed the military use of 'video nasties' and the clinical strategy of killing from distance. In the Gulf most of the media bought into the jargon that a clean technology would allow the military to conduct a war with minimum casualties and maximum efficiency. (A similar fiction was also perpetrated by the American military during the invasions of Panama and Grenada). The military learned very quickly how to manage the press and, as the B.B.C.'s Martin Bell puts it, how 'to train us up and make us one of them'. At military briefings senior uniformed officers such as General Richard Neal of the US Marine Corps explained the allied progress with the latest high technology visual aids. The use of 'smart bomb' videos, as Robin Lustig suggests, caused 'problems', for while the sight of bombs 'hitting their targets...made good television...it was equally clear they weren't giving the whole picture'. What was not made clear was that 'a mere seven per cent of the bombs dropped on Iraq and Kuwait were precision guided.' And of the 88,000 tons that were dropped by the allies seventy per cent missed their target, even though the US military at the briefing sessions insisted that these weapons 'were remarkably precise' and could distinguish between civilian plant and military personnel. The idea, that such bombs could make humanitarian decisions was naturally absurd but 'so overpowering and overwhelming' were the visual images in 'their relative clarity' that journalists tended to accept the fiction that civilian casualties were being kept to a minimum. The fact remains, says Lustig, 'that for most of the six weeks war, the journalists in the war zone' were unable 'to provide any evidence of Iraqi casualties'. According to the defence analyst Christopher Lee the quality of assessment at the allied briefings by western reporters was extremely limited. 'I would have liked people on the ground to have pressed for more about enemy casualties', he says. 'I think it was the one area...where they should have pressed hard and hard'. Instead, the 'cosy relationship' which the military cultivated allowed them to trap the press 'in the parlour of the spokesman'. Disappointed at the lack of critical investigation Lee firmly believes that public opinion was not adequately represented in the press briefing room. The media, he says, 'gave an impression of just re-writing what the spokesman had said, and they didn't publicly press home questions day after day' concerning the levels of 'Iraqi casualties even if they knew what the answer was going to be'. Instead, the press responded to the use of 'smart bomb' videos by choosing to 'applaud' the briefing officer. This, says Mark Laity of the BBC, 'was unprofessional' but hardly surprising. Many of the journalists in Kuwait were not trained as defence correspondents and they lacked a lot of analytical 'and general knowledge that was needed'. Reporters were critically unable to 'spend enough time trying to establish the cost of the war in human life'.

If the absence of Iraqi casualties on our T.V. screens had something to do with a deliberate decision to censor scenes of bloodshed and carnage - one thinks for example of the direct hit on the Baghdad shelter bunker in al-Amiriya - it may also represent an entirely different condition of absence. The firepower unleashed by the Allies disappeared vast numbers of Iraqi soldiers. Robert Fox of *The Daily Telegraph* who returned to the battlefield when the fighting was over spent two days travelling 235 kilometres along the front line with officers from the British Army's Fourth Armoured Brigade but 'could find little trace of the many Iraqi soldiers who...must have died there'. The Iraqis had died out of sight, he says, 'consumed in the most terrible way'. The weapons deployed in Kuwait contained 'so much fissile capacity' that the Iraqi soldiers were 'incinerated'. As Fox puts it:

> Looking into the top of a T55 tank and I've done it dozens and dozens of times afterwards, you see just a little pile of metal ash and in several of those cases if not many of those cases, there must have been people there. It was eerie, it rather depressed people to know that this was a battlefield without bodies, without any trace, without any memorial of what had happened. The thing that is frightening about the dead is that many of them were simply consumed by fire and the sand.[40]

In the Kuwaiti desert the twentieth century's deepest fear of itself was defined as a glorious victory by politicians and the military over the forces of tyranny. If, during World War 2, the firebombing of Dresden had produced, in the words of Kurt Vonnegut, 'the largest massacre in European history', then in the Gulf conflict the consequence of mass technology was to turn people into 'charred firewood'.[41] Norman Mailer's account of the comprehensive terror of the gas chambers and the baseness of a scientific system that results in the mass disappearance of millions of people appeared to have made no impression whatsoever on the mind and memory of Gulf militarists and politicians. Mailer's evocation in his essay 'The White Negro' no longer seemed of concern to the West.

> Probably we will never be able to determine the psychic havoc of the concentration camps and the atom bomb upon the unconscious mind of almost everyone alive in these years. For the first time in civilized history we have been forced to live with the knowledge that...we might still be doomed to die in some vast statistical operation in which our teeth would be counted and our hair would be saved, but our death itself would be unknown, unhonoured and unremarked - a death which could not follow with dignity as a possible consequence to serious actions we had chosen, but rather death by a 'deus ex machina' in a gas chamber or a radioactive city.

If 'The Second World War presented a mirror to the human condition which blinded anyone who looked into it' then the Gulf sought to remove the disability.[42] The burial of the Vietnam Syndrome became an overriding political imperative for the American military. The bombing of the Iraqi army offered a vital fulfilment for machine-made dreams and 'smart' technologies that military failure in Vietnam had prevented. Furthermore, the prospect of a disappeared enemy was totally consistent with the various strategies of sexual regeneration that underpinned the doctrines of the 1980s. Just as the military were attempting to remove all evidence of the Iraqi soldier from the deserts of Kuwait so the American government, since 1975, had attempted, by more covert strategies, to belittle the achievement, eliminate the memory, vilify the politics and disappear the resistance of the people of Vietnam.

The idea of nature as a toxic or contaminated terrain is a mainstay of Puritan hostility to the wilderness, those uncultivated places wherein dwell the legions of the antichrist. It is his polluted habitat that needs to be cleansed with the purifying fire of the righteous. The fear of contamination that haunted America during Vietnam and pervades many of its retrospectives - one thinks of the fate of Nick in Cimino's *The Deer Hunter* - crops up again in the fastidious displays of regeneration through violence that we see in the Gulf. One wonders certainly whether the logic that justified the use of such extraordinary firepower was part of an attempt to eliminate the threat of viral contamination which close proximity to the Arabs implied. A scorched earth policy might not prevent Saddam Hussein polluting the Gulf when he flooded the oil wells but a policy of 'fissile' violence might allow the military to vindicate the tactics of hygienic bombing, first introduced in the Vietnam War. A Saigon University professor, Ly Chanh Trung, commented on this approach of the military in a 1967 article in the Vietnamese magazine

Dat Nuoc;

> Observe the American pilots, tall, handsome, athletic, with such precision equipment as the electronic computer. They eat breakfast at some military installation or aircraft carrier; then they climb into such marvelous toys as the B-52, Skyhawk, F-105, etc., fly away for a few minutes, push a few bottons and fly back. Death is the immediate result of all this button pushing activity, but it's down there at the other end, mere dots on a map. But they have no contact with the blood or the dust; they don't hear one groan, one call for help. They have no contact with the corpses of men, women, and children blown apart or burned like a cinder down below, unless anti-aircraft rounds turn them into corpses like the other corpses. But that's the hazard of their profession which they accept when they draw their salary, as in any other profession. If they make it through their mission safely, they return to their base, eat, drink, relax, play sports, and on Sunday they go to church and listen to a sermon on Christ's Sermon on the Mount: 'Blessed are the meek. Blessed are the compassionate. Blessed are the peaceful'.[43]

In Vietnam, space was the condom for sexual technologists who feared infection while 'ethics', as Philip Caputo remarks, seemed 'to be a matter of distance'.[44]

At the outset of Operation Desert Storm the American army broke through the Iraqi front line by using earthmovers and ploughs shaped like giant teeth mounted on Abrams tanks. Thousands of Iraqi soldiers were buried - some still alive and firing their weapons - in more than 70 miles of trenches. In the first two days of ground fighting in Operation Desert Storm, brigades of the 1st Mechanised Infantry Division, 'The Big Red One' (the sexual innuendo implicit in the graffiti speaks for itself) used this innovation to 'clean out' the trenches and bunkers being defended by more than 8000 Iraqi soldiers. Most of the Iraqi soldiers were 'buried beneath tonnes of sand, according to participants in the carefully planned and rehearsed assault'. Every American soldier in the assault was inside an armoured vehicle and impervious to Iraqi small arms fire. Since no one personally knew what was happening to the Iraqis in the trenches a body count was impossible. 'Once we went through there, other than the ones who surrendered, there wasn't anybody left', said Captain Bennie Williams, who was awarded the Silver Star for his role in the assault. Colonel Lon Maggart, commander of the 1st Brigade confirmed this. He captures the surgical mood of the 80s when he says of the assault: 'I know burying people like that sounds pretty nasty but it would be even nastier if we had to put our troops in the trenches and clean them out with bayonets'[45]

Notes

1. Said, Edward (1991), 'Empire of Sand', *Weekend Guardian*, p. 5, 12-13 January.
2. State of the Union Address, United States Information Service, 30 January, 1991, pp. 1-3.
3. Said, Edward 'Empire of Sand', p. 5.
4. State of the Union Address, United States Information Service, 29 January 1992, pp. 1-3.
5. State of the Union Address, (1991), p. 9.
6. Ibid, p. 8.
7. Said., p. 5.
8. State of the Union Address, (1991), p. 3.
9. Sanford, Charles, L. (1955), 'An American Pilgrim's Progress', *American Quarterly*, Vol. iv., Winter.
10. Pinter, Harold (1990), 'Yanquis Go Home!', *The Independent on Sunday*, p15, 27 May.
11. State of the Union Address, (1991), p. 3.
12. (1992), 'Hanoi's Bag of Secrets', *Newsweek*, p. 31.
13. State of the Union Address, 29 January 1992, pp. 1-2.
14. Quoted in Chomsky, Noam (1986) 'Visions of Righteousness,' in Berg, Richard and Carlos Rowe, John (eds). *Cultural Critque*, no. 3, p. 10, Spring.
15. Chomsky, Noam (1992), *Deterring Democracy*, Vintage, London, pp. 69, et seq.
16. Taylor, Philip M. (1992), *War and the Media: Propaganda and Persuasion in the Gulf War*. Manchester University Press, Manchester, p. 1.
17. State of the Union Address, 30 January 1991, p. 3.
18. Pilger, John (1992), *Distant Voices*, Vintage, London, p. 107.
19. McKeever, Robert J. (1989), 'American Myths and the Impact of the Vietnam War: Revisionism in Foreign Policy and Popular Cinema in the 1980s', Walsh, Jeffrey and Aulich, James (eds.) *Vietnam Images: War and Representation*, Macmillan, London, pp. 50-52.
20. Schell, Jonathan (1987), *The Real War*, Pantheon Books, New York, p. 43.
21. Chomsky, Noam, *Deterring Democracy*, pp. 148, 149, 254.
22. Wimmer, Adi, 'Rambo: American Adam, Anarchist and Archetypal Frontier Hero,' *Vietnam Images*, p. 188.
23. Pilger, John (1990), 'Nam', *Weekend Guardian*, p. 13, 24-25 February.

24. Walsh, Jeff (1988), 'First Blood to Rambo: A Textual Analysis', Louvre, Alf and Walsh, Jeffrey (eds.) *Tell Me Lies About Vietnam*, Open Universty Press, Milton Keynes, p. 56.
25. Fuller, Graham (1987), 'Oliver's army routs Rambo', *The Guardian*, p. 15, 14 February.
26. Rushdie, Salman (1986), 'A foaming attack of ideological rabies', *The Guardian*, p. 7, 26 May.
27. State of the Union Address, 30 January 1991, p. 1.
28. Fukayama, Francis (1990) 'Forget Iraq - history is dead', *The Guardian*, p. 23, 7 September.
29. Bigsby, C. W. E. (ed.), (1975), *Superculture: American Popular Culture and Europe*, Elek, London, p. 15.
30. Gott, Richard (1989), 'The Bear Turns Bullish', *The Guardian*, p. 23, 20 November.
31. Steiner, George (1990), 'Shadows at the Heart of the Carnival', *Observer*, p. 47, Sunday, 20 February.
32. Bradbury, Malcolm (1990), 'Frontiers of Imagination', *The Guardian*, p. 21, 15 February.
33. Chomsky, Noam, *Deterring Democracy*, pp. 109, 110.
34. Myers, Thomas (1988), *Walking Point: American Narratives of Vietnam*, Oxford University Press, New York, p. 11.
35. Anderson, Kurt (1985), 'A pinched and Hermetic Land', *Time*, p. 33. 15 April.
36. Fathers, Michael (1990), 'Goodbye Rambo, Good Morning Vietnam', *The Independent on Sunday*, p. 45, 11 February.
37. See Delli Carpini, Michael X (1990), 'U.S. Media Coverage of the Vietnam Conflict in 1968', Klein, Michael (ed.), *The Vietnam Era: Media and Popular Culture in the U.S. and Vietnam*, Pluto, London, p. 42.
38. Chomsky, Noam *Deterring Democracy*, pp. 120, 133, 145, 152.
39. Said, Edward, 'Empire of Sand', pp. 4-5.
40. 'File on Four' (1991), British Broadcasting Corporation Transcript, pp. 1-18, 9 April.
41. Vonnegut, Kurt, *Mother Night*, Jonathan Cape, London, pp. 10-11.
42. Mailer, Norman, *Advertisements for Myself*, Putnam's Sons, New York, p. 338.
43. Luce, Don and Sommer, John (1969), *Vietnam - The Unheard Voices*, Cornell University Press, Ithaca, pp. 198-9.
44. Caputo, Philip (1984), *A Rumor of War*, Ballantine Books, New York, p. 218.
45. Sloyan, Patrick (1991), 'Iraqi troops buried alive say American officers', *The Guardian*, p. 24, 13 September 1993.

6 Vic Williams, conscientious objector and the peace movement

Jeffrey Walsh

During the two world wars there existed in Britain a tradition of conscientious objection to warfare on moral, religious or political grounds. Within the 1914-18 conflict there were 16,500 conscientious objectors of whom 1,500 were Absolutists who refused to participate in any way at all in war: also in the Great War 69 conscientious objectors died in prison and 39 went insane.[1] In her study of conscientious objectors during 1939-45 Rachel Barber cites the figure of 60,000 documented cases many of whom suffered psychological trauma after incarceration;

> Conscientious objectors, then, usually managed to survive their sentences in prison with good humour and courage. Although they were rarely victimized or persecuted within the prisons, they suffered for years afterwards the stigma of having a prison record. But perhaps the worst aspect of their prison sentence was the sheer waste of manpower and talent which most were only too willing to use in civilian life.[2]

Historically the First World War generated some striking instances of dissent as resistance grew to conscription. The conduct of the war itself, patently becoming more futile as time went on, together with the vast scale of slaughter, gave added credence to those public figures who opposed it. The Independent Labour Party, led by Keir Hardie, argued for pacifism, while Fenner Brockway, writing in *Labour Leader*, called upon all men eligible to fight to form a No Conscription Fellowship. Intellectuals opposing the conflict, including the socialists Phillip Snowden and Ramsey MacDonald, vociferously supported such conscientious objectors as Clifford Allen and Stephen Hobhouse by speaking and writing publicly about their struggle.

Writers and artists, too, during the Great War protested against the pointless slaughter: D.H. Lawrence and Siegfried Sassoon typified their articulate oppositional voices, as did members of the Bloomsbury Group, including Clive Bell, Duncan Grant, David Garnett and Lytton Strachey. English culture, in the early decades of the century, generated much debate about the constraints war placed upon individual freedom, and a spectrum of radical intellectuals dissented from what they considered to be the inhumanities of militarism. It is instructive, taking account of this past historical tradition of protest, to compare the very different cultural situation that existed when Vic Williams, the subject of this essay, decided he could no longer betray his conscience by fighting in the Gulf.

England in 1991 was a very different country from the land in which Clifford Allen and Stephen Hobhouse carried out their principled objection to mass warfare. English culture and its political contexts had been transformed by the success of Conservative governments since 1979. Whereas there had been a powerful pacifist movement throughout the 60's and 70's, epitomized in CND and the peace wing of the Labour Party, both the domestic and international situations had changed dramatically. Following comprehensive defeats in the polls the Labour Party sought to transform its image in order to make itself more electable; its leader Neil Kinnock recanted his earlier commitment to CND, while other prominent Labour politicians such as Roy Hattersley publicly endorsed the Gulf war. (Even Joan Ruddock, formerly the head of CND, retained her front bench position as a Labour shadow minister during the Gulf conflict).

As a result of the political consensus to liberate Kuwait and defeat Saddam Hussein, opponents of the war soon became marginalized, and their activities either ignored or misrepresented. Internationally, too, the end of the Cold War seemed to herald a new era of neocapitalism in which visions of the brotherhood of man were widely discredited. At the time of the Gulf war, then, the consciousness of pacifism was under duress; the major opposition party was in disarray, bereft of its socialist idealism, and the powerful religious movements so evident in 1914, similarly offered little sustenance to the peace movement that opposed the war in Iraq.

Within the broad sweep of historical circumstances, though, there is often the exception that proves the rule, and the story of Vic Williams constitutes a counter-narrative to the abandonment of Labour Party, CND and radical principles; his experiences prove that there was an active peace movement in Britain during 1990-91 which coherently opposed the bipartisan political endorsement of the Gulf war. In this wider historical sense, then, the case of Vic Williams is exemplary and representative of events, ideologies and attitudes that transcend his own actions and motives. His decision to go absent from his unit, the 27th Field Regiment, Royal Artillery, based in Dortmund, Germany, on 28 December, 1990, the day before he was due to leave for duty in Saudi Arabia, triggered off a sequence of happenings that became a catalyst for organized protest.

Any evaluation of Vic Williams's case centres upon the integrity of his decision to leave his regiment rather than fight in what he considered to be a morally unjust war. His previous career shows him to have been an effective and committed soldier with little interest in politics. Born in 1962, Vic Williams lived in Disley, a pleasant, rural part of Cheshire, about fifteen miles from Manchester. He gained seven 'O' levels at school, and proceeded to study at advanced level; after the divorce of his working class parents in 1979 he left sixth form college and worked in catering and in a chemical factory. In 1986 he joined the army where he proved an adept and keen radar operator in the Royal Artillery. His career in the army, where he was promoted to Lance Bombardier, did not suggest a rebellious personality, and at his court martial his good military record and disciplined attitude to his duties were praised. In protesting against the Gulf war Vic Williams seemed to act out of character. From interviews given when he was on the run and some others given subsequently, Vic Williams has tried to explain why he felt he had no option other than to quit his regiment and his friends and then to speak out against the war.

Initially Vic Williams claims to have had no difficulties in approving of the role of the British army as part of a defensive operation which would defend Saudi Arabia against further Iraqi aggression after the invasion of Kuwait. His doubts, he says, arose when it became apparent that UK Military involvement would be stridently offensive rather than defensive. This change of tack was crystallized for him when, on a training exercise, hostile attitudes of a racist kind were evoked towards the Iraqis. It became obvious to him then, when Iraqis were stigmatized as 'a lower form of life' that a bloody and savage war was imminent. During the training period gradual changes occurred over a number of weeks which suggested a strategic difference in the role conceived for the United Nations' forces. Senior officers, acting on the orders of their C.O., significantly shifted the emphasis away from deterrence and peacekeeping. Soldiers were encouraged to ignore the public explanation of their activities, that they were making ready to preserve the peace, and to practise instead their real but necessarily hidden aim, to teach the Iraqis a lesson they would not easily forget.

Vic Williams appears to have struggled increasingly with doubts that continued to disturb him: he claims also to have spoken to a civilian priest about his growing disillusionment, and also to his sergeant major. Both men, although not unsympathetic, did not seem to comprehend his problems, were unable to help, and were unaware of the formal procedures necessary for the presentation of his case. After a sleepless night on the eve of his departure for Saudi Arabia, Vic Williams packed hurriedly, and drove away from the barracks at Dortmund. He eventually crossed the Channel, and stayed with relatives in the North West and Midlands.

At one time he was on the point of giving himself up when he parked opposite the guardroom of the Royal Artillery barracks. Now he fully intended to face up to the authorities, to take his punishment and then continue leading a normal life again. Such a course of action, though, as he contemplated it, seemed futile as he was convinced it would not solve anything and would certainly not do anything to stop the war which now looked inevitable. Shortly after this incident, on the night when the air war started, a remarkable coincidence happened. Vic Williams was driving on the outskirts of the capital in South London, preparing to unpack for a night's sleep, when the BBC news reported on his car radio that bombing raids on Baghdad had begun. Angry at this news, and acting out of reflex, he turned the car round and headed instinctively for central London. After crossing Westminster Bridge, he turned right down Whitehall where he saw a demonstration against the war taking place. In retrospect he rationalizes that his actions at this juncture were partly driven by his unconscious and partly by logic. Somehow he believes, he correctly judged that things would be happening in London, and if there were anti-war protests, then he should become involved because of his strongly growing convictions that the war was morally wrong. Outside the Ministry of Defence building a man who was a member of the protest group, Reservists Against the War, listened to Vic Williams's story. He offered to put him in touch with a solicitor and with MPs and other pressure groups who opposed the war. From this chance encounter with someone who remains a friend Vic Williams actively entered anti-war politics.

Lance Bombardier Williams became a focus of media attention when he addressed a massive anti-war rally in Hyde Park on 2 February, 1991. The man who had earlier volunteered to join the Gulf peacekeeping force, who had also declined a medical downgrading which would have kept him out of a combatant role in the conflict, because of a partial hearing deficiency, and who approved of the role of British troops in Ireland, now spoke out vehemently against the aerial bombardment of Iraq and the killing of civilians. In the course of this address he informed the crowd that many soldiers were convinced that there was no justification for the Gulf conflict. He strove to make his point more effectively by paraphrasing the words of many of his fellow soldiers, 'This must stop. It is wrong. We are no better than Saddam Hussein with what we are doing in the Middle East.' Ironically these words were skilfully used against him later at his courtmartial when they were taken out of context, and their nature as paraphrase distorted to make them appear Vic Williams's own words.

In British newspapers his actions were extensively reported, and he was interviewed nationally on *News at Ten*. Other programmes such as *Free For All* debated his anti-war stance, and there was international coverage in such countries as Norway, Japan and Australia. The most intellectually serious treatment of Vic Williams's case on British Television, though, was the documentary in the BBC 1 series, *The Heart of the Matter*, which was shown on 9 March. During this programme Joan Bakewell interviewed Vic Williams, and another dissenting military voice was heard. This belonged to a veteran of the Falklands war, Commander Robert Green, formerly staff officer (intelligence) to Admiral Sir John Fieldhouse. The core of Commander Green's argument was that in modern war the destructive potential of advanced weapons technology, which detaches the operator from the havoc he creates, makes it doubly important that soldiers think for themselves. Far from being a liability, soldiers who ask awkward questions and act according to conscience are valuable because they ensure that the conduct of war is underpinned by an ethical spirit of inquiry. Commander Green's remarks, amplified later in an article,[3] are certainly relevant if we consider what happened at My Lai during the Vietnam war, or on Mount Longdon during the Falklands conflict. The 'bolshie' soldier fulfils the role of spoiler and lie detector, an agent of correction against the organizational certainties of the military. After Vic Williams gave himself up at Rochester Row police station in central London on 9 March 1991, such issues of conscience and morality were again addressed at his court martial where he faced a possible sentence of twenty four years' imprisonment.

During the hearing Vic Williams, who was eventually sentenced to fourteen months' imprisonment and who was demoted to Gunner after his arrest, was charged with desertion and conduct prejudicial to good order and military discipline. At the court martial, described by one solicitor as 'one of the most important military trials since the end of the second world war', a number of important legal and moral issues were raised concerning the obligations and rights of service personnel in a combat situation. On the prosecution side it was argued that Gunner Williams, as a member of Her Majesty's forces, broke his oath of allegiance to the crown by going absent without leave before embarking for the Gulf. Lieutenant Risius, prosecuting, also submitted that Vic Williams damaged army morale and contravened Queen's Regulations by speaking out publicly against the war both on television and at the Hyde Park rally. He contended that a serving soldier makes binding commitments to serve his country, and such a pact freely entered into is absolute. A soldier is clearly aware of his obligations to the state and by criticizing government policy and opposing the war publicly Vic Williams was disloyal both to his country and to his regiment. The prosecution case was underpinned by recourse to principles of duty, patriotism and legal obligation whereby service to one's country is not negotiable: a soldier makes a kind of covenant and is expected to conduct himself in a manner worthy of such a moral code.

For the defence the civilian solicitor James Nicholl, and the barrister, Helena Kennedy QC, the first woman to represent a soldier at a British court martial, advanced arguments founded upon unassailable human rights. While admitting that Vic Williams had gone absent without leave, they suggested that he was not a deserter, but someone whose actions were motivated by conscience. Believing the war to be wrong, he had no alternative other than to act in the way that he did. His act of disobedience was, in Vic Williams's eyes, justified because he felt it to be morally right. In speaking out publicly against the war, Vic Williams, also following his conscience, opposed a war which he believed was unjust. The defence sought to present their client as a man who was impelled to act as he did out of integrity and a sense of moral purpose.

The legal axis of the defence argument was that Vic Williams did not have 'reasonable access' to those avenues open to him in order to exercise his legitimate rights as a conscientious objector. The Judge Advocate, presiding over a panel of five officers, stated that it was 'not in dispute that Vic Williams was *not* specifically made aware of the procedures for conscientious objection.' In practice, these procedures, outlined in a restricted document, are made known only to officers: because the document is presumably thought to be highly sensitive, it is drafted as a general routine order, and is not easily available to the lower ranks. This has the effect, probably intended, of limiting the options and choices of those whom it is designed to help. Clearly there are ethical and legal implications in the apparent concealment of the document.

Perhaps the deep contradictions underlying the document's significance are irreconcilable: an army needs to be a mean machine yet should also have a heart and a conscience.

Whereas the treatment of his court martial by the British press was, at first, restrained and factual, some press coverage changed its tone after the verdict was announced. Although many of the quality papers, notably *The Guardian*, retained their objective style of reporting, often tabloids, such as *The Sun* and the *Daily Star*, now seized their chance to impugn Vic Williams's motives. A common theme running through such articles is that Gunner Williams was simply a coward who cloaked his cowardice with fine words. Perhaps the most vituperative of these tirades was written by Julie Burchill in *The Mail on Sunday*.

In her piece she eschews logic by combining an unpleasant attack on Vic Williams with rambling polemic about Oswald Mosely, Third World Aid, the fight against Nazism, the International Brigades and irresponsible contemporary journalists. If there is an argument in her ragbag of a commentary, it is that British military involvement in the Gulf was patriotic, necessary and distinguished by compassion, whereas Vic Williams, supported by such left wing journalists as John Pilger, lacked the humanity of fellow British troops who defended Muslim women against further rape in Kuwait.

Burchill's article is exemplary of the manner in which popular journalism prefers to rant and rave rather than construct measured arguments based upon evidence. Using a kind of crude metalanguage, she contrasts the traditional British 'language' of 'decency' against what she takes to be Vic Williams's perversions of truth. She focuses upon some of his words which she takes totally out of context; 'It's nothing to do with us. It's not our business; we don't even speak the same language or have the same religion. It's not up to us to put it right.'[4] Burchill castigates Vic Williams for having a 'sick mind', and for stigmatizing his fellow soldiers as 'mindless'. Ironically, her own use of language is intemperate, especially when she describes Vic Williams as 'as bad as Saddam Hussein himself'. At the centre of her emotional broadside is a wounding dismissal of his motives;

> Williams is, rather, The Soldier who Thought of Himself; as a few do, he probably joined the army believing he'd never have to fight. In the old days cowards admitted to being cowards. Now, when every personality defect has some sociological get-out clause, they don't. They make throwing a wobbly into a crisis of conscience.[5]

Continuing to inveigh against Vic Williams as 'a hero of the left', she rhetorically contrasts his actions with 'the straightforward, clear-eyed, almost embarrassed kind of heroism' of the soldiers who fought, yet she produces no evidence to substantiate her character assassination. Had she bothered to research the topic of conscientious objection carefully, she would have found that the evidence proves the opposite, that conscientious objection is not easy; it leads to pain, humiliation, scapegoating, and the inevitable charges of betrayal and cowardice. This point is made by Robert Green who analyses the decision made by Vic Williams in a positive way.

> All I can do is pass on my findings as an ex-officer with 20 years' military experience. Vic accepted that the primary role of the armed forces is to sort out failures of diplomacy by legalized violence. He had joined to take part proudly in the application of reasonable military force within the context of the Nato alliance upon which his country's security depended... Yet he felt so strongly that what the army expected him to do in the Gulf was wrong, that he decided to sacrifice a secure career and withstand all the military, political and social sanctions that exist in a nation with such a strong martial tradition. I think that stand took a special blend of moral and physical courage.[6]

Green's position is confirmed by reference to history when John Rae, in the most authoritative study yet of conscientious objectors between 1916-19, reflects upon why men decided to become objectors. He surveys the causes of conscientious objection, and concludes 'there is no conclusive evidence that cowardice (which loomed so large in the popular imagination) was one of them'.[7] In the charges made by the army against Vic Williams no mention was made of cowardice.

What happened to the Peace Movement?

The standard histories of the Gulf War, such volumes as Lawrence Freedman's and Efraim Karsh's *The Gulf Conflict 1990-91* or Dilip Hiro's *Desert Shield to Desert Storm*, tend to relegate the impact of anti-war opposition to footnotes in wider debates about the morality of the war. Although there have been at least two collections of essays written from the perspectives of those who opposed the war, Phyllis Bernis and Michael Moushabeck's *Beyond the Storm* in the United States and Victoria Brittain's *The Gulf Between Us* in Britain, the influence of peace protesters has rarely been explored in any comprehensive way. It is surprising that a nationally based peace movement did not emerge in the United States in view of the historical precedent from the Vietnam era.

Several reasons have been given for this, ranging from poor organization, misguided tactics, lack of effective slogans, living in the past, and apathy and conservatism in the population.[8]

Other more sinister explanations have been advanced for the lack of coordinated public resistance to the war in the United States. Grace Paley for example, suggests that the main purpose of the Gulf War was 'to bathe the American conscience in blood so as to give it a taste for blood...'. To accomplish this, she theorizes, the Bush administration and its allies suppressed dissent by silencing the voices of those who spoke out: a process of subtle repression thus eliminated the old war resister's mentality,

> Now I will tell you about the ways we organized against this war - how roughly 3,500 events were successfully hidden from other Americans and the world; how it was shaken by the terrible accumulating speed of the Gulf War, It's as though the war itself were one of those smart weapons, the market system's directed trajectories tested in vicious electoral campaigns and used in this case to eliminate the Peace Movement and its natural and historical accomplishment, the Vietnam Syndrome. At this moment of triumph, with 300 Americans and 100,000 Iraqis dead, the President announced that he had indeed extinguished the Peace Movement and ended the Vietnam Syndrome.[9]

A similar conclusion, although one specifically linked to the role of the American media and, in particular, television, was reached at a conference held in New York during the war.[10] Media bias, slanted reporting and exclusion of dissident or alternative viewpoints was blamed for creating a kind of cultural myopia. One survey found that over a five month period, during the build up of US troops, only one per cent of television coverage dealt with popular opposition to the Gulf escalation.

In view of these examples of censorship it is important to acknowledge that there were massive anti-war demonstrations both in the United States and throughout the world. On the weekends of 13 and 20 January, for example, protests were held throughout the United States, Europe and Britain. In France over 200,000 people demonstrated on 12 and 13 January; in Germany over a quarter of a million people marched to oppose the war. In Italy and Spain opinion polls showed between 52 per cent and 80 per cent opposition to the war: later 2 million Spaniards stopped work in protest. On 16 February the Indian Government announced that it would withdraw refuelling facilities from US Air Force cargo flights to the Gulf.[11] Such international actions proved conclusively that those in favour of increased military action against Iraq did not have things all their own way.

In Britain the war retained, as in the United States, a consistently high popular rating, yet there were many groups and individuals who opposed it, some from the beginning, others when hostilities increased. Because the course of a war is unpredictable and the wider international contexts change rapidly, groups that oppose a war often appear marginal, disorganized, their actions provisional and lacking in strategic coherence. The experience of Vic Williams during 1991, however limited and fragmentary, allows some examination of the loose anti-war coalitions that existed in Britain during the Gulf conflict. Of course one individual, no matter how eminent, can have only minor and passing significance as great public events unfold historically, yet the story of Vic Williams illustrates how elements of the Labour Party, the media and radical political groups formed alliances and interacted both ideologically and organizationally.

On a national level the Labour Party, at the time of the Gulf crisis, showed itself to be uneasy, at times split and riven by ideological contradictions. Although its front bench spokesmen, notably Neil Kinnock, Roy Hattersley and Gerald Kaufman, maintained disciplined support for the coalition's efforts, two junior social security ministers, Tony Banks and Clare Short resigned from office in opposition to the war, and one, Robin Cook, spoke out against the conduct of the war. Some Labour MPs were tireless in their criticism of bombing raids, the growing increase in civilian casualties and the apparent lack of commitment by the United States to explore diplomatic solutions: among this group were Gavin Strang, Bill Hamilton and Tam Dalyell. When Parliament voted to support the use of force in the Gulf, over fifty Labour MPs either voted against the motion or abstained. The full list was printed in outrage by *The Sun* opposite a page which advised girls 'Flash your knickers for Our Brave Boys'.[12]

The most prominent Labour MPs to oppose the war, the tireless Tony Benn and Jeremy Corbyn, who had criticized Saddam's poison gas attacks in 1988, joined with CND's leadership notably Marjorie Thompson and Bruce Kent, in forming a Committee To Stop The War in the Gulf which gave daily briefings and sought to counter official press conferences. At rallies held in Hyde Park, Trafalgar Square, RAF Fairford and in Manchester and other provincial cities, CND and religious leaders raised issues of conscience concerning civilian and military deaths. Cardinal Basil Hulme and Dr John Habgood, for example, criticized the US air force for their admission that they dropped napalm on Iraqi trenches; Marjorie Thompson denounced all kinds of violence in the Middle East including Iraqi scud attacks on Israel; Lambeth councillors condemned the war as barbaric.

Because of the frequent lack of 'hard news' during the conflict, journalists often waged a kind of ideological civil war among themselves, which is clearly represented in Brian Macarthur's collection of articles, *Despatches from the Gulf War*. Two public events at the cessation of hostilities epitomized the polarities of feeling generated by the war within the British media. On successive days *The Sunday Times* published its classic of establishment triumphalism on 3 March, and next day Media Workers Against the War held a high profile rally in London. In *The Sunday Times* the newspaper's big guns, Norman Stone, Robert Harris and Norman Macrae, denounced the pinkish 'pacifist coterie'. With God and victory on their side, Stone and Co. were in self congratulatory ecstasy; scornful adjectives pilloried left wing demons and right wing doubters such as Auberon Waugh and Enoch Powell alike; they were dismissed as dismal Johnnies and spineless pessimists in contrast to the prescient Norman Macrae, the septuagenarian journalist who coined the spiteful phrase 'turkey shoot'. In the scale of blame Edward Heath and Dennis Healey were the ultimate traitors. This tone of recrimination was echoed only less stridently in other papers where Peregrine Worsthorne, Paul Johnson and Max Hasting rejoiced that history had vindicated their stance.

In the other less populated camp the leading critics of British intervention were next day articulating their continuing doubts about the prosecution of the war, about the heavy toll of casualties, about Mutla Ridge, Amiriyah, about further destabilisation of the Middle East and other likely adverse political effects. Alongside the venerable peace warriors, John Pilger and Paul Foot, stood two correspondents of *The Guardian*, Victoria Brittain, its assistant Foreign Editor, and Edward Pearce, a prominent political analyst. In the eyes of Norman Stone, its arch critic, *The Guardian* tragically betrayed its fine intellectual traditions by toadying to Saddam, 'At any stage where the West buckled and sent its lick spittles to a man the world knows to have been a combination of Hitler and Stalin, *The Guardian* was there, not to offer support, but at least as Fairy Godmother'.[13] Other institutions accused of betrayal by *The Sunday Times* were Newsnight, Panorama, Today and Channel Four News.

While he was speaking out against the war, and during and after his court martial, Vic Williams received encouragement and support from a number of committed people. Although such groups and individuals shared no common political beliefs, and included old style pacifists, Labour radicals, religious activists and Trotskyists, they were fighting on his behalf. During the period when he was evading arrest for 62 days he was helped and comforted by Marjorie Thompson of CND, by Reservists Against the War, by Tony Benn, Jeremy Corbyn and other Labour MPs, and by numerous people not so well known who aided and sustained him through difficult times. Of particular help was the Quaker organization *At Ease*, a voluntary helpline which gave counselling on all military matters including disciplinary problems and issues of conscientious objection. At this point Vic Williams wrote to his commanding officer explaining his views that the war was wrong, and resisted attempts to persuade him to return to Germany where he would face the minor charge of going Absent Without Leave. Seemingly the coverage of Vic Williams's case initially by *The Guardian's* David Pallister and then by other journalists, was attracting adverse publicity that the army wished to avoid.

The two most influential organizations to call for leniency towards him and to explain publicly the moral principles underlying his objections to war were The Vic Williams Defence Campaign which comprised CND, Reservists Against The War, Committee for A just Peace in the Middle East, and Socialist MPs, including Jeremy Corbyn, Tony Benn and Bob Cryer. These groups organized petitions, lobbied vigorously, issued statements, wrote pamphlets, sold T-shirts and held vigils outside Woolwich Barracks and High Point prison. There was also a well attended vigil held as St. Martins in the field touchingly on Vic Williams's birthday, 1 December. There was even a gig played in his cause by the Robb Johnson Band and The Price in Southall.

When he was in prison Vic Williams expressed a wish to study law, perhaps influenced by the example of the two excellent lawyers who had defended him, James Nicholl and Helena Kennedy. After the celebrations marking his release were over he decided to take a degree in law to help others like himself who had undergone harrowing experiences. Looking back upon his actions, he has no regrets and remains convinced that he did the correct thing. His conscience, he believes, is clear; and he bears no grudges and shows little bitterness for having gone to prison for his beliefs. Although he feels that his court martial was unjust and that he was made an example of, he thinks positively about the hundreds of letters and cards received from well wishers at home and abroad. The overwhelming impressions that stay with him are of generosity and idealism. Overall he is convinced that he has gained from his experiences rather than lost.

In retrospect there are two overriding issues raised by his case: one is political, the other humanitarian. John Dettmar of *The Independent*[14] inferred that Vic Williams had allowed himself to become a dupe of peace groups such as the Socialist Workers Party, who were the sponsors of Reservists Against the War, a charge that Vic Williams strenuously denies. At his court martial he refused to plead as mitigating circumstances that he was manipulated against his will by extremists. His own politics are left inclined, but, like most people's, inconsistent, sometimes based upon instincts and feelings stemming from his northern working class roots. Regarding the humanitarian dimensions of his court martial and subsequent imprisonment, Amnesty International argued that he was denied reasonable access to the status of conscientious objector because he was not told of his rights. The army it claims had not fulfilled its proper legal and moral obligations towards him. Amnesty International framed the specific circumstances of Vic Williams's court martial within broader democratic and constitutional conventions such as Article 18 of the Universal Declaration of Human Right and the International Convention of Civil and Political Rights.[15] Significantly Amnesty International adopted Vic Williams as a prisoner of conscience.

One of the most interesting features of the Vic Williams story is that it has an optimistic ending. He is now at the University of the South Bank reading law where he subsidizes his meagre grant by doing part time work at the weekends. Two of his favourite relaxations are listening to music, of which he has an impressive collection of vinyl and tapes; and, understandably, reading about other conscientious objectors. He is proud of a small collection of books about soldiers who took actions similar to his own by refusing to fight. One veteran of the Somme, Bert Steward, a former agricultural correspondent of *The Daily Herald*, now presumably in his nineties, sent him a signed copy of his autobiography, *One Journey*. Pride of place in his library, though, is a photocopy given to him by Vic Williams's friend, Tony Benn: this is a handwritten journal, as yet unpublished, of the First World War conscientious objector and later Labour MP, Emrys Hughes.

Notes

1. Rae, John (1970), *Conscience and Politics, The British Government and the Conscientious Objector to Military Service 1916-19*, Oxford University Press, London, p. 71.
2. Barker, Rachel (1982), *Conscience, Government and War: Conscientious Objection in Great Britain 1939-45*, Routledge and Kegan Paul, London, p. 96-7.
3. Green, Robert (1991), 'The Case of Gunner Vic', *The Tablet*, 21 September.
4. Burchill, Julie (1991), 'The foreign values of a selfish soldier', *The Mail on Sunday*, p. 21, 15 September.
5. Ibid.
6. Green, Robert, op. cit.
7. Rae, J., op. cit., p. 86.
8. Helm, Sarah (1991), 'US peace campaigners struggle to find a voice', *The Independent*, p. 5, 21 February and Elbaum, Max, (1991), 'The Storm at Home', in Bennis, Phyllis and Moushabeck, Michel (eds.), *Beyond The Storm : A Gulf Crisis Reader*, Olive Branch Press, New York.
9. Paley, Grace (1991), 'Something about the Peace Movement' in Brittain Victoria (ed.), *The Gulf Between Us : The Gulf War and Beyond*, p. 62-3, Virago Press, London.
10. See Bryson, Chris (1991), 'Ricochets from another shooting war', *The Guardian* Media section, p. 23, 4 February.
11. Brown, Derek (1991), 'Indian government denies US Air Force refuelling rights, *The Guardian*, p. 2, 18 February.
12. 'MPs who cried off at crunch', (1991), *The Sun*, p.3, 17 January.
13. Stone, Norman (1991), 'So much for the pacifist coterie on the pink cloud', *The Sunday Times*, p. IX, 3 March.
14. Dettmar, John (1991), 'How peace army was handed a propaganda victory', *The Times*, 12 September.
15. Amnesty International (1991), United Kingdom, Conscientious objection to military service - Vic Williams, London, October.

7 The politics of pop and the war in the Gulf

Deborah Johnson and John Storey

Some definitions of political pop

> Hey don't the wars come easy
> Hey don't the peace come hard[1]

This is one version of the relationship between politics and pop. There are others. What is certain is that the relationship is complex and multi-layered. Politics enter at different moments in the making of pop: production, distribution, performance, consumption, etc. Each moment produces its own politics. 'We're going to make a record about sexism.' 'We don't want our music distributed by a "fascist" record company.' 'We won't play Sun City.' 'I buy this music because it's about real life.' In these and many other ways pop can be defined as political. At the level of 'common sense', political pop is simply pop that is *political*: it is pop music which contains overtly political commentary on the world. In this definition, the Ruthless Rap Assassins are political when they sing 'That's My Nigger' in a way that Madonna is not when she sings 'Holiday'. But how adequate is such a distinction? Both songs are after all ideological forms through which we negotiate our relation to the real. Each in its different way articulates particular human experiences; moreover, is music about racism more political than music about the politics of pleasure? The answer may seem self-evident; but part of the purpose of this chapter is to suggest that sometimes it isn't.

Politics is about people; therefore political pop must reach people; it must be popular. There is a difference between Bob Dylan performing 'Blowin in the Wind' on a civil rights march and someone singing the song in their bedroom. To be popular means to reach a mass audience. Consumption is never passive: eighty percent of records fail to make a profit.[2] Precisely why some records are popular and others are not is always difficult to determine. For John Street, it is 'in the way private feelings trapped by the song are linked to the public world which shapes the listener's experiences'.[3] It is not entirely clear why the coming together of private feeling and the public world should be experienced as pleasurable. But what is clear, is that within pop music, as within other media, there is a constant interplay between individual fantasy and collective experience. These experiences may be anything from how it feels to be in love, to how it feels to be on the dole. The collective experiences articulated by the audience webs each individual into shifting consumer communities. Playing with experience, pop music produces experience. Yet music can do different things with the raw material of life: it can both challenge and reinforce. Some pop stars sing of the wonders of love; others of its terrible pain. Like other cultural forms, pop music is in this sense an ideological form: it produces images of the world. Good or bad, a pop song makes us see the world in a particular way. There is no song which does not in some way affect the way we feel about ourselves and others. No matter how apparently trivial, to paraphrase Bertolt Brecht, pop music is never without consequences.[4] In this sense all pop is political. Sometimes the politics are subtle, easily missed. For example, when the Dance Underground emerged in the late 1980s to many critics here was a youth subculture devoid of any politics. For these critics 'stop everything and dance' means simply escapism. But escapism is never simple; there is always a reason for going and a reason for going *there*. Such decisions are profoundly political: to think otherwise is to simplify the consumption of pop. The slippery term escape, so often applied to the texts and practices of popular music (and popular culture generally), always means an escape from and to something. Once escape is recognised, the question of pop doesn't suddenly become an unequivocal answer, but a series of further questions: why escape? what is being rejected? what replaces it? The answers to these and other related questions are political.

Politics is also about power. Pop music can be party political. Politicians have long realised this. They have often dreamed of turning the taste of communities of pop into the voting constituencies of party politics. The prospect of the votes of the young has tempted many a politician into pop. In 1965 Harold Wilson's courting of the Beatles resulted in their being awarded MBEs. As Robin Denselow explains: 'in his early campaigns he was only too pleased to be photographed puffing his pipe alongside these charming, cute and utterly safe-seeming moptops who were working such wonders for the British balance of payments'. [5] Of course the relationship soured somewhat in 1969, when John Lennon returned his award in protest at Britain's support for America's war in Vietnam. But while it lasted, it was political pop. There are many other illustrations of such relationships. Jimmy Carter tried to use Bob Dylan, both Reagan and Mondale tried to use Bruce Springsteen, and Neil Kinnock appeared in a Tracy Ullman video. All examples of political pop.

Politicians involve themselves in pop in other ways: for example, the demand for censorship. In 1977, the year of the Royal Jubilee, pressure was exerted to ban the Sex Pistols 'God Save the Queen'. The song was banned and went straight to number one. In other countries, censorship is much more harshly implemented. In South Africa, all lyric sheets have to be submitted for official scrutiny before a song can be recorded. To avoid this, political expression often becomes a question of the style of the music, rather than the words performed. But State intervention runs riot: whilst Pink Floyd's 'The Wall' was banned when Soweto school students adopted the line 'We don't need no education', forms of so-called 'homeland' music are encouraged because it is thought to connote that the true home for native South Africans lies somewhere at a safe distance from white dominated cities. [6] This is another instance of political pop.

Pop can be political if the musicians say it is. Taste communities can become political constituencies. West Coast rock was ideologically premised on opposition to America's war in Vietnam. It addressed its audience as actual or potential members of an 'alternative' society. Part of the sense of belonging involved an attitude to the Vietnam War. The prevalence of this anti-war feeling was such that in the context of the counterculture all songs were in a sense against the war. What we mean is this: the fact that Country Joe and the Fish sang songs against the war was enough to make all their songs seem implicitly against the war. Opposition to the war was the central articulating principle of the counterculture. (We use articulate here in its double sense, meaning both to express and to make connections.) Music expressed the values and aspirations of the counterculture, whilst at the same time acting as a consolidator and reproducer of the culture. Beneath a variety of slogans - 'Make Love, Not War', being perhaps the most famous - it engaged in a counter-hegemonic struggle over the meaning(s) of the war. [7]

Sometimes the situation is more complex. For example, on a recent American tour, U2 found that they had to explain the politics of their song, 'Sunday, Bloody Sunday'. In performance after performance, Bono attacked what he regards as the senseless politics of Irish Americans who constantly refer to 'the war back home' with enthusiasm and excitement. 'Sunday, Bloody Sunday', he explained, is not a song in celebration of the IRA. Yet, despite Bono's protests to the contrary, the audience seemed determined to claim it for the American version of the Irish Revolution.

The music industry has its own definition of political pop. Political pop as sales category. Certain pop - rap or the work of Billy Bragg, for example - is marketed as political. Since the mid-sixties, record companies have been comfortable making money out of politics. By 1968 the music of the counterculture began to be marketed under slogans such as: 'The Revolutionaries are on Columbia'; 'The man can't bust our Music' (Columbia); 'It's happening on Capital'; 'Psychedelia - the sound of the NOW generation' (MGM).[8] This is incorporation on a grand scale. When it comes to individual songs their attitude is often quite different. Selling the music of a subculture, or of a particular genre, or even the work of a particular performer, as political is fine, but selling the individual political song is something quite different. In the unpredictable and everchanging world of pop, individual political songs (cut loose from a movement, a genre, a profitable performer) are something record companies would rather not handle. The big transnational record companies universalize their interests and profits by dealing in universals. The politics of profit which try to dictate the terms of the international market consider the political pop song usually too specific to make money. From the perspective of the record industry, political pop, unless it can be catalogued in a particular way, is financially far too risky. At home, these risks are of offending, of seeming too opinionated, of crossing the line between entertainment and dull social comment. Abroad, the risks are that the audience will not connect with the ideas and experiences dealt with in the song. Political pop (as defined by the industry) is a risk. But political pop can make money. For example, The Farm's 'All Together Now', a subtle anti-war song, was a massive hit.

Another definition of political pop is pop *organized* politically. In 1976, Eric Clapton voiced his support for Enoch Powell's version of racism. Outrage within pop quickly solidified into the anti-racist umbrella organisation, Rock Against Racism (RAR). RAR was a united pop collective which staged concerts and festivals. Together with the Anti-Nazi League, RAR was successful in curbing the growth of organised racism.[9] Political pop in the 1980s (using this definition) began with the release of the 'No Nukes' film and triple album featuring the performance of members of Musicians United For Safe Energy. The appearance of Crosby, Stills and Nash on the same bill as Springsteen, suggested a symbolic suturing of the counterculture rock of the 1960s and the political rock of the 1980s. The Sun City Project established in 1985, united pop musicians in opposition to apartheid in a declared refusal to play the Sun City entertainment complex in South Africa. The result was a single, a video, and an album, all featuring performers such as Bob Dylan, and Springsteen. Live Aid, perhaps the key political pop event of the 80s, reached an audience in excess of two billion. It gave famine both money and publicity. The following year Amnesty International's *Conspiracy of Hope* tour featured Dylan, Tom Petty, Peter Gabriel, Jackson Browne, Lou Reed, Joan Baez, Sting, and U2, on a week long tour across America from San Francisco to New York. As a result, Amnesty International doubled its membership in the USA. Two years later it organised the *Amnesty International World Tour*. The event was headlined by Springsteen.

Pop is political in this definition to the extent that it is able to establish constituencies for specific political campaigns. U2's tour of the USA, the year following the *Conspiracy of Hope* tour, certainly seemed to suggest the possibility of success. Audiences turned up with anti-apartheid banners and Amnesty International posters calling for the release of political prisoners around the world. Bono's comments certainly support an optimistic assessment:

> When we first came here five years ago, there was this incredible entrenchment, and a broken spirit, made up for by an arrogance and a right-wing prevalence through the colleges and schools, and a feeling not just that rock 'n' roll couldn't change anything. But now there is a turning of the tides.[10]

We could of course be cynical and suggest that some of the performers who have supported campaigns have done so simply to sell records. Well-founded or not, such cynicism does not invalidate the witnessing of the deeply moving reception Nelson Mandela received at Wembley in April 1990. However the performers were defining their presence that day, the audience clearly wanted to be part of a utopian-political moment when pop music mattered enough for the world's most famous political prisoner (released only two months earlier) to thank a pop music audience because they 'chose to care'.[11]

For most people, the label political pop is probably reserved for pop which has a recognisable political message. This might include, for example, the explicit politics of NWA's 'Fuck the Police', or the implicit politics of UB40's 'Food for Thought'. Sometimes songs shout their politics, at other times they whisper them compellingly. During an interview with Robin Denselow, Billy Bragg commented, 'pop music has always kidded itself that it's a radical force for change. That's rubbish. It's entertainment. But it is a chance to get specific ideas across'. [12] This is a difficult claim to unpack. If pop music is not a force for change, why use it to get specific ideas across? What Bragg seems to be suggesting is that political pop must always, first and foremost, recognise itself as a form of entertainment. In short, if it doesn't entertain it doesn't get its politics across. Street cites the example of the Council Collective's 'Soul Deep', released in 1984 to raise money and support for the cause of the striking miners. It was not a great hit argues Street, because it was not a great pop song. The song was 'a rather worthy record', lacking 'inspirational qualities' and thus a *political failure* because of its 'musical dullness'. [13] He compares the song unfavourably to the Special AKA's 'Free Nelson Mandela'. Whilst the former relies upon commitment to a specific cause, the latter draws upon basic notions of equality. [14] The Special AKA name Nelson Mandela, detail the length of his imprisonment, and ask 'are you so blind that you cannot see?' What they do not do is get involved with whom 'you' in the song actually is, as compared to the Council Collective's 'where is the backing from the TUC?' There are certain things that pop can do politically, and in order to understand this, musicians must realise the limitations of the form. This is more or less Bragg's point: pop music is always primarily sold for its sound. If the politics fit the sound, then the sound will sell the politics. Put simply, without a good tune, political lyrics run the risk of not being heard.

For some critics of pop, this is always the problem of mixing politics and pop. The world of pop is often seen as a world in retreat from politics: a world of sex, drugs and rock 'n' roll. Politics are wasted on pop. If your interest is political expression, turn instead to a serious musical form like folk. Mostly, people don't dance to folk, they listen. The world of folk is an arena of ideas - politics. The world of pop is a pleasure palace of festivals and concerts, dancing and desire, discos and pubs, youth clubs and parties. Dylan moved from serious singer to 'Judas' when he swapped his acoustic for an electric guitar, or so the story goes. Is it really the case that pop is inherently a less political form than folk? Or does it simply mean that pop operates within a different generic system, one which is geared to a mass audience? We would argue that this difference *makes* the difference: its potential political effectivity can be measured in its potential to take its politics to a global audience. This is illustrated nowhere more clearly than in the massive, highly organised pop fund-raising events which have become commonplace over the last decade.

To call pop political is to bring into play a diversity of meanings. Pop can be political *simultaneously* in lots of different ways. As Street puts it, 'the politics of music are a mixture of state policies, business practices, artistic choices and audience responses'. [15] Each of these elements places restrictions on the politics of pop. Yet, limitations are not always negative; they also form the framework within which consumption of, and pleasure in, pop takes on meaning. The whole system is in constant revolution; nothing stays the same for very long in pop. Pop politics are often vague, open to negotiation and (mis)interpretation and ultimately dependent on audience articulation. Pop music accompanies most of today's social movements. It is a channel of communication through which to unite an audience. But it is the audience who ultimately make or constitute the meaning in pop. For example, dancing to 'Free Nelson Mandela' or giving money to Band Aid, does not necessarily signify a political commitment to a specific cause. The politics of pop can be the expression of emotion through the experience of a song or a momentary pleasure in (vicarious, for now) resistance. It can be determined by social context - in the disco or at a concert - or social environment - with friends or alone. In essence, the politics of pop rarely stand still to be scrutinised. However, when music is censored or banned, discouraged or encouraged by the state or the pop music industry, the relationship between politics and pop becomes overt. This can in fact be scrutinised.

Censorship, the Gulf War, and the politics of pop

> It is almost a truism now to say that the United Kingdom of Great Britain and Ireland is among the most heavily censored of all the industrial nations. [16]

War can make pop political. The Gulf War was no exception. At the beginning of the war the press carried stories of pop censorship. The BBC was accused of compiling a list of records to be denied airtime for the duration of the war. 'Yes, there is a list, but we can't issue it', a BBC spokesperson announced on 22 January.[17] Another BBC spokesperson was a little more forthcoming:

> We're giving guidance to producers. We're not saying these records should never be played at all during the current situation. But it would be wrong to play, say, Roberta Flack's 'Killing Me

Softly' right after a war report of casualties in the Gulf. [18]

The BBC preferred to talk of a 'caution list' for DJs, rather than a list of banned songs. It was simply a question of 'caution and sensitivity'; certain records would not be played at 'inappropriate times'. Whether censored or cautioned, DJs were issued with a list which consisted of seventy songs (see appendix). Was this censorship or sensitivity? Many in and out of pop music thought the former: censorship wrapped in a sweet bouquet of misleading words - 'caution' not 'ban'. Tim Neale, the Head of Radio Training at the BBC, was quick to reinforce the point that there was 'no ban on bands'. [19] The issue was simply 'sensitivity': songs that were considered to have the potential 'to cause unnecessary offence' were searched out of the library and placed on the list.

> The BBC has not banned any...records. The BBC takes listeners' sensitivities seriously, especially in time of war or disaster. The placing of particular songs needs special care; any song involving death or war unintentionally played close to a news bulletin could be inappropriate or hurtful. [20]

Looking through the 'caution list' it is difficult to see any overall governing logic determining inclusion or exclusion. Selection seems to have been made on the basis of three separate considerations: a macabre literalism, a mistrust of anything vaguely anti-war, and a bizarre sense of the discursive range of the war. For example, in the first category, the list includes a number of love songs: 'Waterloo' (Abba), 'I Will Survive' (Arrival), 'Bang Bang' (Cher), 'Light My Fire' (Jose Feliciano), 'Boom Bang A Bang' (Lulu), 'I'm On Fire' (Bruce Springsteen). In the second category, for example, and here we can't help wondering whom it is they are in fear of offending: 'We've Gotta Get Out Of This Place' (Animals), 'Army Dreamers' (Kate Bush), 'Give Peace A Chance' (John Lennon), 'Imagine' (John Lennon), 'Ruby Don't Take Your Love To Town' (Kenny Rogers), 'War' (Edwin Starr). Inclusions on the basis of the third category demonstrate a very particular sense of the politics of the war: for example, 'Walk Like An Egyptian' (the Bangles), 'Israelites' (Desmond Dekker), 'Midnight At The Oasis' (Maria Muldaur). There are some very surprising omissions (given the BBC's literalism): for example, the Cure's 'Killing an Arab' and the Clash's 'Rock The Casbah'. Some songs although not included on the list were also treated with 'caution' (meaning: denied airtime). One example was Carter's 'Bloodsport for All', a track critical of racism in the armed forces, but not specifically about war. [21] The song was not 'banned' because it was anti-military, but because it was 'tasteless'. The BBC claimed to be playing the B-side instead. Jimbob of Carter USM was surprised by the reason given for the decision; 'I don't know why they're playing the B-side instead, cos it finishes with the words, "Fucking arsehole bastards". You'd think they wouldn't like that much either'. [22] One of the ironies of the BBC's policy was that it ran counter to the policy of the British Forces Broadcasting Service (BFBS) set up to entertain the British troops in the Gulf. The most requested song, and the first played by the BFBS, was the Clash's 'Rock The Casbah'. [23] Among the other most requested: 'The Air That I Breathe' (Hollies), 'Bang Bang' (Cher), 'Eve of Destruction' (Barry McGuire). [24]

It is difficult to say really what the 'caution list' hoped to achieve. It seems that in a comic version of 'McCarthyism' the BBC got carried away and 'banned' anything that seemed related to war, and yet still managed to leave off the most obvious tracks. Like the real thing, the BBC's comic McCarthyism affected the behaviour of others. Though other radio companies had no obligation to comply with the BBC's list, most quickly developed a similar policy of their own. There was a general air of caution most strikingly brought home in the case of Jazz FM's DJ, Giles Peterson, who was reportedly sacked for dedicating part of his show to 'Peace in the Middle East'. [25] Pop television was also affected. Performers who attended the British Phonographic Industry (BPI) awards ceremony - the Brit awards (February '91) - were warned by Jonathan King, 'don't mention the war'. This, he said, was because it was 'too boring'. [26] Lisa Stansfield dared to break the ban, when she said, collecting her award for Best British Female Artist: 'I'm really happy to get this award, but I'd feel a lot better if the war stopped right now'. Hardly a devastating critique of British or American imperialism, but enough to ensure that when the show was broadcast her remarks were cut. [27] Similarly, at the Great British Musical Weekend, Billy Bragg was told he could say whatever he liked about the war - he made a five minute speech in which he urged people to join the peace movement - as long as he appreciated that it would be cut out before the show was shaped for general consumption. The broadcast did not include his final words: 'Say no to war'. [28]

Censorship seemed to be almost everywhere. My Jealous God's 'Petrol Bomb', due to be released during the war, was delayed. [29] Bomb The Bass, Massive Attack and Burn This all had to change their names. [30] Conflict and Ghost of an American Airman claimed they had TV shows and concerts cancelled due to the supposed 'sensitivity' of their names. [31] There was also self-censorship. Queen recorded two versions of their 'Innuendo' video; a second edited version (with World War Two scenes removed) for use on the BBC. [32] The KLF also obliged the BBC by recording a special BBC version of '3AM Eternal' - minus opening gunfire. A spokesperson for the KLF explained: 'The band felt the situation was a bit special, and they made a seven-inch version with the machine gun taken out, just for the BBC'. [33] The original version continued to be sold in record shops. The war also prompted absences of a different kind: Whitney Houston, Vanilla Ice, A Tribe Called Quest, Cinderella and Donny Osmond, all withdrew from British tours as a result of concern over security following the outbreak of war. [34]

With so much interference in the music world it is surprising that any protest songs were released during the war at all, but pop attempted to play its part in the anti-war movement. The Orb released 'Peace in the Middle East' under the name Apollo XI.[35] Lenny Kravitz, Guns'n'Roses, Red Hot Chilli Peppers, Dave Stewart, Peter Gabriel, Tom Petty, joined together with a host of other stars to record 'Give Peace a Chance'. The lyrics were re-written by Sean Ono Lennon. The final verse reads: 'Everybody's talkin' 'bout Amazon's/Trees gone/Cancer cells/From the sun/Middle East/Crazy Beast/ Rock'n'Rollers/ Sing for peace'. [36] Billy Bragg sang the original version to 70,000 peace demonstrators in Trafalgar Square. The Brixton Academy hosted the *War And Peace Benefit*, featuring The Shamen, The Orb, Rebel MC and others, 'converging to fight...imperialist rhetoric'. [37] The political potential of sampling was heard to great effect in the pop political critique of the war. Bush was perhaps more sampled than most. It is easy to highlight contradictions and hypocrisies of war when direct samples can be used to illustrate both. The KLF 'America No More' (the B-side of 'America: What Time Is Love'), is something of a masterpiece in the political art of sampling. It begins with a news broadcast during Vietnam, cutting to Nixon's comments, and then, later, to Bush talking about the Gulf: the samples are interspersed with synthesised bombs dropping, gun shots and helicopters. The song's politics are not vague, as the ending demonstrates. The last sample - 'Praise Jesus Christ. If Jesus Christ were here tonight, you would not dare to drop another bomb'. The song ends with a countdown and consequent explosion. Test Department produced a similar sound and effect. 'New World Order' examines various questions raised by the Gulf conflict. Were 'we' there for 'more than just the price of a gallon of gas', as Bush stated? Synthesised bombs and helicopters come and go as Bush comments, 'What we're doing is going to chart the future of the world for the next hundred years'.

Of course, some pop musicians supported the war effort. As Operation Desert Storm got into full swing, Mark Knopfler got together with Little Richard and Luther Vandross to record 'Voices that Care' for the troops in the Gulf. [38] Whitney Houston recorded 'The Star Spangled Banner' (an interesting contrast to Jimi Hendrix's anti-Vietnam version recorded live at Woodstock in 1969). And MC Hammer accepted his award for best rhythm and blues album at the American Music Awards with the comment: 'I'd like to dedicate this award to the troops in the Persian Gulf'. [39] The media's attempt to manage political dissent and encourage support for the war effort in the Gulf, was seen nowhere more clearly than in the pop world. Whilst the war filled newspapers and television screens, pop radio was expected to pretend that everything went on as normal. Yet many in pop music were sceptical of what the news media were presenting as the 'Gulf facts'. Whether or not The KLF were making a political statement when they painted over a billboard reading The Gulf Facts, is hard to say. What is certain is that in an atmosphere of war paranoia, the act resulted in Bill Drummond and Jim Cauty being detained at Battersea police station for four hours. [40]

Many of the records attacking the war were inevitably (because of censorship and the short duration of the conflict) released after the end of hostilities. Yet those musicians who wanted to speak out against the war were not completely denied the opportunity. The music press constantly had interviews and comment sections which specifically discussed the issues of the war. For example, while some sought to demonstrate their machismo in boasts of how they would go to the Gulf if requested, others wondered about the relationship between the British imperialism of old and the reasons for 'our' involvement in the war: a nagging doubt that maybe 'we' had something to do with the cause of the war. [41] This is something that the Disposable Heroes of Hiphoprisy articulate in 'The Winter of the Long Hot Summer':

> We tried to remember the history in the region
> The French foreign legion, Imperialism
> Peter o'Toole and hate the Ayatollah
> were all we learnt at school
> Not that we gave Hussein five billion

Musicians had different theories as to why the West had become involved in the conflict. Very few believed the hypocrisy that democracy was to be 're-established' by restoring the Sabah family to power. Danielle Dax, for example: 'I find it confusing that the West should get on its high moral horse about Iraq invading Kuwait while ignoring what China's been doing in Tibet. There's a different set of rules when it's economically in the interests of the West to interfere'. [42] The Ruthless Rap Assassins ('Flow It Out'), place the war in the context of other military interventions and non-interventions:

> The Gulf War crisis, who was to blame
> Was it Bush or was it Saddam Hussein
> When Russia went to Afghanistan
> No one did a thing, did anyone give a damn
> If Saddam Hussein's an invader
> Then so was Ronald Reagan when he annexed Grenada
> Did the West protest when Reagan bombed Libya
> Did they fight South Africa to free Namibia

For most, the war was about oil. Caron Wheeler (former Soul II Soul singer, now solo) suggested: 'neither Hussein nor Bush give a shit about the rest of us. This is their war over oil'. [43] Much of this is epitomised in 'Black Bandages' by the Falling Joys:

> Black oil Burn out
> Black fight Black Death
> Black bandages
> Black hope escape
> Black night Kuwait
> It's Blackfire
> It's backfired

The track is cut with a sample from a news broadcast detailing economic sanctions against Iraq. Blur, the Godfathers and Carter, all expressed the belief that many of the declared reasons for fighting were hypocritical because of the West's previous economic and military involvement with the Iraq regime. [44] Iraq had in effect been armed by the West as a bulwark against the perceived threat posed by Iran. Peter Coyne, the vocalist with the Godfathers, in an interview in *Sounds*, made the point: 'It's not just a matter of somebody invading another country. Hussein's been sponsored by most of the Allies. We're fighting a war which we created ourselves because of money and greed. All the money spent on a day's war could clear up the underfunding of hospitals in this country. It's disgusting.' [45] Caron Wheeler makes much the same point: 'the British Government are spending £4 million a day [on the war effort]. Strange how there's always cutbacks on hospital spending during peacetime, but the money seems to manifest when it suits them.' [46] A sentiment expressed by the Ruthless Rap Assassins in 'Think'; the song makes the case for a connection between economic difficulties at home and hypocritical military adventurism in the Gulf:

> You know the shit was heavy cos they started a war
> You know who got the blame they called him insane

> But just who was it sold him weapons and planes
> The National Health's in trouble lack of money is why
> But still they spent millions sending people to die

The Ruthless Rap Assassins' point, that the money Britain mis-spent during the war, defeating what was in large measure its own military-economic investment, should have been used to improve the social fabric of Britain, is made with reference to the USA by the Disposable Heroes of Hiphoprisy in 'The Winter of The Long Hot Summer':

> On January 2nd the Bush Administration
> announced a recession had stricken
> the nation...
> Meanwhile a budget was placed in our hands
> as the deadline came to an end
> so much for the peace dividend
> one billion a day is what we spent
> and our grand children will pay for it till the end
> When schools are unfunded
> and kids don't get their diplomas
> they get used for gun boat diplomacy

For other musicians the cost is to be measured in other ways. Beth Watson's 'Waiting at the Border', for example:

> I'm trying not to think about
> The price of desert storm
> And while I know that
> We will win here
> There'll be many people dead...
> Though the air war might continue
> Still Hussein just isn't listening
> To the reign of mass destruction

Despite the BBC's comic and unfunny attempts at censorship, different positions on the war (both for and against) were presented and debated in pop music - the nature of the super powers, the war's cost financially, ecologically, and in terms of human life, the legacy of imperialism and the experience of soldiering in the Gulf. The latter two are heard in The The's 'Sweet Bird Of Truth':

> you know I can almost smell the blood washing against the shores
> Of this land that can't forget its past
> Oh, the wind that carries this plane is the wind of change

Heaven sent and hell bent
Over the mountain tops we go
Just like all the other GI Joes...
Should I cry like a baby?
Or die like a man?

Conclusion: the limits of control

As we said earlier, pop politics are often vague, open to negotiation, and ultimately dependent on audience articulation. Throughout the course of the war, attempts were made to control the flow of the political into pop, and pop into the political. But political pop is a moveable feast, rarely remaining still to be eaten whole analytically. However, when music is censored or banned, discouraged or encouraged by the state or music industry, pop becomes political in a way that can be scrutinised analytically. During and for the period immediately following the war, politics and pop had an open relationship. This took different forms: on the one hand, the 'banning' of records, enforced name changes, cancelled gigs, delayed releases, censored opinions; and on the other, pop on peace marches, peace benefits, debate within the music press, and, of course, music for and against the war. The line of the BBC was never hegemonic. Many musicians simply refused to be silent. While the BBC attempted to impose 'sensitivity' on the pop music industry, the music press continually sidestepped the urge to dance in harmony with the war effort; providing pop musicians with an arena in which to express themselves about the war. Here musicians debated opinions on the war which often subsequently became expressed on vinyl. Many of the songs released were 'B' sides or album tracks, rather than high exposure single releases. Much of the political pop of the war, therefore, relied and still relies on determined audience articulation. Nevertheless, the war did produce a diversity of political pop, often diverse in ways that were hardly anticipated ('Boom Bang A Bang' becoming a political pop song), and as the *Melody Maker* rather sardonically pointed out (thinking mostly of the American acts - Donny Osmond, etc. - who cancelled tours of Britain because of the war), 'the Gulf War was bad for the world but good for music'. [47]

Appendix

The BBC 'caution list' [48]

Abba: Waterloo
Abba: Under Attack
A-Ha: Hunting High And Low
Alarm: 68 Guns
Animals: We've Gotta Get Out Of This Place
Arrival: I Will Survive
Joan Baez: The Night They Drove Old Dixie Down
Bangles: Walk Like An Egyptian
Beatles: Back In The USSR
Bee Gees: Staying Alive
Pat Benatar: Love Is A Battlefield
Big Country: Fields Of Fire
Blondie: Automatic
Boomtown Rats: I Don't Like Mondays
Brook Brothers: Warpaint
Kate Bush: Army Dreamers
Cher: Bang Bang (My Baby Shot Me Down)
Eric Clapton: I Shot The Sheriff
Phil Collins: In The Air Tonight
Elvis Costello: Oliver's Army
Cutting Crew: I Just Died In Your Arms Tonight
Skeeter Davis: End Of The World
Desmond Dekker: Israelites
Doors: Light My Fire
Dire Straits: Brothers In Arms
Duran Duran: A View To A Kill
Jose Feliciano: Light My Fire
First Choice: Armed And Extremely Dangerous
Roberta Flack: Killing Me Softly With His Song
Frankie Goes To Hollywood: Two Tribes
Eddy Grant: Living On The Frontline
Eddy Grant: Give Me Hope Johanna
Hollies: The Air That I Breathe
Elton John: Saturday Night's Alright For Fighting
Millie Jackson: Act Of War
Johnny Hates Jazz: I Don't Want To Be A Hero
John Lennon: Give Peace A Chance
John Lennon: Imagine

Jona Lewie: Stop The Cavalry
Lulu: Boom Bang A Bang
McGuinness Flint: When I'm Dead And Gone
Bob Marley: Buffalo Soldier
Maria Muldaur: Midnight At The Oasis
Mash: Suicide Is Painless
Mike & The Mechanics: Silent Running
Rick Nelson: Fools Rush In
Nicole: A Little Peace
Billy Ocean: When The Going Gets Tough, The Tough Get Going
Donny Osmond: Soldier Of Love
Paper Lace: Billy Don't Be A Hero
Queen: Killer Queen
Queen: Another One Bites The Dust
Queen: Flash
Martha Reeves & The Vandellas: Forget Me Not
BA Robertson: Bang Bang
Tom Robinson: War Baby
Kenny Rogers: Ruby Don't Take Your Love To Town
Spandau Ballet: I'll Fly For You
Specials: Ghost Town
Bruce Springsteen: I'm On Fire
Edwin Starr: War
Status Quo: In The Army Now
Status Quo: Burnin' Bridges
Cat Stevens: I'm Gonna Get Me A Gun
Rod Stewart: Sailing
Donna Summer: State Of Independence
Tears For Fears: Everybody Wants To Rule The World
Temptations: Ball Of Confusion
10cc: Rubber Bullets
Stevie Wonder: Heaven Help Us All

Notes

1. Sainte-Marie, Buffy (1992), 'The Big Ones Get Away', from the album, *Coincidence And Likely Stories*, Ensign Records.
2. Frith, Simon (1993), *Sound Effects: Youth, Leisure, and the Politics of Rock*, Constable, London, p. 147.
3. Street, John (1986), *Rebel Rock: The Politics of Popular Music*, Basil Blackwell, Oxford, p. 7.
4. Brecht, Bertolt (1964), *On Theatre*, Methuen, London, pp. 150-151.
5. Denselow, Robin (1990), *When The Music's Over: The Story of Political Pop*, Faber and Faber, London, p. 92.
6. See *Rebel Rock*, pp. 19-20.
7. See Storey, John (1988), 'Rockin' Hegemony: West Coast Rock and Amerika's War in Vietnam' in *Tell Me Lies About Vietnam*, eds. Louvre, Alf and Walsh, Jeff, Open University Press, Milton Keynes.
8. Ibid.
9. See Widgery, David (1986), *Beating Time*, London: Chatto and Windus.
10. *When The Music's Over*, p. 260.
11. See Storey, John (1994), 'Side Saddle On The Golden Calf' in *One Step Forward: The American Media in the Age of Reagan and Bush*, Klein, Michael (ed.), Pluto, London.
12. *When The Music's Over*, p. 221.
13. *Rebel Rock*, p. 80.
14. Ibid., p. 79-81.
15. Ibid., p. 23.
16. Cubitt, Sean (1990), 'Innocence and manipulation: Censorship, consumption, and Freedom in Britain' in *Identity, & Style*, Tomlinson, Alan (ed.), Routledge, London, p. 102.
17. *Socialist Worker*, 26 January 1991.
18. *Select*, March 1991.
19. *Independent*, 2 February 1991.
20. Ibid.
21. *Sounds*, 26 January 1991.
22. *Select*, March 1991.
23. *New Musical Express*, 16 February 1991.
24. *Observer*, 27 January 1991.
25. *Vox*, February 1992.
26. *New Musical Express*, 16 February 1991.
27. Ibid.
28. *Sounds*, 26 January 1991.

29. *New Musical Express*, 2 February 1991.
30. *Melody Maker*, 9 February 1991, *Vox*, February 1992.
31. *Melody Maker*, 9 February 1991.
32. *Melody Maker*, 21 February 1991.
33. *Melody Maker*, 26 January 1991.
34. *New Musical Express*, 2 February 1991, and *Vox*, February 1992.
35. *Melody Maker*, 9 February 1991.
36. *Melody Maker*, 26 January 1991.
37. *New Musical Express*, 26 January 1991.
38. *Vox*, February 1992.
39. *Independent*, 31 January 1991, and *Melody Maker*, 9 February 1991.
40. *New Musical Express*, 16 February 1991.
41. *Melody Maker*, 21 December 1991.
42. *Select*, March 1991.
43. Ibid.
44. *Sounds*, 26 January 1991 and 16 February 1991, and *Melody Maker*, 21 December 1991.
45. *Sounds*, 16 February 1991.
46. *Select*, March 1991.
47. *Melody Maker*, 21 December 1991.
48. The list is compiled on the basis of reports in *Select* (March 1991), *Socialist Worker*, (26 January 1991), *Observer* (27 January 1991), and the *New Musical Express* (26 January 1991).

8 War in the British press

John Taylor

To censor or self censor?

War is an anxious time for newspapers. Official censorship, news-blackouts and other gagging devices bear more directly than usual on the industry and, because of the immediacy of news flashes and film on television, sales and readership tend to fall. An NOP poll showed that in Britain during the Gulf war, a quarter of adults said they read fewer papers, and 57 percent claimed to have been watching more television. Reflecting a long term decline in the use of newspapers as the main source of national news, the majority of people either watched TV or preferred radio to the papers. The only national paper to figure in the top-ten news sources was the *Daily Telegraph*.[1]

In addition, press stories were widely seen as unreliable. According to Robert Worcester, chairman of the opinion pollsters MORI, 'only one person in three said they had faith in their own daily newspaper to tell the truth. In fact, over a third of *Sun* and *Daily Star* readers and near a third of *Today* and *Daily Mirror* readers said they had 'no trust at all' in their own paper's war reporting.'[2]

But in wartime, national dailies have even more to worry about than falling sales, and widespread disbelief in their news value. The first anxiety actually stems from the fears of government and the military: over and above their interest in keeping battle plans secret, they believe that realistic TV pictures and photographs will show the full horror of war, and that such pictures will badly affect civilian morale, threatening to open hostilities on the home-front. This fear of documentary realism means politicians take an unusual interest in TV and the press, and demand that reporters support the war by repeating the official story lines.

The second anxiety is related to the first, but originates in the press itself: it has a well-founded fear of government legislation. The easiest way the industry can avoid this is by practising self-censorship. There is nothing inherently bad about this practice - it does not mean that the press is always hiding the 'truth'. On the contrary, the press is busily repeating and reinforcing its own type of truth, and at the same time protecting itself from the types of truth imposed by the even greater restraints of official censorship.

In this essay, I shall look at the way the story of the Gulf war was told in some of the national dailies. The newspaper industry in Britain is extremely rich in titles, with eleven national dailies in England and Wales, and another four or five in Scotland; there are ten Sunday papers in England, and numerous local evening and free papers. The only distinctions which need to be made here are between three broad market niches: the quality broadsheets such as the *Daily Telegraph*, *Times*, *Guardian*, and *Independent*, whose readers tend to be older, middle-class men (and which make up only 16 percent of the market); the middle-market tabloids such as *Today*, *Daily Express* and *Daily Mail*, whose readers tend to be aspiring working-class men and women; the downmarket tabloids, such as the *Daily Star*, *Daily Sport* and the *Sun*, whose readers tend to be young working-class men, and the *Daily Mirror* with its appeal across a wider age-range, and to women (the *Sun* and *Mirror* alone account for about half the newspaper readership).

In reporting the Gulf war, there were major differences and similarities between the national broadsheets and tabloids. The greatest gap lay between the 'liberal conscience' *Guardian* and the populist *Sun* and *Daily Star*. Each newspaper imagined its readers to have quite different attitudes towards the war, centring on the role of the British forces in the coalition and on nationalism. After the 'Baghdad bunker bombing' in February three influential journalists made their different views known to the *UK Press Gazette*: Peter Preston, editor of the *Guardian*, believed readers wanted to know everything, and expected to 'argue' about the war; Ron Spark, chief *Sun* leader writer described the readership of the *Guardian* as 'bizarre' for having doubts, and said any newspaper should 'support the cause'; Sir Peregrine Worsthorne, a well-known conservative, was also critical of papers that were 'adversarial' saying that the 'public reacts [to this] with more hostility than gratitude'. He believed 'the public wants less, not more'.[3] After the war, audience research showed that large numbers of the population were ready to accept less information, and did not mind covert news management in wartime as long as they would be told the truth later.[4] This research seems to accord with Worsthorne's judgement: in an article in the *Sunday Telegraph*, he argued that the media were getting more and more out of step with public opinion, and that public opinion was moving away from supporting 'a right-to-know' towards greater support for 'right-to-privacy'.[5]

These opinions have a long history, and were all aired in 1982, during and after the Falklands campaign. Then the press and broadcasting media were invited to give their views to the Select Committee of the Ministry of Defence, which brought out a report on 'handling the media'.[6] The report was firmly on the side of views such as those later expressed by Spark and Worsthorne, and underlined several factors which had a bearing upon news accounts of the Gulf war. Firstly, it brushed aside press complaints about news management, since the national interest lay in winning the war. Secondly, it said 'the harsh realities of war', especially TV pictures, would lower morale on the home front. Thirdly, it congratulated the press for its 'good taste and tone', avoiding unpleasant scenes that might have caused offence to the families of serving men and women.

The Falklands campaign, and the similar experience of the USA in Grenada in 1983, ensured that the international machinery for controlling realism was in place by 1991. Legal constraints upon the British press in peacetime were already formidable. In wartime, these could be extended, but this proved unnecessary: the deterrence of the 'D' notice system of 'advice' to editors on sensitive matters was sufficient. The press was expected to police itself.

Self-censorship did not come easily to the press (for commercial and ideological reasons), but between 1982 and 1991, the 'right-to-know' was supplanted by the 'right-to-privacy'. A series of air-crashes and other disasters led to gross intrusions into the private grief of individuals. The main issue was invasion of privacy. All the newspapers used photographs of victims suffocating at the Hillsborough football ground disaster (17 April 1989), and later the *People* offended the Royal Family with a shot of Prince Harry peeing in the park (19 November 1989). Robert Maxwell sacked the editor, but the press was warned to 'clean up its act' or face government legislation. As a spur to the industry, the government set up the Calcutt Commission which gave the press a last chance to prove that voluntary self-regulation through self-censorship would work. Newspaper editors attempted to forestall Calcutt with their own code of practice which claimed to protect privacy (28 November 1989). Whilst this did not prevent sensational news reports or eliminate all potentially offensive pictures, the minds of editors were focused upon avoiding legal restraint through the practice of good taste. To help them, Calcutt said the Press Council should be disbanded and replaced by a tougher independent Press Complaints Commission, which started work in January 1991.[7]

Given the recent threats of legislation and the official control of access to the front line the press was in no position to delve behind the approved versions of the Gulf war.[8] But official censorship did not throw the industry into disarray, with nothing to say or show. On the contrary, it facilitated the flow of information, and the newspapers were full of stories from the front, many of them accompanied by photographs as evidence. The military cleverly incorporated front-line journalists into the war by aiding their identification with the forces, giving them uniforms and granting requests to retain them at the end of tours of duty.[9] It is well known that identification and the reliance upon official channels of information closes the gap between official demands and press practice. In these circumstances, journalists were not only willing to accede to the military in matters of operational secrecy but, without overt direction from their 'minders', produced stories and pictures which suited the official line on the progress and purpose of the war.[10]

The press was squeezed by legislation, the fear of more legislation, and the established skill of the government and military in handling the media. At the 'What the Papers Say' Awards in February, the Home Secretary Kenneth Baker reminded journalists about Calcutt's recommendations for new offences of intrusive journalism, and at the same time congratulated them on their coverage of the war, especially for exercising their judgements 'correctly'.[11] This meant the war was being fought with civilians in mind and with commitment to the lives of allied troops. Home support depended on this confidence, which was being reinforced in 'thumbs up' images and texts.

Realism and dreams

Journalists were not simply duped by officials, but had their own requirements which derived from the ways the press tells stories. Storytelling is directed by two forces which flood the newspapers - realism and dreams. The force of the real is expressed through eyewitness accounts and photojournalists' pictures, which are widely perceived as documentary proof, and evidence of newshounds' presence.[12]

The actuality of pictures helps to prove (or to test the validity of) the text, because readers can see what happened for themselves. This material is hard news, and is often extremely disturbing, being visceral and bloody, cruel and inhuman.

At the same time, and at the other extreme, the harsh realities of life are softened by advertisements which offer immediate and unending pleasures, the gratification of all the senses and the promise of eternal youth. The texts and photographs which make up advertisements are often fantastic, but this does not diminish them; on the contrary, the liberties taken with realism are often a sign of the intensity of dreams about commodities.

Occasionally, the worlds of hard news and advertisements collide. The stories and pictures of unbearable hardships, such as 'famine victims,' will be placed unintentionally next to wonderful plates showing thin but pampered 'models', though we rarely see them or ourselves as 'fashion victims'. Sometimes, the same picture may be used to illustrate hard news and the dream world of holiday advertising. A photograph of soldiers on their armoured vehicle in the Gulf was used by the *Daily Star* under the headline 'The Rats Bite!' (25 February - the year is 1991 unless otherwise stated); it was later used to advertise five hundred free holidays in Florida for members of the Gulf forces, donated by Thomas Cook Travel (*Independent on Sunday*, 3 March). In practice there is no absolute divide between the realism of hard news and the magical promises of pleasure. Some advertisements play on our fears of death and decline, or of being on the 'outside,' while many news stories in the editorial pages of the papers are full of sensual delight, or other pleasures such as humour (which may be a cruel delight in seeing the high and mighty take a fall through scandal or stupidity).

The forces of realism and dreams translate into the rampant forces of sex and death, which are among the most powerful motivating forces in newsworthiness (and in advertising). The press has long-established methods of using these forces as the hook to tell captivating human interest stories, and was able to continue its normal practice under the regimes of censorship and self-censorship.

Human interest

The human interest story releases a great deal of copy, and serves to draw the titles closer to each other than their market position would suggest. It provides reader-identification through local colour and atmosphere, and as such, it is literally and metaphorically close to home. It is underpinned by an ideology which escapes official censure as long as it is not too intrusive on privacy: it pretends that the differences between people are less significant than their common humanity. It uses a number of well-known narrative devices, assuming that people are attracted by, or at least susceptible to, stories which derive their authority from two kinds of appeal - the heartwarming and the heartbreaking.

Heartbreaking stories play upon families broken up, waiting wives and, finally, the loss of loved ones, stories about the first injured, lost or killed; the story of the youngest victim; young widows; especially cruel deaths, or otherwise bizarre incidents attached to death, such as the bitter irony of dying in friendly fire. Heartbreaking stories appear on the front covers of both the broadsheets and the various tabloids, often accompanied by the words such as 'nightmare' or 'horror'. In the Gulf war, the *Sun* accompanied the story of the nine 'British heroes [killed] in bomb blunder' with photographs of two of them in dress uniform, and the banner headline 'So Young So Sad' (28 February). The *Guardian* carried a full report, including photographs of four of the soldiers, on an inside page under the headline. 'Families count cost of "friendly" fire'. (28 February).

Heartwarming stories are often associated with lucky escapes and love, and also with sex. For instance, later in 1991, the 'perfect couple' Jill Morrell and released Beirut hostage John McCarthy were pictured side by side in *Today*: the headline ran 'The Look of Love,' but it was topped by the words 'Joy of Sex' printed in red, and announcing an inside feature (26 September). Of course, the two headlines affect one another, and it is common practice to have various headlines underscoring each other, or providing some ironic contrast.

In keeping with this practice, though emphasising family life, the *Sun* ran a heartwarming story showing a soldier returned from the desert and holding up his baby son. The headline said 'Rats My Boy', which managed to make a linguistic 'joke' as well as keep up the references to British action by the Desert Rats during the Second World War, which was an important touchstone or historical reference for the *Sun* (12 March).

Sometimes, heartrending and heartwarming stories appear on the same front page. An example of this practice is the *Daily Mirror*'s account of the storm of January 1990. Under the headline which said 'Death toll reaches 46...,' the *Mirror* printed photographs of two girls - one of whom survived and one who died; the headline was 'Tears of Heartbreak and of Joy' (27 January 1990). In a similar vein, during the Gulf war, *Today* reported the homecoming of a captured Tornado pilot with the words 'Flying into Love...'; however, under the photographs of the man reunited with his wife, it continued the headline with the downbeat message '...but third-rate welcome for our 17 dead heroes' (8 March).

The forces of life and death are strongest when combined in ironic contrasts as in the above examples, though the *Sun* is especially practised in combining sex and death on the front page. Its headline in January read '300 Iraqis Die in Tank Blitz,' but the only photograph was of a (clothed) 'Page Three girl', looking sexy in a stereotypical way. *Sun* readers would then have discovered that, cruelly, this 'model of bravery' was dogged by death and 'fighting a nightmare battle against cancer' (31 January). Thus on a single page, and through the careful choice of words and pictures, the *Sun* managed to provide the thrill of a tank battle, a reference to the Second World War in the term 'blitz', a frisson of sex in a picture, and a chill at the presence of cancer.

Sex and death stories run as strongly through the broadsheets as they do the tabloids. After the court martial of a naval officer and a Wren found naked together on a Gulf warship, the *Daily Mirror* (punning as usual on words and historical reference) said 'England Sexpects' (14 June). But the story was given much greater coverage and told in fuller detail in the *Daily Telegraph*, though on an inside page and under a more sober headline ('Wren and Navy officer found naked in cabin reprimanded').

Death stories are equally well represented throughout the titles, especially when they combine personal 'tragedies' with issues which often embarrass the government. Such was the case of the nine soldiers killed together in a single incident, which was first reported with fatalistic cries such as 'What a bloody shame...' (*Daily Star*, 28 February). But acceptance quickly turned into the well-known newspaper mode of 'watchdog outrage', when editors adopted angry tones after a report into the incident showed that the men had been killed by 'friendly' fire, and no government official had even bothered to apologise (*Daily Mirror* and *Daily Telegraph*, 25 July). Again, in standard newspaper practice, the story was picked up the following May, when the inquest declared the deaths had been 'unlawful' killing by USAF forces. This verdict was so momentous, with the promise of further revelations of government weaknesses in the face of USA intransigence and unconcern, that the *Guardian* carried it on the front page, with a large photograph of distraught and determined relatives outside Oxford County Hall (19 May 1992). However, its headline was more restrained than the *Daily Mirror*'s 'Dishonour and Disgrace - US Top Gun pilots guilty of unlawful killing, says jury' (19 May 1992).

Another important characteristic of the human interest story is its special kind of politics. It is not simply a neutral window on a diverse world but embodies a particular way of seeing: it rejects the possibility of basic structural inequalities in favour of the random and non-historical forces of luck, fate and chance.

The fate of ordinary individuals is worked out against a backdrop of several converging elements: the hardware of war, the military chiefs who deploy these materials and the political arenas and prime political actors. These forces, people and institutions are consistently described as (and shown to be) in control. The war could be represented in this simple way: first, world leaders tried to control Saddam Hussein through law; failing in this, they passed responsibility to their military commanders who through technology and 'intelligence' were expected to minimise fate and the disastrous effects of Saddam's random or irrational decisions.

All the newspaper stories used politico-technical rationality as a driving force of the narrative. Diplomacy never became too cerebral because it was personalised: Bush was thoughtful and resolute, whereas Saddam was bad and mad.[13] The equivalence of this in the military was its hardware, which was state-of-the-art. This, too, never became too cerebral because we saw thrilling images of machines and missiles in action.[14]

However, the super-rational force of the coalition was imperfect. It reduced Saddam's power but could not erase it altogether, and especially could not always outwit (what was presented as) his cruel and cynical mind. So the allies blamed the destruction of the Amiriya shelter in Baghdad, which killed at least 300 Iraqi civilians, on Saddam's ruthless use of human shields rather than their own faulty intelligence. Less easily explained away were the deaths of Iraqi civilians in Fallouja and the deaths of allied troops from so-called 'friendly fire'. These deaths were 'tragedies' put down to 'the fog of war' or 'the heat of battle', but again the low number of such incidents only served to emphasise how allied control was near to absolute, and that random fate was largely eliminated.

Speaking for readers

Despite these shared assumptions about what makes a news story, the different titles will tell it in the 'voice' of their imagined ideal readers. This difference was clear in the above example, though the papers can make mistakes, especially in wartime. We saw this in the different captions which accompanied the same photographs of a shell wrecking an Iraqi bunker. In speaking for its readers, the *Daily Mirror* said 'Rats Get Stuck In': this no-nonsense headline swamped the information (printed under the picture) that Americans had blown up this position. The *Guardian* headline was vaguer: it read 'Allies race to snap pincer on

Guards' - but the paper was immediately criticised by readers for using non-*Guardian*, warmongering language (26 February).

The easiest way for tabloid editors to refer to the shared knowledge of readers was through film or television, mixing cowboy films with references to Vietnam and the Second World War. For instance, the ultimatum to Iraq was 'High Noon' (*Daily Express*, *Sun*, 23 February); photographs of a 'fun album' of soldiers relaxing on the 'front line' were headlined 'It ain't half hot mum!', referring to a popular TV programme (*Daily Mirror*, 19 January); maps claiming to show the likely plan of attack described the areas as 'The Killing Fields' (*Daily Mirror*, 1 February); the *Sport* headlined 'Rambo Rescue' under a picture of a couple in bed (18 January); the captive Tornado pilots, once freed, were described as having been 'To Hell and Back' (*Daily Mirror*, 5 March); a damaged Tornado flew home 'On a wing and a prayer' (*Today*, 25 January).

In contrast to the tabloids, the shared knowledge of broadsheet readers was not so rooted in popular programmes, films or songs. However, headlines (which tended to be longer) still drew on military clichés, and were still triumphalist in tone. For instance, the headline in the *Independent* at the start of the 'aerial offensive' was 'Iraqi defences crumble as allied bombers pound on' (18 January).

There was also an air of excitement over possible business opportunities which the war could create, as in the *Independent on Sunday*'s 'British Aerospace flies into the front line' (27 January), and 'The oilman's war- how the West can win the battle for black gold' (3 February).

Jingoism and doubt

Despite the similarities, there were also marked differences between the broadsheets and the tabloids, and between national and local papers. After three weeks of saturation coverage, particularly on television, Brian McArthur asked the professional journalists who read the *UK Press Gazette* whether the Gulf war was still 'an automatic front-page splash?'[15] He concluded that the national broadsheets were continuing to cover it on the front page; the tabloids were not always leading with the war; the local papers habitually looked for local angles, but were more diverse and ready to abandon the war as a lead story.

At the same time, the lower-market tabloids were much more jingoistic than the other papers. As the war started, the *Sun* dedicated its front page to a picture of the Union flag with a portrait of a soldier at its centre; the *Sun* said 'Support our boys and put this flag in your window' (16

January). Throughout the war, the *Sun* flagged itself as 'The paper that supports our boys and girls'. The nationalism of this newspaper obscured the international nature of the coalition, and the fact that British forces comprised a small part of the total. Ideal readers, whose 'voice' the papers attempt to ventriloquise, are not the same as actual readers, of course, who recognise a gap between their perceptions and those offered to them by the papers. This gap was measured by a survey of readers of all papers which showed that tabloid readers were fully aware of the jingoism and triumphalism of their papers. The survey showed that 'As many as 41 percent of *Sun* and *Star* readers agreed that their papers glorified the war too much, as did 35 percent of *Mirror* readers, 25 percent of middle-market tabloids, but only 7 percent of quality-paper readers'.[16] However, the widespread media coverage of British exploits, particularly in the tabloids, led to the belief among this sample that British airmen had flown a high percentage of the air sorties: 'Thirteen percent...believed that the British had flown more than 50 percent, 29 percent said 30-50 percent, 21 percent said 20-30 percent, 19 percent said 10-20 percent, 16 percent said 5-10 percent, and only 3 percent said less than 5 percent. The correct answer was about 3 percent...'.[17]

The perception of the war as a British affair was continued in the jingoistic *Daily Star* in its report of the Gulf War Victory Parade. In terms which referred directly to the autobiography and film version of the life of Douglas Bader, a famous pilot in the Battle of Britain in 1940, the *Star*'s headline was 'The Day Britain Reached for the Sky' (22 June). The front page picture showed a five-year-old boy in military uniform waving a flag at the fly-past; the back page picture showed Tornados flying over the dome of St Paul's Cathedral, which was an icon of endurance from the Second World War. In contrast, the *Guardian*'s report was of 'mixed feelings', but it decided that in the end 'Pride' lightens doubt and drizzle at Gulf parade' (22 June).

The biggest gap between the broadsheets and the tabloids was in the amount of criticism or at least doubt they were willing to print. The *Guardian*, for instance, carried critical commentaries from independent reporters, such as John Pilger,[18] Noam Chomsky,[19] and Philip Knightley.[20] The *Independent* ran stories by Robert Fisk, who stayed outside the pool system and was one of the first to 'express scepticism' concerning the official coalition line.[21]

Middle-market tabloids were also critical of the way news of the war was being managed. For instance, the *Daily Express* told its readers that there was a gap between the 'Bloodless video games' which the Americans were fond of showing to demonstrate their 'smart bombs' and actual war: 'computer images [were] hiding the real horror of conflict'

(21 January). Interestingly in this case, but not uncommon in newspaper practice, there was a gap between the written text and the accompanying pictures. The report by Chris Buckland emphasised that despite the unprecedented bombing campaign, 'not a single body has yet been photographed, and not a single injured soldier seen on TV'. But the story was illustrated with a photograph of General Schwarzkopf combined with a still image from the video taken by a laser guided missile 'bombing an Iraqi ammunition dump'. The photograph appeared as a perfect 'thought bubble,' an idea of precision bombing which was supposed to exist both in the General's mind and in the real world.

If these papers sometimes expressed doubts, the bottom range of tabloids were never so uncertain, consistently reporting the war in bloodthirsty and simple terms. The *Star* said 'No Mercy' (18 January); the *Sun* said '96 Hours to Wipe 'Em Out' (11 January); the *Mirror* said 'We'll Bomb them Till They're Not There Anymore' (19 January). The attitude of these papers was 'the Iraqis asked for it'.

Blaming Saddam

The difference between the broadsheets and tabloids over the effects of such a huge bombardment was most clearly seen in reports of the destruction of the shelter at Amiriya. The Americans always maintained that the shelter was a bunker and a military 'command and control centre'; the Iraqis always said it was a shelter for civilians. Television networks in London received horrific, uncensored footage from Baghdad, which they then cut according to their established practice of good taste and tone. The following day, the press had decided on the degree of distance they were willing to put between themselves and the official line. The *Independent*'s photograph was of the outside of the smouldering building, but it placed the words 'Shelter a military target' in quotation marks, and also reported the 'Myth of pinpoint bombing' (14 February). The *Guardian* headline ran 'US insists it hit army bunker,' but created a much greater visceral impact by headlining 'bodies shrunk by heat of fire,' with a picture 'frame-grabbed' from the TV of 'rescue workers' carrying out the remains of a body wrapped in a blanket (14 February). In complete contrast, the tabloids blamed Saddam Hussein for the deaths of the Iraqis. Over pictures of grieving relatives and covered bodies, *Today* said 'Entombed by Saddam'; over a picture of an injured child, the *Star* said 'Sacrificed' (14 February).

Blaming Saddam was characteristic of the tabloid coverage, and fitted well their view of the war as directed primarily against the 'madman'

'Butcher of Baghdad' (*Daily Star*, 3 and 23 August 1990). The historical and immediate economic reasons for the invasion of Kuwait were by-passed in the tabloids in favour of declaring Saddam to be the 'New Hitler of the Middle East,' annexing 'world oil' at the point of a gun (*Today*, 3 August 1990). *Today* 'proved' that Saddam was like Hitler by placing side by side two photographs - one showing the Iraqi leader with an English boy he had taken hostage, and the other showing Hitler with a boy of similar age: 'Hitler also used children...' (25 August 1990).

The common tabloid practice of reducing world historical events to the personalities of current top politicians continued throughout the summer and autumn of 1990. These simple opinions were also broadcast by President Bush and Saddam Hussein, who each claimed the issue was black-and-white, a contest between 'good and evil'.[22] The theme of leaders of the so-called 'New World Order' agreeing to stop Hussein/Hitler was readily picked up in the tabloids. In September, the *Mirror* used a photograph of President Bush and Gorbachev together, pointing at the camera but made to say the headline, 'We're After YOU Saddam' (10 September 1990). As the ultimatum expired in January, and war came closer, the *Mirror* distilled 'The Heroes' into individual British fighters, whilst 'The Villain' was Saddam (15 January).

Saddam was turned into the epitome of the slippery, untrustworthy Arab, 'The Great Pretender,' as the *Mirror* called him (24 August 1990). So when on the eve of war he was reported as saying 'We'll pull out!', readers were already familiar with his shiftiness, and encouraged to back the US declaration that 'the war goes on' (*Birmingham Evening Mail*, 15 February). Saddam continued to prove his worthlessness by refusing to face up to the allies in a square fight, acting the 'coy virgin' and avoiding combat. He alone was responsible for reducing his soldiers to 'Cannon Fodder' (*Mirror*, 2 February). He alone used random 'terror' weapons - Scud missiles which were widely reported as unpredictable and of little military significance but which proved the Iraqi leader to be an international terrorist (*Today*, 23 January).

The broadsheets were not so clear that individuals alone make world historical events but they were similar to the tabloids in turning Iraqis into demons. Viewing the destruction of Kuwait City after its 'liberation' in February, Robert Fisk, writing for the *Independent*, said 'something evil has visited Kuwait City'. He asked, 'What kind of people burn museums and libraries?' (28 February). This type of thinking was more crudely expressed in the jingoistic tabloids, but according to Edward Said its presence is endemic among 'civilised' Westerners, who see Arabs as 'essentially sadistic, treacherous, low'.[23]

This belief was used to make some sense, or excuse, the massacre of the fleeing Iraqis at the battle of Mutla Gap. It was not the only explanation, since military considerations were supposed to be uppermost: as Michael Dewer said in the *Guardian*, without any regret, 'it has been a messy ending, but war is a blunt instrument' (11 April). The massacre made sense as part of the general outrage at the way the occupying Iraqi army had behaved in Kuwait, signifying its low moral worth and justifying the 'turkey shoot'.

We can see this in the report which accompanied the terrifying 'horror' picture of a dead Iraqi leaning forward in his burnt-out vehicle which was published in the *Observer* after the allied war had ended (3 March). The headline was 'The real face of war,' and its use seemed to be a response to official censorship, and a risk (given the 'correct' use of taste and tone) calculated to dispel the air of unreality about a war with no pictures of the dead. Certainly, the picture did signify at this level, and did create some debate within the broadsheets (the image was not printed in the tabloids) about what the picture editor of the *Guardian*, Eamonn McCabe, called the 'Dilemma of the grisly and the gratuitous' (4 March).

However, just as interesting, though ignored in the furore over the picture, was the accompanying report by Julie Flint. After the recapture of Kuwait City and first hand evidence from Western journalists of atrocities, it became impossible to pretend that Saddam alone was bad and the citizens of Iraq made up an unwilling army of basically decent people. Flint could not condemn the massacre at Mutla because she had witnessed Iraqi horrors in Kuwait: 'The Nazis killed the people, but not like this. It is not just Saddam. The whole regime is a monster'. The tone of the story shifted from pity at the massacre to outrage that the dead had earlier looted the city and (who knows) perpetrated rapes and vile murders. At that moment, blame was detached from Saddam and extended to all his countrymen.

The *Observer* had broken ranks and ended the tacit agreement amongst the media that the worst effects of bombing could not be seen. In the Second World War, images of burned bodies were used to show the savagery of fascism, not the savagery of the allies. If this picture signalled an end to the war, it struck a note of ambivalence, and allowed into the British press a discussion of what had been done in the name of Western values: the Pentagon's estimate of defenceless victims from allied bombing was put 'in the range of one hundred thousand'.[24] The only excuse on offer was that Saddam was Hitler and the troops retreating from Kuwait were wicked, but the question remained whether this was a justified action.

At this moment, the *Observer* summed up so much about the quality press unease about the war, and also its determination to make the war fit deep-rooted Western beliefs about Saddam and his soldiers. Even so, the story was unable to settle upon a simple ending, and therefore was unable to make sense of the event. The confusion of tone is a perfect analogue to the confusions engendered by the whole war - fought for oil, for free Kuwait, for the New World Order, for USA self-esteem, for the United Nations, for Western imperialism, for stability in the region, for the end to tyranny in Iraq - all of these aims at the same time. Given the multiple, competing and undecided war aims, it is not surprising that the story should remain open-ended, or become a never-ending story, with local settlements and narrative closures of the most tentative kind. The only fixed point in the narrative has become the personalisation of history into a grudge match between political leaders, a stand-off between the good West and the evil Arab. As Edward Said wrote in 1978, the 'mind-forg'd manacles' of 'orientalism' are 'a reminder of the seductive degradation of knowledge, of any knowledge, anywhere, at any time. Now perhaps more than ever'.[25] This degradation exists in the way the press told (and continues to tell) the story of the Gulf war, but it neither begins nor ends there. The processes of censorship and self-censorship of the press, though critical, are symptomatic of the wide degradation of what passes for 'knowledge' in Western democracies.

Notes

1. Worcester, Robert (1991), 'Who Buys What - For Why?' *British Journalism Review*, p. 48, Summer.
2. Ibid.
3. Anon (1991), 'The Role of the Press at War', *UK Press Gazette*, 18 February.
4. See Morrison, David E. (1992), *Television and the Gulf War*, John Libbey, London.
5. Worsthorne, Sir Peregrine (1991), 'The Press v the People', *Sunday Telegraph*, 10 February.
6. House of Commons Defence Committee, (1982), *The Handling of Press and Public Information during the Falklands Conflict,* vols HC 17-1 and HC 17-11, HMSO, London.
7. See Snoddy, Raymond (1992), *The Good, the Bad and the Unacceptable*, Faber and Faber, London. For reports on Calcutt's *Review of Press Self-Regulation*, which recommended a tougher code on reporting, large fines for infringements, criminal offences to safeguard privacy and injunctions to halt publication, see the press for 15 January 1992.
8. Henderson, Casper (1991), 'The Filtered War', *Banned*, Channel 4, London. *New Statesman Society*, (1991) BFI, pp. 16-17, April. See also (1991), 'Stop Press : the Gulf War and Censorship', *Article* 19, 15 February, and (1991), 'Warspeak : Media Management in the Gulf war', *Index on Censorship,* April/May.
9. McNamara, Martin (1991), 'Muffled Response Teams', *UK Press Gazette,* 25 March.
10. See Nohrtedt, Stig A. (1992), 'Ruling by Pooling', in Mowlana, Hamid, Gerbner, George and Schiller, Herbert L. (eds), *Triumph of the Image, The Media's War in the Persian Gulf - a Global Perspective*, Westview Press, Boulder, pp. 118-27.
11. Anon, (1991), 'Baker Praises Gulf War Coverage', *UK Press Gazette*, 25 February.
12. Morgan, Jean (1991), 'Iraq Pack may be made Saddam's Pawns...but Eyewitness Accounts are Vital', *UK Press Gazette,* 11 February. See also Taylor, John (1991), *War Photography - Realism in the British Press*, Routledge, London.
13. Robins, Kevin (1991), 'The Mirror of Unreason', *Marxism Today*, pp. 42-4, March.
14. Levidow, Les and Robins, Kevin (1991), 'Vision Wars', *Race and Class,* pp. 88-92, April.
15. MacArthur, Brian (1991), 'To Splash or not to Splash', *UK Press*

        Gazette, 11 February.
16. Shaw, Martin and Carr-Hill, Roy 'Public Opinion and Media War Coverage in Britain', in Mowlana, Hamid, Gerbner, George and Schiller, Herbert L. (eds), op. cit., p. 150.
17. Ibid., p. 152.
18. Pilger, John (1991), 'Myth-Makers of the Gulf War', *Guardian,* 7 January.
19. Chomsky, Noam (1991), 'A Stand on Low Moral Ground', *Guardian,* 10 January.
20. Knightley, Phillip (1991), 'A New Weapon in the News War', *Guardian,* 4 March.
21. Fisk, Robert (1991), 'Free to Report What We're Told', *Independent* 6 February. See also Taylor, Phillip, *War and the Media, Propaganda and Persuasion in the Gulf War*, Manchester University Press, Manchester, p. 66.
22. Aksoy, Asu and Robins, Kevin (1991), 'Exterminating Angels: Morality, Violence and Technology in the Gulf War', *Science as Culture,* No. 12, pp. 322-36.
23. Said, Edward (1978), *Orientalism*, Penguin, Harmondsworth p. 287.
24. Chomsky, Noam, 'The Media and the War: What War?' in Mowlana, Hamid, Gerbner, George and Schiller, Herbert L. (eds), op.cit., p. 52.
25. Said, Edward, op. cit., p. 328.

9 The media and the military: An historical perspective on the Gulf War

Terrance Fox

The news media have, on occasion, been guilty of losing perspective on events. In their restless way they signal first one development in foreign affairs, then another, usually following the public commentary of presidents and their critics. Nevertheless, our free press, when it accompanies the nation's soldiers into battle, performs a unique role. It serves as eyewitness; it forges a bond between the citizen and the soldier; and, at its best, it strives to avoid manipulation either by officials or by critics of the government through accurate, independent reporting. It also provides one of the checks and balances that sustains the confidence of the American people in their political system and armed forces.[1]

The relationship between the news media and the military has been an evolving one over the two hundred year history of the United States. The natural tension which exists between an institution which depends upon the secrecy of its plans and operations designed to protect the country from foreign enemies, and another which was given special constitutional protection by the founders in order that it may be free to call attention to tyranny, and which endeavours to expose all manner of operations engaged in by any arm of the government, is most intense during times of conflict. One is defender of the status quo; the other an agent of change and innately adversarial.

The Persian Gulf War represents both the crowning logistical and technological achievement of the news media, and arguably the first successful execution of a comprehensive press plan by the US military. A segment of US military opinion still holds the press responsible for the US loss in Vietnam, despite the refutation of that charge by as authoritative a voice as Alexander Haig, former Reagan administration Secretary of State, Supreme Commander of Allied forces in Europe under Presidents Ford and Carter and Vice Chief of Staff of the US Army, who served in Vietnam as a unit commander. Despite Haig's counsel and the denial of press complicity in the US defeat by a variety of other authoritative voices, the 'Press Lost Vietnam' syndrome appears to be influential in the press plan developed by the US military and operationalised in the Persian Gulf.

Former Assistant Secretary of Defense for Public Affairs, Phil G. Goulding, observes that the tendency of subordinates to hide instances of incompetence or corruption from superiors is probably no more pronounced in the military services than in any other public or private sector bureaucracy. The view expressed by the Twentieth Century Fund Task Force on the Media and the Military encompasses not only the type of information referred to by Goulding, but also routine information, and includes a constitutional imperative: 'The public's need for timely information about its government's military operations is implicit in the constitutional guarantees that underpin our society, including the First Amendment.'[2]

In analysing the constitutional guarantee of a free press, a relatively consistent interpretation of the guarantee as an instrumental one appears to dominate the documentary record, that is, the guarantee is viewed as being *for something* rather than constituting an end to itself. Views such as that of the Task Force then, must logically include such aims as facilitating an informed electorate as well as guarding against the deception alluded to by Goulding. 'An informed electorate' is in itself instrumental; such an electorate will be better prepared to choose their leadership and will theoretically select the most qualified individuals to lead them. Facilitating an informed electorate will include both uncovering incompetence and deception and providing information on the stewardship of the operationally responsible officials.

This implies an objective description of events which will allow members of the electorate to decide whether they endorse the performance of a given elected official engaged in the process. However, many sources argue that an objective description of events is not possible and that reporting from the battlefield has a negative impact upon home-front morale. This view reflects the pervasive sentiment, widely held by respected authorities such as Samuel P. Huntington and Admiral Elmo Zumwalt, that press coverage of the Vietnam War and specifically the Tet Offensive was influential in turning the American public against the war.[3] When the Vietnam War media experience is grafted on to the extensive, essentially positive coverage of the Persian Gulf War, it becomes clear that media coverage is influential in shaping public opinion, but the assumption that the effect is necessarily an adverse one is cast into serious doubt. Despite the conclusions of some contemporary scholars, content seems to play a persuasive role in determining the reaction of individual audience members.

It has become fashionable to point to the increasing cultural gulf which separates the military professional from his media counterpart: the end of the draft; the pervasive 'Press Lost Vietnam' myth perpetuated among senior military officers; the lack of exposure of media professionals - an increasing number of whom are female - to any aspect of the military. I would argue that the military of 1990, compared to the military of 1960, despite the cessation of the draft, more accurately reflects society as a whole.

The historical role of the US media in prior wars

The role of the press in the American Revolution was more that of creator than chronicler. The state of pre-technology communications in the colonies made the fledgling print organs the primary medium of transmission of the revolutionary message.

The colonial army was primarily a series of militia forces, recruited by each colony as it was petitioned to do so by the Continental Congress, harbinger of the fledgling central government of the last decade of the 18th century. Though the citizen army was composed primarily of uneducated rural youth, the relative homogeneity of the colonial cultures and the 'artisan' image of the printer contributed to an environment in which there was no significant occupational gulf between the two.

Print media coverage was characterized by sensationalistic bombast. The pamphlet must have seemed ideal as the chosen method of political discourse, though newspapers reached a greater percentage of the population. Nevertheless, the Revolutionary War had a lasting salutary effect on the influence and popularity of the newspaper, establishing a newspaper-reading tradition that continues to a significant extent to this day.[4]

The two developments which most dramatically impacted Civil War media coverage were the invention of the telegraph by Samuel Morse in

1844 and the advent of the so-called 'Penny Press' of 19th century America in 1833.

The press contingent which accompanied the Northern armies from one battle to another numbered over 300.[5] Phillip Knightley, in his epic work *The First Casualty*, uses the figure 500, an indication of the turnover among field reporters. The *New York Herald* contingent numbered 63, the *Times* and *Tribune* over 20 each and smaller papers had their own correspondents.[6]

Censorship took the form of prior restraint or topics which correspondents were forbidden to address, field censorship or reviewing copy at the point of dispatch, censorship of dispatches at the point of retransmission by the headquarters staff in Washington or outright prohibition of correspondents in the area of responsibility by the field commander. Instances of the former are too numerous to cite. Military control of the telegraph lines and the role of Washington as a central point of reception of combat reports facilitated censorship by senior officers.

Historians disagree on the relative merit of the Northern press corps. While Folkerts and Teeter find them 'fairly well educated, with several graduates of Harvard, Yale and other universities among the corps,'[7] Knightley asserts the majority 'were ignorant, dishonest, and unethical.'[8] The general picture which emerges is one of a heterogeneous press corps composed of reporters in their late twenties, comparatively well educated - many with university degrees, from all sections of the country including many of foreign descent, who had previously served as teachers, lawyers, poets, clerks and bookkeepers, and numbered among their lot misfits and malcontents as well as supremely talented individuals.[9]

The Union Army was composed of both career and non-career officers and an enlisted force that, while attracting some volunteers, was primarily a conscript one. Relationships between the military officer corps and the representatives of the press were initially cordial, but deteriorated as the war progressed and various censorship measures were introduced.

Despite idiosyncratic anomalies, the relationship between the military and the media during the Civil War was generally positive, and there is little recorded evidence of tension between correspondents and enlisted forces, a pattern that would be replicated in military actions that followed. The fifty years between the end of the Civil War and the start of World War I witnessed an explosive growth of the media. The corps of journalists accredited to the American Expeditionary Forces numbered 60, and a number of others were not on any official roll.[10] In addition to accreditation, the AEF used a censorship system under the control of a central headquarters, with a veteran journalist, Fredrick Palmer, wielding the blue pen. Correspondents were not allowed unfettered access to the forces but were shepherded on escorted tours.[11] The AEF that landed in Europe numbered 75,000 and was largely a conscript force. It eventually numbered over two million troops.[12]

The relationship between the war correspondents and the American doughboy bordered on hero worship, since many of the gentlemen and ladies of the press were justly famous for their journalistic endeavours in magazines or other media and must have appeared the epitome of sophistication to the naive conscripts. Peggy Hull, an unaccredited correspondent who exploited her personal relationship with General Pershing, and Irvin Cobb were especially popular with the troops.[13] The numbers are revealing: less than 100 correspondents and over two million men; a ratio of one to 20,000 made it likely that the average doughboy never came face-to-face with a war correspondent during the average six months he spent in Europe between his arrival and the Armistice.

The technological environment that greeted the US entrance into World War II represented a colossal advance over that which had existed only 23 years earlier. In a counterpoint to the First World War, America accredited 2,600 journalists in the European and Pacific Theatres during World War II, roughly 40 times the number in WW-I when supplemented by unaccredited freelances and the combat correspondents of the *Stars and Stripes* and *Yank*, the GI newspaper and magazine.[14] The manpower commitment of the military services eventually reached approximately 12 million in all the far-flung areas of operation, so the individual soldier's opportunity to encounter a war correspondent in the course of his duties was reduced to one in 4,000.[15]

The character of the correspondent corps remained remarkably similar to that of WW-I. The 'star' quality of the war correspondent was again evident, and men and women of letters abounded on the roster of journalists, and the correspondents formed a contingent that, like their World War I counterparts, were older, better educated and immensely more sophisticated than either the enlisted men or the officer corps of the military forces whose activities they chronicled.[16]

The largely draftee force was, by comparison, young, naive and incredibly uncosmopolitan. Most had never been outside their home state before the war. They were led by an officer corps presided over by a layer of seasoned veteran professional career warriors and a second echelon of young, brash citizen reservists. I submit that, when education, personal characteristics and experience are taken into account, the gulf which separated the correspondent corps and the military force was wide indeed.

The military censorship plan initiated in the lead up to WW-II was thoroughly organised and scrupulously administered. It consisted of field censorship in each unit and a headquarters echelon which gave final approval to copy. Prior to D-Day, the Allied Command spelled out the principles of the censorship effort. 'Operational Memorandum Number 27 stated that "the minimum amount of information will be withheld consistent with security." Press censorship activities would be conducted in the light of four basic objectives: security, speed, consistency and assistance to war correspondents.'[17] After Pearl Harbor, the censorship office developed guidelines called *The Code of Wartime Practices*, but the Code called for a continuation of the voluntary controls and it elicited adherence from all major news organizations throughout the war.[18]

The World War II correspondent, unlike his World War I counterpart, came much closer to creating a chronicle of events as he saw them. The 1918 journalist was mindful of the emergence of the US, with its entry into the war, as a world power. His Civil War colleague felt a responsibility to shore up civilian morale and his Revolutionary War forebears, existing in a vastly different journalistic environment which sanctioned, even expected partisanship, performed the vanguard role he envisioned had been thrust upon him. Desmond's assessment probably reflects the prevailing view of the performance of the correspondent corps in World War II: 'Most commentators, while aware of flaws, seem to have regarded it as the most accurately and fully reported war in history...correspondents acquitted themselves extremely well.'[19]

The press and Vietnam

If communications experienced 'colossal advance' in the 20-year interregnum, the similar period between the end of the Second World War and the advent of the Vietnamese conflict was marked by explosive growth. Both communications technology and the size of its audience advanced dramatically.

CBS Correspondent Morley Safer, in *Dateline 1966*, expressed the qualitative nature of the advance:

> This is television's first war. It is only in the past few years that the medium has become portable enough to go out on military operations. And this has raised some serious problems - problems, incidentally, which every network correspondent and cameraman in Vietnam is keenly aware of.
>
> The camera can describe in excruciating, harrowing detail what war is all about [emphasis added]. The cry of pain, the shattered

face - it's all there on film, and it goes into millions of American homes during the dinner hour. It is true that on its own every piece of war film takes on a certain antiwar character, simply because it does not glamorize or romanticize. In battle men do not die with a clean shot through the heart; they are blown to pieces. Television tells it that way.

It also tells what happens to civilians who are caught in the middle of battle. It tells what happens to soldiers under the stress of the unreal conditions in which they live. American soldiers are not always 100% sterling characters, just as American policy is not always exactly what is right for the world or for Vietnam's smallest hamlet.

The unfavourable has always been reported along with the favourable - but television tells it with greater impact. When the U.S. blunders [sic], television leaves little doubt.[20]

The makeup of the 464 correspondents accredited to both the South Vietnamese government and the US Military Assistance Command, Vietnam (MACV) is a matter of conjecture. The 464 covered a US force that numbered 500,000, or a ratio of approximately one to 1,100.[21]

Knightley sees the composition of the press corps in a pluralistic vein:

There were specialist writers from technical journals, trainee reporters from college newspapers, counter-insurgency experts from military publishers, religious correspondents, famous authors, small town editors, old hands from Korea, even older hands from the Second World War, and what Henry Kamm of the *New York Times* called 'proto-journalists', men who had never written a professional word or taken a professional photograph in their lives until the war brought them to Saigon. They all wrote stories that were used and presumably read or took photographs that were bought and reproduced.[22]

The record is replete with evidence of the presence in Vietnam of many very able, extremely qualified, well experienced - even distinguished - journalists. Almost by default, the press corps represented an older, better educated and trained group than the enlisted element in Vietnam; however it is doubtful if the same generalisation can be extended to include the commissioned force.

While the enlisted element was composed predominantly of young draftees containing a higher proportion of racial minorities than the general population, the commissioned force was largely college educated; many officers had advanced technical and other professional training, and their average age was considerably older than that of the enlisted force and most probably equalled or exceeded that of the press corps.

The role or function served by the media in the Vietnam War is still a matter of dispute. Perhaps the experience of that war is so recent that we are unable to arrive at any rough consensus, and the subject remains a contentious one.

Samuel Huntington, in a Trilateral Commission study in 1975, argued that the American political system of the 1960s and 1970s suffered from an imbalance between its governing institutions - chiefly the presidency - and its oppositional institutions. Central among these oppositional institutions, which he saw as gaining enormously in power during the Vietnam era, Huntington named the media, with special emphasis on television. Huntington wrote: '... In the 1960s, the network organizations, as one analyst put it, became a highly creditable, never-tiring political opposition, a maverick third party which never need face the sobering experience of governing.' Huntington later argued that crises like those of the 1960s and 1970s resulted from a hostility to power and authority deeply entrenched in American political culture and expressed strongly by the media.[23]

While there may be continued disagreement on the role and function of the media in Vietnam, there is little doubt it was carried out in a atmosphere virtually free of overt censorship. The military asked journalists to follow a set of guidelines and voluntary compliance was almost total. The result of a severe violation of the guidelines was likely to be revocation of credentials or, for correspondents who were outside the country at the time, denial of a visa to re-enter South Vietnam.[24]

The physical environment in which the correspondents operated was perhaps the most comfortable and civilized ever accorded a press contingent. Accredited journalists had access to all the amenities available to rear-echelon military officers, were accorded reserved space on military transport flights and were provided with press camps at the major outlying military centres, with telephone communications and daily flights to Saigon. In addition, helicopters from individual units were often assigned exclusively for use of correspondents. The helicopter was especially suited to the requirements of television journalism. A correspondent could fly out to the scene of some action, get film of the encounter and fly back to Saigon on the same day to get the film on its way to the US for next day airing on the six o'clock news.[25]

The final word has yet to be written on the role and performance of the media in Vietnam. The 'Press Lost Vietnam' syndrome is a pervasive one, and even the complete turnover of a generation of officers will not excise the myth. It remains probable that senior officers, as a group the most adamant about the adverse effects of Vietnam media coverage, passed the virus of mistrust on to their successors, and that they will, in turn, pass it on to their successors, and so on, so that acceptance of the conviction becomes, in effect, a rite of passage, a badge of membership in the fraternity.

The press and the Persian Gulf War

The Persian Gulf War represented logistical achievement for both the military and the media. Television networks and local electronic and print media around the country mobilized personnel and equipment and recreated press accommodation half a world away, including satellite uplinks and facilities for the transmission of graphics and copy. The military buildup has been characterized as moving the equivalent of Oklahoma City to the Saudi Arabian desert. Airlift accounted for 7,248 plane loads, and sealift moved 949 ship loads to the theatre of operations, including 12,400 tracked vehicles and 114,000 wheeled vehicles.[26]

The period between the end of the Vietnam War and the hostilities in the Gulf is similar in length to the period from the end of WW-II to the start of the Vietnam War but the advance in communications technology during the later interlude may appear, upon cursory examination, to be less dramatic than that during the former. I would submit that this is not the case. The technology of film existed during WW-II, so the public saw images of the war in newsreels, just as they would see in Vietnam. The differences lie in time and convenience. One could view the Vietnam War from the comfort of his or her living or dining room, and the videotape was only 24 hours old, rather than the weeks-old footage WW-II audiences saw in *The March of Time*.

In the Persian Gulf, satellite communications made instant live transmission possible from the other side of the world. The same technology allowed television networks to transmit live audio and video from deep within the belligerent camp. Cable television was available in all developed countries and most of the Third World, and the signal of CNN was sent to all states which subscribed to its service. These three factors, I would argue, represent a technological and sociological challenge as traumatic as that caused by the advances experienced between WW-II and Vietnam.

When President Bush ordered American troops deployed to Saudi Arabia as part of Operation Desert Shield in August, 1990, a 17-member press pool and 6 Public Affairs Officers accompanied the contingent, albeit after some initial resistance from Defense Secretary Richard

Cheney. The six officers established the Joint Information Bureau (JIB), the chief censorship agency in the combat theatre.[27] The establishment of news pools had been one of the chief recommendations of the *Sidle Panel*, an ad hoc committee created by Joint Chiefs of Staff Chairman, General John Vessey, after the Grenada invasion to make recommendations for accommodation of news media representatives during combat operations.[28]

Subsequent discussions between DOD, media leaders and representatives of the Saudi Arabian government failed to produce any substantive agreement on modification of the pool system. The censorship guidelines spelled out 12 categories of information which should not be reported: numbers (troops, aircraft, etc.), future operations, revelation of locations of forces, rules of engagement, intelligence collection methods and results, friendly troop movements, identification of aircraft origin, effectiveness of enemy countermeasures, information on downed aircraft, special operations force tactics, attack tactics, and vulnerabilities of US forces.[29]

Despite the restrictions placed on newsgathering, over 1,600 media representatives were present in the theatre of operations by the conclusion of the war, reporting on the activity of the 539,000 US troops committed to the liberation of Kuwait, one for each 300 Desert Storm participants.[30]

The press pools eventually numbered 24 and were deployed to cover units in the field, each pool escorted by a Public Affairs Officer. Their reports, after they had been cleared by the censor, were made available to the remainder of the army correspondents.[31] The video and copy filed by correspondents in the rear areas was not subject to censorship, but was required to conform to the guidelines that had been established by the military.[32] The media, especially television, made extensive use of military briefings in their coverage. The briefings often included video of 'smart weapons' detonating on targets, and the logic inherent in television news summaries dictated that the scenes would be replayed many times during a broadcast day. In addition, the daily military briefings from Saudi Arabia and the Pentagon filled approximately three or four hours of air time and featured some charismatic characters, notably Schwarzkopf and Lieutenant General Tom Kelly.

A distinctive feature of television news coverage was the employment of 'talking heads', analysts, usually but not always high-ranking retired military officers. Admiral William Crowe, former JCS Chairman, and ABC consultant, Anthony Cordesman, were the experts cited most frequently.

Possibly the most controversial aspect of the media coverage was the presence in Baghdad throughout the war of a CNN crew. Peter Arnett remained throughout the duration of the combat and often transmitted live to CNN through satellite uplink. Arnett had an Iraqi censor standing at his shoulder just off camera during these live broadcasts.[33]

Perhaps an equally vexatious problem from a military intelligence standpoint is posed by live television transmission of enemy missile attacks on friendly territory which provide the enemy access to bomb damage assessment information to some limited degree.

With the exception of CNN's Baghdad coverage, the information transmitted by the media was largely controlled by the military. As Charles S. Lewis, a Hearst bureau chief observed, General Norman Schwarzkopf controlled 'the information spigot'. 'The press was held captive,' said Lawrence Grossman, former NBC and PBS president. Grossman suggested the flow of information at the press briefings given by the military directed the media's attention to and helped determine priorities for reporting, for example, first to a SCUD attack then to the Iraqi destruction of oil wells and subsequently to a successful bombing raid (illustrated with mission video), and so on.[34]

The 1600 plus member press corps that was the object of the military's 'disinformation' campaign differed markedly from the Vietnam group of correspondents.[35] While many were seasoned journalists, the activation of reserve units from around the country prompted media managers to send local representation to cover human interest stories involving hometown citizen soldiers. The net effect was to create a press corp that was younger, less experienced and probably better educated than in Vietnam and contained a sizeable proportion of women.

The 539,000 strong US military contingent was composed of both regulars and reservists, but they shared one characteristic; they had all volunteered to serve in their respective military force. As a result, the enlisted force was older, more experienced and better educated than its counterpart in Vietnam. The weapons used often required computer literacy, and even the more prosaic equipment demanded technological astuteness.

The education level of the commissioned officer corps has advanced since Vietnam. The all-volunteer military has become a thoroughly institutionalised force with aspirations, attitudes and requirements regarding working conditions and compensation similar to those found in the larger society.

Despite the relative lack of familiarity with military issues on the part of many members of the press corps, there was probably more similarity between the two groups in the Persian Gulf than in any previous war in US history. A report prepared by the Gannett Foundation underscores the point. In interviewing journalists who had served in the Persian Gulf, they found a vast majority (86 per cent) who said their informal contacts with military personnel had proven somewhat helpful, and a substantial minority (37 per cent) who characterized such contacts as very helpful.

The Twentieth Century Fund Task Force on the Military and the Media takes an opposing view and points to the lack of combat familiarity on the part of journalists and the influx of women into the profession. The report ignores the identical trend in the military, where a greater percentage of women perform an increasing range of combat-related jobs.[36]

The role the press played in the Persian Gulf War and the role they envision the media serving in such an environment do not coincide. A US public overwhelmingly supportive of the war effort wanted the press to function as a chronicle as it had in WW-II, and the information it was allowed to gather dictated that this was the type of media coverage delivered to the public. The press aspired to a sentinel role such as it had performed in Vietnam. The opportunity to perform this function was denied the media by the pool system and the accompanying censorship. A statement in the Gannett Foundation's report is indicative both of the values and aims of the two groups and of the gulf of misunderstanding separating them: 'In the end, media coverage of the Gulf war was shaped far more by the military's concern with achieving a decisive victory than the media's paramount goals of comprehensive and accurate reporting.'[37]

Historical analysis and observations

The judgement represented by the Gannett Foundation detailed above implies that the fundamental objectives of the media and the military are mutually exclusive. I would argue that this is not the case, that the two institutions share ultimate objectives. The media seeks to report two 'paramount' categories of information: instances of incompetence and deception, and information bearing on the stewardship of the operationally responsible officials. No responsible military leader would disagree with the right of the public to such information. Likewise, no responsible media leader would intentionally seek to publish or transmit any information that would unnecessarily place US forces in harm's way.

In WW-II 2,600 correspondents were accredited during a four year period to report on the activities of 12,000,000 GIs deployed worldwide; in WW-I less than 100 covered 2,000,000 doughboys in Europe; in Vietnam the ratio was approximately one journalist per 1,000 military personnel; in the Persian Gulf 1600 plus reporters covered 539,000 troops for six months in an area confined to the Saudi Arabian peninsula. In each case, the media wielded enormous influence in forming public perceptions of the war.

Despite the protestations of unprecedented management of media access, the historical record suggests that the treatment of the media in the Persian Gulf war is consistent with that afforded the press in most previous conflicts. The Vietnam War, on the other hand, represents the anomaly. If there is a parallel between media coverage of the Persian Gulf and Vietnam Wars, it lies in the near-identical stylized television presentations dictated by systemic media logic that dictates the form in which a news item will be 'fed' to the audience.

The formal adoption of Airland Battle Doctrine by the US Army, and by implication the entire military establishment, in 1986 represents a watershed event in US military history. There are those who charge that Airland Battle is informed by the Cold War experience. Even if such a charge is conceded to be a valid one, the strategists and theorists who developed the doctrine were veterans of the Vietnam conflict and the concepts have been sufficiently abstracted that they become relevant in environments which differ markedly from the urban terrain of the European plain.[38]

The primary implications for media planners lie in two areas: the concept of the non-linear extended battlefield and the level of lethality. The former implies unprecedented logistical challenges and the latter raises ethical questions concerning the extent to which a journalist should be required to imperil his or her life in gathering information. Although it is not generally recognised, the essential elements of Airland Battle Doctrine as they impact on the media were present in the Persian Gulf.

Advances in satellite technology represent the second challenge posed by the experience in the Persian Gulf. The chief user, CNN, is a US media company which supplies other states with cable television programming via a network of satellites. Bernard Shaw, chief anchor for the Atlanta-based network, raised potential ethical questions when he implied the existence of an extra-national obligation for journalists.

These two factors represent a radical alteration of the conditions under which conflict will be prosecuted in the future, so radical, I would argue, that both media and military representatives must accept that the Vietnam experience has only historical significance and represents a model for the conduct of the media/military relationship as outmoded as that provided by the war between the states.

Notes

1. Twentieth Century Fund Task Force on the Media and the Military, (1985), *Battle Lines*, Priority Press Publications, New York, p. 13.
2. Twentieth Century Fund, *Battle Lines*, p. 6.
3. *ibid*, p. 11.
4. Schlesinger, Arthur M. (1958), *Prelude to Independence: The Newspaper war on Britain 1764-1776*, Alfred A. Knopf, New York, p. 296.
5. Cutler Andrews, J. (1955), *The North Reports The Civil War*, Pittsburg Press, p. 60.
6. Knightley, Phillip (1975), *The First Casualty*, Harcourt Brace Jovanovich, New York and London, p. 2.
7. Folkerts, Jean and Teeter, Dwight L. (1989), *Voices of a Nation*, Macmillan Publishing Company, New York, p. 211.
8. Knightley, *First Casualty*, p. 21.
9. Andrews, *The North Reports*, pp. 60-61.
10. Hohenberg, John (1964), *Foreign Correspondence: The Great Reporters and Their Times* Columbia University Press, New York and London, p. 237.
11. *Ibid*, p. 235.
12. Knightley, *First Casualty*, pp. 122-123.
13. *Ibid*, p. 126-127.
14. Desmond, Robert W. (1984), *Tides of War: World News Reporting 1940-1945* University of Iowa Press, Iowa City, IO, pp. 448-449.
15. Twentieth Century Fund, *Battle Lines*, p. 27.
16. Desmond, *Tides of War*, p. 449.
17. The Gannett Foundation, (1991), *Media at War: The Press and the Persian Gulf Conflict*, Gannett Foundation Media Centre, New York.
18. *ibid*, p. 10.
19. Desmond, *Tides of War*, p. 461.
20. Twentieth Century Fund, *Battle Lines*, p. 67.
21. Braestrup, Peter (1978), *Big Story*, Yale University Press, New Haven and London, p. 9.
22. Knightley, *First Casualty*, p. 402.
23. Hallin, Daniel C. (1986), *The Uncensored War*, Oxford University Press, New York and Oxford, pp. 4-5.
24. Gannett Foundation, *The Media at War, p. 14-15*.
25. Twentieth Century Fund, *Battle Lines*, p. 64.
26. Pagonis, Lieutenant General William G., US Army, and Raugh Jr., Major Harold E., US Army, (1991), 'Good Logistics is Combat

Power,' *Military Review LXXI*, pp. 32-35, September.
27. Gannett Foundation, *The Media at War*, p. 16.
28. Sidle, Major General Winant, US Army, Retired, (1991), 'A Battle Behind the Scenes: The Gulf War Reheats the Military-Media Controversy,' *Military Review LXXI*, pp. 55-56, September.
29. Gannett Foundation, *The Media at War*, p. 17.
30. Sidle, *Military Review*, p. 57.
31. Gannett Foundation, *The Media at War*, p. 18.
32. Sidle, *Military Review*, p. 59.
33. *ibid*, p. 36.
34. *ibid*, pp. 31-32.
35. *ibid*, p. 30.
36. Twentieth Century Fund, *Battle Lines*, p. 9.
37. Gannett Foundation, *The Media at Work*, p. 20.
38. U.S. News and World Report Staff, (1992), *Triumph Without Victory*, Times Books, New York, pp. 158-64.

Figure 1   'War in the Desert, Day 6', *Daily Star*, Tuesday, January 22, 1991

Figure 2   From 'Spoils of War', written and drawn by Carol Swain in *Ceasefire* (1991)

Figure 3   From 'Punch', written and drawn by Jackie Smith in *Ceasefire* (1991)

Figure 4   A young Jordanian holds aloft a placard that depicts the US President as Hitler during a pro-Iraq demonstration through the street of Amman 14 September 1990: Ramzi Haidar

Figure 5 *The Monument* or *The Victory Arch*, Baghdad (1989)

Figure 6 Frederick Hart, *Three Fighting Men* : Karal Ann Marling

Figure 7   Glenna Goodacre, *Women's Vietnam Memorial* : Associated Press (1993)

Figure 8   *Portrait of Saddam Hussein*, Iraq, 1993. Ian Katz

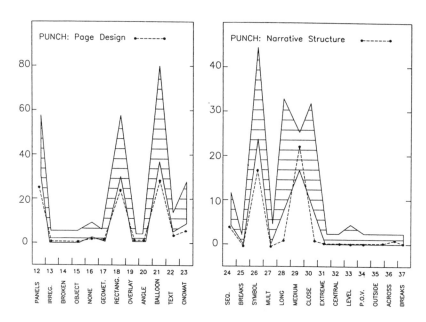

Table 1 David Huxley, Standard British Humour Comic (1993)

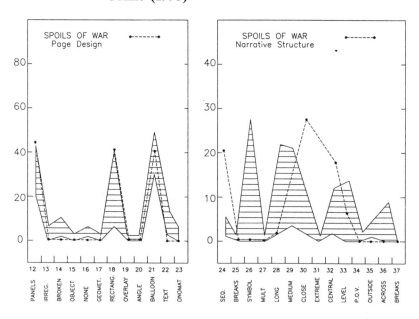

Table 2 David Huxley, Standard British Adventure Comic (1993)

10 Pools, minders, unilaterals and scud studs: War reporters in the news

Robert Hamilton

1. The lessons of history

Sir Robert Thompson

It was pointed out to me in 1962 that only the American Press could lose the war and the whole problem was how to deal with the American Press. The advice I gave was to ignore it and to get on with the job, and let what was being done speak for itself, because it would get through in the end.

General Sir Walter Walker

If I think it boiled down to the fact that you have to win not only the hearts and minds of your people, but also the hearts and minds of the Press. We had a number of sensitive operations in Malaya, and I had never less than some forty journalists with me at one time. I always let them into my plans, and they never failed me once. I wonder to what extent the Americans do this. Monty was a great believer in this during the last war.

Sir Claude Fenner

You must also have a sanction you can apply in the last resort and the Press must know it.

The Chairman

There is none in Vietnam.[1]

These remarks were made at a conference held in 1970 in London on the lessons of the Vietnam War. The participants were all military men with experience of post-war conflicts of national liberation from Borneo, Malaya and in Sir Robert Thompson's case, the British Advisory Mission to Vietnam (1961-65). They highlight a problem the military have had since the Crimean War and William Howard Russell. Namely, how do you control the press in times of conflict? The problem intensified during the Vietnam War with the creation of the myth of the press operating in-country without restrictions or sanctions. Despite the Chairman's comments, there *were* sanctions in Vietnam and some journalists did have their accreditation suspended. Barry Zorthian head of the US Press Mission (1964-68) stated that relatively few journalists violated the ground rules:

> In the four years (1964-68) that I was in Vietnam with some 2,000 correspondents accredited...we had only four or five cases of security violations...of tactical military information. Our leverage was the lifting of credentials and that was done in only four or five cases and at least two or three of these were simply unintentional errors on the part of the correspondent. There was only once or twice that [ground rules] were deliberately challenged, and the correspondent's credentials were immediately lifted.[2]

In the main, the ground rules consisted of restricting information that would be of use to an enemy. Orders of Battle, Unit Identification and Operations in the Field were subject to news embargoes and sanctions. These can be considered to be legitimate military concerns in that information of this order released before missions would alert the enemy and place men and material at risk. Apart from this, Zorthian instigated a policy of 'Maxim Candor'[3] in his dealings with the press, briefing them as honestly as possible in the hope that they would 'get on the team and get with the program'. For a variety of complex reasons, the policy failed. However, it is interesting to note that as early as 1962 someone pointed out to Sir Robert Thompson that 'only the American Press could lose the war' and certainly, this has been perceived by the US military as a major contributing factor for their defeat in Vietnam. With this in mind, the military have sought new means to control and sanction the press in times of conflict, and in particular, two measures have been introduced: 1) the Pool System and 2) enhancement of the role of Public Affairs Officers or 'Minders'. In the Gulf War, Douglas Kellner states:

> From the beginning of the US deployment, the Press was prohibited from having direct access to the troops. Journalists were instead organised by the Military into pools that were taken to sites selected by the Military itself, and then reporters were allowed only to interview troops with the Military 'minders' present.[4]

In Vietnam, the press could travel to battle zones almost with impunity, and as Public Affairs Officers in the field acted as liaisons, not minders, they could conduct interviews without much interference. In the Gulf, the military sought to reduce such access by controlling directly where the media went and what they heard, to control the raw material of news at source. Other journalists were formed into Media Reporting Teams (MRTs) and assigned to specific units.[5]

During the Falklands, the military observed that journalists living at close quarters to soldiers would sometimes come to a 'better' understanding of the Military point of view. David Morrison and Howard Turner have noted:

> Close living and working with the troops forced some journalists to reconsider their opinions of the military. Hastings admitted that one reason for his successful coverage of the venture was that he 'spoke the same language'. 'I like soldiers', he told us. 'I get on well with them, and I spend a lot of my working life with them'. He compared this with the attitude of Pat Bishop who, Hastings said, 'conceded from day one that he doesn't like soldiers and he doesn't like the Services'. They were therefore unlikely 'to pull a finger out for him...'. Most of the journalists came to admire the Military; some even made friends.[6]

Depending on the nature of the relationships between units, minders and the media, access to the news could be made difficult or relatively easy. 'Close living' could also influence the tone of a story. To gauge the effect of theses structural changes one only has to look at the lack of critical reporting of the Gulf War to see how successfully the military 'handled' the press. The lessons of Vietnam had been well learnt.

2. Out of sight out of mind

'If I had to sum up current thinking on precision missiles and saturation weaponry in a single sentence', said W. J. Perry, a former US Under-Secretary of State for Defence, 'I'd put it like this: once you can see the target, you can expect to destroy it'. This quotation perfectly expresses the new geostrategic situation and partially explains the current round of disarmament. If *what is perceived is already lost*, it becomes necessary to invest in concealment what used to be invested in simple exploitation of the new Stealth weapons.

The inversion of the deterrence principle is quite clear: unlike weapons which have to be publicised if they are to have a real deterrent effect, Stealth equipment can only function if its existence is clouded with uncertainty.

Paul Virilio, *War and the Cinema*.[7]

Anyone who has seen the footage of the destruction of the retreating Iraqi Army on the road to Basra will understand the full impact of W. J. Perry's statement. Once the Iraqi tanks, hardware and transport vehicles were spotted, they were targeted by electronic means and destroyed. The development and deployment of so-called 'smart weapons', using video and laser-guided systems (first used towards the end of the Vietnam War), also led the US to the development of deliverance systems which could not be detected by radar, such as the F117A Stealth Bomber, which is virtually undetectable.

This sight/concealment duality had implications for the reporting of the Gulf and allowed the Air War (and to some extent the Ground War) to be 'clouded with uncertainty'. Not a single journalist was given permission to accompany air crews on bombing sorties as they had in Vietnam (for example, see Larry Burrows' photographs for *Life Magazine*). Reporters, therefore, had to rely on military briefings and controlled interviews with returning pilots, to ascertain the success or failure of the air strikes against Iraq, again allowing the military to have strict control over the release of material for public consumption.

The media were treated to sanitised videos during briefings which, apart from the hostile questioning after the awful destruction of the civilian shelter at Amiriya,[8] were held in a friendly, almost jolly atmosphere of collusion between the military and the media. Of the briefings, Douglas Kellner remarked

> These videos were replayed for days, producing the image of a precise bombing and coding the destruction as positive. Norm

Schwarzkopf's video cassette shows demonstrated that US bombs always hit their targets, do not cause collateral damage, and only take out nasty military targets. This was intended to change the public perception of war itself, that the new technowar was clean, precise, and surgical, that the very nature of war had changed. War was thus something that one could enjoy, admire, and cheer about. War was fun, aesthetic, and fascinating. The videos created a climate of joy in destruction in its audiences, as when reporters clapped and laughed when Horner said: 'And this is my counterpart's headquarters in Baghdad', as a video showed a bomb blowing up the Iraqi air force headquarters.[9]

Quite unlike the atmosphere of mutual distrust during the daily briefings in Vietnam which became known as the 'Five O'Clock Follies', one can observe in the briefings in Riyadh the media's objectivity being slowly eroded like sand in a desert storm, and enhancing the feeling that the military and the media were out to defeat Saddam Hussein together, in a clean and bloodless conflict.

Given such strict control over hard military news, the media, in its unquenchable thirst to fill its pages with Gulf stories, looked to politicians, diplomats, military experts and human interest stories (see John Taylor's essay in this volume). One way of using up column inches was to focus on the reporters themselves, unlike Vietnam where stories on war reporters tended to have some news value. Whether it be the visit of Walter Kronkite during the Tet Offensive of 1968, the disappearance of Sean Flynn and Dana Stone in Cambodia or the death of Larry Burrows, they were of some import. However, during the Gulf, many of the 'reporter' stories, especially in the tabloids, heroised the reporter simply by virtue of his being there. One such story appeared in the *Daily Star* of 22nd January 1991 on the BBC correspondent in Baghdad, John Simpson. Under the headline 'Please Don't Make Me Out To Be A Hero' the story continued:

> Speaking about his ordeal last night he pleaded: 'Please don't make me a hero. All I do is speak a few words on camera'.
> Despite his modesty, the newsman had proved his bravery before the war started:
> 'I was told by the BBC that I would have to evacuate before the shooting began' he said, 'but I threatened to resign so they let me stay.'
> Simpson admits he suffered some tense moments in Baghdad. On one occasion a bullet narrowly missed him and on another, a cruise missile circled his hotel.[10]

The story is accompanied by an illustration and a photograph of Simpson being given a welcome home hug, by his girlfriend (human interest). The illustration (Fig.1.)[11] shows Simpson in his hotel room in Baghdad as a cruise missile flies past his window, recreating the event mentioned in the article. The illustration and the tone of the story, whilst acknowledging his modesty, set out to demonstrate his bravery under fire and in the camp of the enemy, placing him both in danger and in opposition to Saddam Hussein. It is made clear whose side he is on.[12] Furthermore, at the bottom of the same page, there was a short piece on CNN reporter Peter Arnett, entitled 'Peter the Great'. It says

> Brave Cable News Network reporter Peter Arnett is the only journalist left in the Iraqi capital of Baghdad. He is managing to send out live telephone reports, although filming has been banned.[13]

The story is again framed in terms of bravery, but it ignores two important aspects of Arnett's remaining in Baghdad. Firstly, he was not, as he claimed on air, the only western journalist in Iraq. There was also Alfonso Rojo of the Spanish newspaper *El Mondo* and *The Guardian*. Secondly, it fails to mention the public row between Arnett and Rojo over the former's refusal to allow the latter use of CNN's telephone, making it difficult for Rojo to get his copy out of Iraq.[14] Whether or not Arnett was right or wrong to restrict Rojo's access to his communications system, the row points to the fierce competition between journalists to get to the story first. *Battle Lines*, a report on the military and the media published in 1985 states that:

> ...News organisations are relatively small, competing commercial enterprises, operating under economic constraints, heavily dependent on attracting and retaining sufficiently large audiences to draw advertising and thus revenue.[15]

CNN's desire to be first with the news coming out of Baghdad, together with its attendant economic imperative, probably overrode what might be considered a professional courtesy to Rojo. Other journalists went out of their way to make life difficult for their colleagues. In the case of John Simpson, an American reporter gave the Iraqi Ministry of Information an article Simpson had written for *The Observer* simply to place obstacles in the way of his access.[16] This competition further complicates access to the news and in some way aided both the Allies and the Iraqis in their desire to control the reporting of the war.

If the tabloids had a habit of heroising the war reporter, they could also be made into sex objects. One gets a glimpse of this in the *Daily Star's* photograph of Simpson and his partner. While he sits, she is standing above him embracing her returning hero as the object of her desire and making him the object of our admiring gaze. A more concrete instance is that of NBC's Arthur Kent. Kent reported out of Saudi Arabia and perhaps because of his good looks, and the kinds of live games that particularly American TV reporters played - fumbling with gas masks, ducking incoming Scuds and outgoing Patriots - produced a watchable drama that actually had very little hard news content. Kent in particular became a favourite amongst the American female viewing public, becoming affectionately knows as the 'Scud Stud'.[17] In this way reporting of the Gulf War could be reduced to little more than a sexual soap opera, with the reporter as the leading man, playing to thousands of unseen admiring viewers. This is not to play down the importance of the reporting of Simpson, Arnett, Rojo or Kent, but rather to place the war reporter as news in its discursive context that inflected the production of news coming out of the Gulf, and to some extent, reduced its perceived objectivity.

In an attempt to escape the over-bearing attention of the military minders and the restrictive nature of the News Pool system, several journalists withdrew from the pool altogether. Known as 'Unilaterals' they often dressed in borrowed military uniform in order to bypass army roadblocks, and to get to stories without interference from PAOs. Thus, maintaining their sense of separateness, they produced some of the most objective and telling reporting of the war. One indicative example of this appeared in *The Independent* on 7th February 1991. Richard Dowden, travelling with the photographer Isabel Ellsen and Ed Barnes and Tony O'Brien of *Life Magazine*, near the Kuwait border, came across four Iraqi deserters who surrendered to the journalists. After interviewing and photographing them, Dowden handed them over to Arabic speaking Egyptian forces. He wrote:

> At last the Egyptian Colonel led the men away and put them in an army truck. We shook hands warmly and wished each other good luck. Before they went, I asked them how they felt about being captured by journalists. Abu Wahed replied: 'We are pleased. But when I first saw you I thought you were an Iraqi patrol and I say, "Quick, give me the machine-gun" - then I see the truck is not Iraqi. Thank you very much'.[18]

Dowden's luck was able to produce a story that gave some thoughtful insights into the state of morale among Iraqi conscripts, and a letter from an Egyptian General in Arabic giving him better access to forces so often ignored by the western media.

Furthermore, as an example of the discourse of the reporter as news, it demonstrates that operating outside the procedures and structures imposed by the military, often under the 'threat of arrest'[19] could produce good objective reporting, free from military interference or censorship. In a later interview, Dowden stated that the following day the area was inundated with journalists, looking for surrendering Iraqi soldiers.[20]

Despite the important role of the 'Unilaterals', the majority of reporting was controlled by the military. If Vietnam is still perceived as the 'Bad' war, the military and the media ensured that the Gulf War was to be seen as the 'Good' War. Furthermore, if the Gulf represents the ending of the 'Vietnam Syndrome', it must not only be seen as the ending of the American Army's twenty year lack of confidence, to stage and win a major overseas conflict, but as a demonstration that the media will not 'lose' them another war.

3. A different war

> A British photographer died after being shot by a sniper near the Eastern Croatian town of Osijek yesterday.
>
> Paul Jencks worked for the Frankfurt based European Press-Photo Agency.
>
> Some of his photographs appeared in *The Guardian*. He died during surgery at Osijek Hospital shortly after he was shot in the head in the village of Josipin Dvor.
>
> Mr Jencks, a Londoner in his mid-20s, had been covering the Yugoslav conflict for several months.
>
> *The Guardian.*[21]

The above is an example of the war reporter as news coming out of the unfolding and bloody conflict now going on in Yugoslavia. The war reporter is back in the news, not as 'Scud Studs', but on the casualty list and in the obituaries. To date, some 40 journalists have been killed covering the Yugoslav Civil War, more than in the 14 years of Vietnam and certainly 40 more than in the Gulf. There are no pools systems or minders, no reporting restrictions except at the end of a sniper's rifle. And it does not end at the Yugoslav border. Recently, a young Belgrade photographer, Bojan Stojanovic, had to be taken into protective custody in Holland after being abducted by two Serbian assailants.[22] He escaped by jumping from a moving car into the canal. His crime was to have taken a photograph of a Serbian policeman executing a Bosnian Muslim.

Just why the warring factions should see the press as legitimate targets is difficult to ascertain. Robert Fox of *The Daily Telegraph* has suggested that they felt betrayed by the West and that the press is a visible representative of the West and therefore the betrayer.[23] Certainly Serbian government spokesmen have accused the British press of 'distorting the Serbian cause and reporting more often from a Croatian point of view'.[24] Furthermore, some journalists have begun to take sides. Ed Vulliamy of *The Guardian* has stated uncategorically:

> I was a pacifist until quite recently. I don't think anyone wants to see a big war, but when we go past those Serbian artillery positions and watch them shelling civilians and women and children and hospitals and orphanages and what have you, we do think about the US jets coming over and doing the business.[25]

This adds to the growing public and political pressure for Western military intervention as the issues become ever more confused, especially when there are revelations of Croatian atrocities in Moslem villages.

In this paper, I have sought to show how the lessons of the Vietnam War were brought to bear on the Gulf Conflict, especially in how the military handled the media: and I have demonstrated also how the appearance of the war reporter in the news affected the reporting of the Gulf conflict, and press objectivity. And, in turn, I have raised some questions as to how one might begin to interpret the reporting of the war in Yugoslavia. On the two conflicts, Phil Davidson of *The Independent* has stated:

> This (Yugoslavia) came in complete contrast to the last war we'd all experienced or been through - the Gulf War - which was just totally different. That was a clear-cut conflict, we all thought we knew who the enemy was, we had so much superior weaponry we always knew we were going to win. When we got to Yugoslavia from the point of view of the Press, we were totally on our own.[26]

Perhaps the relationship between war reporting and objectivity lies in the ideological gap between the two sentences 'we always knew we were going to win' and 'we were totally on our own'. One has to wonder if the ever increasing media casualty lists are a price worth paying for objective press coverage? And, as the calls for Western military intervention grow ever louder, how will this affect the role of the press and its access to the news?

Notes

1. *Lessons of the Vietnam War*, (1970), Report, The Royal United Service Institution, London, p. 23.
2. *Battle Lines: Report of the Twentieth Century Fund Task Force on the Military and the Media*, (1985), New York, p. 65. Also for the ground rules for journalists see (1965), MACV Directive 360-1 - Public Information Policies and Procedures.
3. See Hammond, W. M. (1988), *Public Affairs: The Military and the Media (1962-1968)*, Washington, pp. 67-86.
4. Kellner, D. (1992), *The Persian Gulf War*, Boulder, p. 80.
5. Taylor, P. M. (1992), *War and the Media: Propaganda and Persuasion in the Gulf War*, Manchester, pp. 51-2.
6. Morrison, D. and Turner, H. (1988), *Journalists at War*, London, p. 26.
7. Virilio, P. (1989), *War and the Cinema*, London, p. 4.
8. See Taylor, P. M., *Op.Cit*, pp. 187-198.
9. Kellner, D., *Op.Cit*, p. 159.
10. *The Daily Star*, 22 January 1991, p. 8.
11. By kind permission of Bob Williams and my thanks to Dennis Hart of Express Newspapers for his help
12. A longer interview appeared with Simpson (1991), in *Today*, p.7, 21 January, under the sub-heading 'The Bravery of a Newsman' and uses the same photograph of his welcoming hug. The discourse is remarkably similar to the *Daily Star* piece
13. *The Daily Star*, 22 January 1991, p.8
14. *The Guardian*, 25 January 1991, p.1
15. *Battle Lines*, *Op.Cit*, p.136
16. Simpson, John (1991), 'The Bombing of Baghdad' in *The Observer*, p. 49, 17 January. The story recounted on the (1991), 'Late Show: Tales From the Gulf', BBC2, 6 June.
17. Other nicknames included 'The Satellite Dish' and 'Arthur of Arabia', 'The Late Show: Tales from the Gulf', (1991), BBC2, 6 June.
18. Dowden, Richard (1991), *The Independent*, p. 1, 7 February.
19. For example, Robert Fisk's experience in Khafji, (1991), *The Independent*, 30 January.
20. 'The Late Show: Tales from the Gulf', (1991), BBC2, 6 June.
21. *The Guardian*, P. 16, 18 January, 1992.
22. *The Guardian*, Section 2, p. 6, 26 April 1993.
23. 'The Late Show: Tales from Sarajevo', (1993), BBC2, 14 April.
24. *The Guardian*, p. 8, 25 January 1992.

25. *The Guardian*, Section 2, p. 15, 18 January 1993.
26. 'The Late Show: Tales from Sarajevo', (1993), BBC2, 14 April.

11 *Ceasefire:* An anti-war comic for women

David Huxley

Introduction

The purpose of this chapter is twofold. Firstly it is my intention to look at one artefact as an example of the opposition to the Gulf War in Britain: a comic written and drawn entirely by women: *Ceasefire*.[1] Secondly, in the course of this examination I will look at two specific stories in the comic to try and determine the ways in which the meanings of the stories are constructed. I hope to demonstrate that contrary to popular misconceptions, comics are not necessarily the facile medium they are often supposed to be - suitable only for children or people who cannot read properly. *Ceasefire* was published in 1991 by Cath Tate who is a practising cartoonist and Carol Bennett who is a partner in the comic publishers Knockabout Books. Knockabout have been publishing 'alternative' and 'underground' comics since the nineteen seventies, which makes them the longest surviving publisher of such material in this country.[2] This is despite the fickle nature of the market for 'alternative' publications and the fact that they have had a series of problems with censorship and custon seizures of imported material.

Carol Bennett had also started the Directory of Women Comic Strip Artists, Writers and Cartoonists in 1990. Its initial aim was to be: '..free to all women in comics. At the moment it takes the form of a loose leaf binder, available to any editor, writer or creator looking for artists. In the future we hope to publish a collection of the works of "Fanny".'[3] The Directory was called 'Fanny' after a friend of Carol Bennett. The potential sexual innuendo of the title raised very few complaints, and then only from men. A rather more complicated problem than this has been the whole idea behind the concept of a separate 'women only' comic. At the 1990 UK Comics convention a women's panel had discussed this problem and according to Carol Bennett: 'The consensus of opinion at UKCAC definitely disliked the idea of segregated comics. The mood was to encourage an open attitude of equal competition for work...'[4] However in practice Carol Bennett decided that the position of women within comics was already disadvantaged enough:

> the 'ghetto' of women creators is so small in an industry where ninety nine per cent of material is produced for 'boys'. Why should we open our pages to print more material produced by male artists? The chances of women getting into print is so very low, even in the poor selection of comics that do take a good mixture of work.[5]

The decision to produce a comic specifically about the Gulf War was taken after a trip to the annual comics festival at Angouleme, near Bordeaux. It was inspired by the reaction to the war in France where Carol Bennett saw: '...students from Paris were out on every corner selling anti-war comics, home produced photo-copied stuff proclaiming their beliefs in calling the war off and sorting it out another way.'[6] Such street selling was just part of a world wide anti-war movement which appears to have been largely ignored by the mainstream media during the course of the Gulf war. Douglas Kellner claims that in America this was not initially the case only because: '...commercial TV networks are profit-machines and at the early stages of a war cannot be certain if the war will be successful and popular.'[7] Kellner points out that after only a ten day period this coverage virtually ceased in favour of attention lavished 'on prowar demonstrations for the duration of the war'.

Women and war

The role of women in war is often neglected and marginalized. This is despite the fact that they have played a major part in many wars, both as active participants and by a series of supportive contributions 'on the home front'. Indeed it is commonly supposed that the part taken by women in both world wars had a tangible and lasting effect on the overall role of women in society. Whatever the facts of that case, it is indisputable that women have also played a significant part in the propaganda war which surrounds any modern conflict. Their contribution, however, has been mixed. During the First World War, women played a major role in recruitment, not least in the distribution of white feathers to 'cowards' who would not enlist. At the same time, although perhaps it has been less publicized, women were involved in strenuous efforts to prevent the war. These include, for example, the work of the Austrian peace activist Bertha von Suttner in the years leading up to the First World War, and the International Congress of Women at the Hague in 1915 where over one thousand women delegates called for an end to the war.[8]

The mainstream media coverage of women in relation to the Gulf War shows that the presentation of women has changed little. Douglas Kellner claims: '...the construction of gender of US military families was extremely conventional, with male soldiers going off to war, while the wife and children stayed behind'.[9]

But Kellner points out that this was combined during the Gulf war with some coverage of women troops (for example in *Newsweek*, 10 September 1991: 'Women Warriors, sharing the danger'). He believes, however, that these stories performed a specific ideological function. Such images of the female US soldier could be juxtaposed with images of veiled Arab women, suppressed and constrained by the Iraqi regime. Thus they became part of the propaganda battle which positioned Saddam Hussein as the mad tyrant and his regime as a backward dictatorship which denied women even their basic rights. This construction can be usefully compared to the earlier image of Saddam in the US media when he was being supported during the war against Iran, and the lack of comparisons between the treatment of women in Iraq and some of the other countries which were allies of America and Britain during the Gulf war.

The nature of modern warfare has meant that civilians, whether men, women or children, have been increasingly likely to become victims of so called 'total war'. Susan Brownmiller has also seen rape as an integral part of war because it is inflicted on women by men to underline their power and control over the enemy.[10] Brownmiller even sees rape as a supporting pillar of patriarchy arguing that it forms part of the wider war of the sexes, where women are continually the enemy, and through the threat of rape are subjugated by men.

Brownmiller's thesis has been an influential one; whatever the complications of the wider arguments it is hard to escape the feeling that her book touched on a truth about the incidence of rape in war, where it appears to have been a depressing commonplace throughout recorded history. Despite this centrality it has often been relegated to the periphery of written histories, or totally ignored. Susan Griffin had earlier associated rape as an individual human crime with the wider institutional crimes of American foreign policy in 1971. The different emphasis of these arguments was commented on by Hesler Eisenstein in 1984:

> Griffin made the connection between the crime of rape, at home, and the American crimes being committed abroad against other countries, especially Vietnam. The idea that rape and imperialism had elements in common was played down in Brownmiller's analysis, which instead made the argument that rape was a symptom of the universal war of men against women.[11]

The fact remains that all wars, to one extent or another, affect women's lives both indirectly and in the most direct ways possible.

Anti-war efforts have continued both during and in between more recent conflicts, sometimes as part of larger organizations and sometimes specifically as part of women's groups. One of the most prominent of the latter groups in recent years was of course the Greenham Common Peace Camp. As we have seen, during the Gulf War there was a wide range of protest against the war of which *Ceasefire* was just one small part. Of course this does not mean that *Ceasefire*, or indeed the Greenham Common Peace camp are necessarily manifestations of feminism per se. Greenham Common caused debates amongst feminists because for some the appeal to maternal values (for example photographs of children on the perimeter fence) represented a retrograde tendency which was in opposition to feminist attempts to challenge the existing social construction of women as mothers and housewives. Because of the fragmentation of the feminist movement it is certainly true that there is no such thing as an archetypal 'feminist', and the issues raised by Greenham Common are extremely complicated in this matter.[12] Equally *Ceasefire* is a piece of work created by twenty three women and it reflects the differing views of twenty three individuals rather than any kind of feminist consensus (even if that were possible). The only common denominator in the work as a whole is an opposition to the war itself.

The role of comics

Comic strips are arguably an excellent vehicle for political satire, and they have certainly been used in that way by artists such as Gary Trudeau in *Doonesbury* and Steve Bell in *If*. Indeed, it could be argued that major political turmoil has occasioned some of Bell's finest work, for example during the Falklands war. Comics often have a strong, dynamic visual content which can also be found in political cartoons, posters or films. But it is possible to control the elements of a comic more precisely than in most films. In a comic narrative everything including the basic script, the way the characters look and behave and how they are seen can all be under the exact control of a skilful artist. In the collaborative medium of film the scriptwriter, director, actors, designers and lighting men, amongst others, will all have had a hand in appearance and potential meaning of a single scene. The precision which is available to comics means that any satire, or indeed propaganda message can be expressed in a most forceful and exact way. According to Umberto Eco:

> [The author] is also conscious, whether we like it or not, that he must operate within a highly stylized language, with precisely drawn boundaries. The critic's task, therefore, is to follow the author through the strip so as to pick out the 'mode' in which he has pre-cast his message.[13]

Because of the complexity of comics as a form this decoding of the author's message can be a task fraught with great difficulty. In the article from which this quote is taken Eco spends five pages of dense text undertaking a preliminary analysis of a single page of the American newspaper comic strip, *Steve Canyon*.

It is also extremely difficult to assess the effect or power of satire, or any kind of humour which is directed at a specific target, whether it be political or not. There are certainly many cases where the targets of such satire have taken their effects very seriously; cartoonists have suffered imprisonment and even been murdered because of their work. This is not just an historical phenomenon; in 1987 the cartoonist Naji Salim Al-Ali was shot in London after he had produced a drawing which satirized Yasser Arafat's girlfriend. The effect of such cartoons on a reader who is not very directly involved with the target of the satire is harder to assess. Indeed the different ways in which any reader will react to a given text are tremendously diverse.

In the case of an anti-war comic like *Ceasefire* its readers will presumably fall, in very broad terms, into the three basic areas of election opinion polls; for, against and don't know. How many of the 'don't knows' could be swayed by such satire is impossible to say. It is possible that *Ceasefire*, because of its distribution to hundreds of specialist comic shops in this country and abroad, and the fact that its cover caused it to be mistaken for a horror comic, may have been at least perused by a high percentage of 'don't knows'. Martin Barker has argued that ideologies are expressed in comics (and indeed other media) only through a kind of 'contract' between the text and the reader.[14] To assess how successful this 'dialogic' system of communication is, it is properly necessary, according to Barker, to know not only something about the author of any given text but also its production history and background as well as the nature and the reaction of its readers. Obviously this would potentially be a massive undertaking, if carried out thoroughly, but it is an indication of the scale of investigation which is necessary before it is possible to move toward anything like concrete conclusions about what can seem to be, at least on the surface, comparatively straightforward texts.

Ceasefire

Ceasefire is thirty two pages long and printed in Canada. It was initially held by customs when shipped back to Britain on the grounds that it was a horror comic. This was presumably because the cover features a stylized, simply drawn screaming figure. In fact the comic studiously avoids the kind of violent or horrific imagery which might often be found in a normal 'children's' war comic.

I want to concentrate in detail mainly on two of the longer stories in the comic: '*Spoils of War*' by Carol Swain and '*Punch*' by Jackie Smith. Concentrating on two specific stories has the disadvantage that much interesting material has to be neglected. The stories vary greatly in tone and length, and include Julie Hollings's satire on the euphemisms of war, such as 'Friendly Fire' ('"ello...my name's Stan...Stan the scud...nice to meet you'). But overall the comic contains twelve separate stories and seven spot cartoons, far too much to be adequately covered in the space available here.

It is probably the case that if examined in isolation both the stories chosen are not obviously by or about women. This is in fact true of the majority of the stories and cartoons in the comic. It may well be that this characteristic is partially an indication of the comparative strength of the position of women cartoonists in recent years which has parallels with the changing roles and status of women in comedy as a whole. Talking about women stand-up comedians, writer Amanda Swift has commented:

> There was a time when women comedians tended to concentrate on issues that were exclusively part of women's experience - periods,

sexism etc. At that time it was very important that they do so, to break the taboos surrounding those things. But now women are becoming established in comedy, we're moving away from that.[15]

This characteristic is also partially to do with the nature of the subject, of course. In 'Fanny's' second issue, where the subject is sex, many more of the stories are self evidently by and about women.

Others would argue that women's progress in this field (as in many others) has been minimal - a combination, perhaps, of 'tokenism' and small concessions. Certainly in America, where the situation is generally perceived to be appreciably better, there is still widespread dissatisfaction with the role of women in comics. This disenchantment was forcibly expressed by artist and author Trina Robbins in the nineteen eighties when she wrote: 'The representation of women in comics is still pitiful. And the improvement has been so incredibly minor that it's like a drop in the bucket compared to how many women were working in comics before the '50s. Its absurd.'[16]

There are some parts of the comic where the contributions could legitimately be described as feminist, in that they utilize ideas and arguments which have come out of feminist discourse to make their point. A cartoon by Cath Jackson shows a vulture on a stone which declares - 'welcome to patriarchy, twin town with fascism, racism and capitalism'. Another cartoon by Lesley Ruda shows the Queen inspecting her troops, all of whom are represented simply by erect penises.

One of the stories in *Ceasefire* which does link women's issues with the war is a neat one page story by Jacqui Adams and Juliet Gosling: '*Home Front*'. It has only six panels, with no word balloons, but a section of text under each panel. It is made evident that this text is representing the voice of someone speaking on the radio by using the convention of wavy 'radio' lines. In the first panel, above the text 'Our soldiers are coming under enormous pressure to achieve their goals...' a woman is shown taking two children to school. In the second panel, above 'Their nerve is unflinching even when surrounded by the enemy...' the same woman is shown being crushed by businessmen on the tube. In the third panel accompanying the text 'Although under extreme provocation they are trained not to react...' the central character is shown being sexually harassed at work. In the following two panels 'Routes to freedom are blocked by the volume of hardware involved' and 'unaided by outside forces they struggle bravely on...' she is shown hemmed in by shopping trolleys and then boarding a bus with her two children. In the final panel she listens to the radio declaring 'Having gained their objective they can now look forward to a well earned rest,' whilst she is busily doing the washing.

Spoils of War

'*Spoils of War*' is a story written and drawn by Carol Swain. The five page story establishes two separate narratives in the first two pages. On the first page a long haired youth, who tells the barber he is seventeen, has his long hair shorn. Dog tags around his neck and glimpses of a queue in the background indicate he is a new recruit to the army. On the second page a journalist in fatigues is reporting from the front. At the juncture where the scene changes to the journalist there is no obvious indication of this fact given to the reader, apart from the actual change of characters and scene. In the first frame, as the reporter addresses the viewer (actually the comic's reader but by implication a television audience) it is possible for a moment to believe that the reporter is talking to the recruit. There is no simplistic indicator, common in many children's comics explaining 'meanwhile' or 'elsewhere'.

The story is drawn in a broad, strongly stylized manner, reminiscent of European rather than English or American comics. This may be due to the fact that Carol Swain trained as a fine artist, and only became interested in comics after the 1987 exhibition Comic Iconoclasm.[17] Her comic strips are drawn in charcoal - in many ways a very 'fine art' medium. By the time her work is reproduced by offset lithography the charcoal loses most of its softer qualities and leaves the pages with a heavy, brooding quality. Combined with her stark, jagged drawing style this makes for an overall impression which is both dramatic and unsettling.

The journalist begins interviewing a major who begins to talk in the military jargon which became so typical of the war: 'neutralisation, friendly fire, mopping up, body count' and so on - phrases which defined the conflict and gave it the veneer of being technologically controlled and 'clean'.

On the third page the story returns to the recruit who removes a 'Faith No More' T-shirt, while the final panel of the page shows the reporter and the major in front of a night sky illuminated by vast explosions.

On the fourth page (see fig. 2) the intercutting between the two elements of the story increases to the point where alternative panels depict single frames from each strand of the narrative. There are still no obvious 'grammatical' indicators to interrupt the flow of the page - indeed the whole story uses no separate text panels or boxes at all. The effect is akin to a film in which the intercutting of two separate scenes increases in tempo as time progresses. This kind of technique - using dramatic 'intercutting' with little or no textual guide - is something which is found in a range of comics which attempt to utilize a more sophisticated kind of narrative structure.[18] These overtones of film and the lack of obvious signposting were quite deliberate on Carol Swain's part, as she explains:

> People watching films seem to be able to cope with complex editing, flashbacks and parallel storylines...and I also don't think it matters if people get slightly muddled with the time and place in stories. I hate 'meanwhiles' etc. because it breaks up the flow of a story, suddenly you're jolted back to the grammar of the medium. Also the jump cutting went well, because in the 'real' world all the T.V. schedules were being thrown into chaos. I can remember people complaining that *Neighbours* was interrupted by the continued coverage from CNN in Baghdad.[19]

By this stage of the story most readers are probably attuned to the rapid changes of scene from panel to panel.

This page also displays the cinematic qualities which some comics are particularly effective at recreating. Indeed it can almost be read as a storyboard for a film. The scenes of the major and journalist remain fairly static, but the views of the recruit being measured jump from a close up to a back view to a high angle. If the strip were used as a story board these latter images could be achieved either by a different camera set up for each frame, or by the camera circling the recruit.

Obviously the device of intercutting invites the reader to make direct comparisons between the two elements in the story. The public face of the war and its effect on the landscape are juxtaposed with the personal transformation of a young recruit. For Carol Swain the purpose is twofold:

> [The intercutting] shows how what we saw of the war was only a part of the whole picture, and also gets some of the jargon of the war in too, because it seemed to go with the theme of the story - of the loss of individuality and choice. The language of the war seemed necessary to sustain the 'belief' in it...[20]

This is important because it shows the way in which Carol Swain is able to combine a series of issues which are expressed not only in the narrative but also in the way in which that narrative is drawn. She is able to ally her main theme of loss of individuality with a recreation of the fragmentation of images which comment on the way in which the war was perceived, as well as highlighting the importance of official language in defining the war and creating the agenda for debate.

On the final page of the story the recruit dons his uniform, still intercut with scenes of the major. The last three frames show the recruit in a line of seven soldiers. They are all in silhouette, close together so that they virtually form an amorphous mass which casts long ominous shadows. Then the major speaks: 'What you see before you is a liberated land and you should be proud...'. The final frame repeats the word 'proud', in much smaller lettering. Behind this single word there is a bleak, almost surreal landscape with a mass of black oil fires. This is a visual echo of the looming black shadows of the recruits which underlines the double or rather triple meaning of the title: 'Spoils of War'.

Punch

'*Punch*' is a six page story written and drawn by Jackie Smith. It makes a strong visual contrast with 'Spoils of War' because its drawing style is very much inspired by mainstream British comic artists. Jackie Smith's influences include Ken Reid, Roy Wilson, George Herriman and Hunt Emerson.[21] The basic premise behind the story also reflects this interest in broad slapstick humour - although with a dark, pessimistic undertone. In the story the Gulf War has become a Punch and Judy show. In the first two pages 'General Punch' disposes of not only the baby but also Judy. However when he is threatened with arrest he pours oil all over the booth (see fig. 3). The crocodile then dies from oil pollution. The policeman reappears with reinforcements only to be threatened by General Punch's nuclear sausages. On the final two pages it is revealed that all the puppets are being controlled by John Major. Although, as a caption points out: 'N.B. Any head of state whose country is involved in the arms trade could be substituted for Mr Major.'

It also becomes evident that 'Mr Major' has sold 'General Punch' his nuclear sausages, although he strenuously denies this charge ('Oh no I didn't!'). Meanwhile the rather perplexed audience is being accosted by a monkey with a tin to pay for the show. When the money is finally divided 'General Punch' ends the strip by asking if he can spend his share on some more sausages. This analogy to the political background of the war, for all its apparent broad humour, is in fact consistently cynical.

The fact that it is drawn in a style which would be at home in the *Beano* seems at first glance to be simply incongruous. But this incongruity is part of the strength of the strip. It is executed in a drawing style familiar to many readers from their childhood, or at least from the bombardment of commercial exploitation which has accompanied *Beano* and similar characters in recent years. Indeed, even if it is not familiar to a reader, the way in which the characters are drawn is intrinsically 'comfortable' - rounded, soft and easy on the eye. Jackie Smith uses traditional brush and ink, the effect of which contrasts sharply with Carol Swain's jagged, harsh charcoal drawings. But whereas Swain's style fits neatly into the overall tone of her strip, Jackie Smith's seems in a sense to work against the atmosphere of her script. But what can happen to a reader during the course of the strip is that they are lulled into a false sense of security. As the strip progresses the broad slapstick of the drawing style and visual effects are undermined as the content of the underlying satire becomes evident.

The construction of meaning

The whole question of the potential meaning of drawing style and the effect of page design and narrative techniques on that meaning can be examined in more detail. As we have seen it is perfectly possible for a drawing style to be in a kind of 'opposition' rather than 'sympathy' with the tone of a comic script. This opposition can then be used to unsettle or confound the expectations of the reader. But the whole layout of a page and the way in which a narrative is expressed can also underline, or modify meanings in this way.

We have seen that Jackie Smith's drawing style echoes very traditional 'comic' comic styles, but does the page layout and her use of the devices of comic strip language with all its symbols and conventions also reinforce this style? To examine whether this is the case it is necessary to compare the structure of the story in much more detail with the 'norms' of more traditional comics. In order to do this I am going to apply an analytical system I devised when researching British underground and alternative comics.[22]

This system of analysis was devised to try to establish whether there was any intrinsic link between the content of comic strips and their formal structure and language. The aim was to create a numerical result or pattern (finally expressed as a graph) which could be used as a standard against which any other comic could be analysed and empirically tested. In particular a series of 'alternative' and 'underground' comics were compared to their mainstream counterparts. The conclusion of this exercise was, in short, that although there was clearly such a thing as an identifiable 'experimental' comic in terms of form and structure, this type of comic cut across the boundaries of 'alternative' or 'mainstream' as defined purely by content. Certain major mainstream comic artists such as Will Eisner or Jim Steranko were just as likely to break the established norms of comic structure as some 'underground' artists, such as Victor Moscosco or Rick Griffin. Equally some 'underground' artists, famous for their challenging or outrageous content, were happy to use absolutely traditional forms - notably Robert Crumb and Gilbert Shelton.[23]

A large number of potential categories were considered for inclusion. After a process of elimination thirty seven of these categories were used, divided into three broad areas of concern: basic form, page design and narrative structure. The first eleven categories of the analysis deal with the basic form of the comic and have not been included in this exercise because they tend to establish only its physical appearance.[24]

The next twelve categories deal with the overall design of the page. Categories 21-23, word balloons, text panels and onomatopoeic words also have a material effect on the narrative structure of the comic. However, they have been included in the page design categories mainly because when the results are expressed in graph form all the categories in page design tend to fall below a high of one hundred , whereas those in the narrative structure tend to fall below a high of only fifty. The categories used are as follows:

Page Design Categories

12. Panels: Total number of panels per five pages.
13. Irregular: not parallel or straight panel lines.
14. Broken: no panel lines on one or two sides.
15. Object: panel lines follow an object or person in the panel exactly
16. None: no panel lines on three or all sides.
17. Geometrical: all geometrical shapes except rectangles.
18. Rectangular: square or rectangular.
19. Overlaid: a panel which overlaps another.
20. Angle: a panel not parallel to the page edges.
21. Word Balloons: overall number.
22. Text Panels: overall number.
23. Onomatopoeic words: total number of onomatopoeic or 'sound' words (outside word balloons).

Narrative Structure Categories

24. Sequences: overall number of sequences (a series of frames which

are set in the same location in one continual period of time).
25. Breaks in chronology: Flashbacks, breaks in chronological flow.
26. Symbolic devices: number of frames which include 'graphic symbols', for example speed lines.
27. Multiple Images: multiple images of a character or object used to a complicated piece of action.
28. Long shot: from landscape to a group of figures.
29. Medium shot: from half to full length figures.
30. Close up: from less than half figure to full face.
31. Extreme close up: part of a face or extreme detail.
32. Non-centrality: number of frames in which characters are significantly cut off by the vertical panel edge.
33. Non-eye level: scene shown from a high or low angle.
34. First person: frame obviously meant to show the point of view of a character in the narrative.
35. Images outside panel: part of a character or object crossing outside the panel lines.
36. Images across panel: as above, except that the 'break out' is so significant that it impinges on the images in another panel.
37. Breaks in picture frame: a complete break in the illusion of the panels (e.g. the 'artist's hand' appears or characters interact with panel lines etc).

Several of the categories in this section can prove difficult to distinguish with absolute accuracy in practice. In particular no. 24, (sequences), just as with the cinema, can be difficult to assess. Sometimes they are clearly delineated in comics by text panel information, but at other times they can be extremely unclear. Equally the differences between 'long' and 'medium' shots or close-ups can be blurred. Category no. 32 (non-centrality) is a characteristic which is not found at all in many early comics, and for the purpose of this exercise it is only counted when a character is significantly cut off by the vertical panel line (i.e. at least half the figure is cut off). Equally category no. 33, non-eye level, is only counted when the angle of the viewer is obviously very high or low rather than only slightly away from eye level.

These criteria were then applied to a whole series of mainstream comics produced by large publishers. From the results it proved possible to create 'bands' of figures which represented the range of elements which appeared in these comics. In order to make the bands narrow enough to be meaningful it proved necessary to separate humour comics from adventure comics and British from American comics. This left four graphs, two of which are reproduced here against which other comics of different types could be compared (see tables 1 and 2).

If the analysis of *Punch* is compared to the standard pattern for the British humour comic (taken from comics such as the *Beano*) it can be seen that it is very similar (see table 1). It only deviates in a very minor way at several points. These are largely due to the fact that its overall number of frames in five pages (twenty seven) is slightly less than might normally by used. This in turn leaves its rectangular panels (category no. 18) and word balloons (category no. 21) very slightly below normal levels. Equally this also accounts for the lesser number of symbolic devices (category no. 26) and 'long shots' (category no. 28) also falling short of normal levels. However the graph indicates that the strip is not only drawn in the style of traditional British comics, but also uses the structure and narrative style of that form as well. This underlines that the 'subversive' nature of the strip is expressed in its confounding not only the expectations of its drawing style, but also its whole structure.

It is also instructive to compare Carol Swain's story '*Spoils of War*' to the standard British Adventure comic. In terms of page design it is extremely close to the norm (see table 2). However when the narrative structure is compared there are dramatic deviations. This is despite the fact that the varied nature of British adventure comics meant that the original results produced the widest bands of the four types of comics studied (British and American humour comics and British and American 'adventure' comics). In particular, because of its intercutting, the strip has twenty separate 'sequences' in its five pages, whereas the very highest level normally found is only six sequences. Indeed the 'cinematic' tendencies in the strip which have already been remarked upon can be said to account for many of these differences. Another striking feature, for example, is the number of times there are characters very much on the periphery of the frame (category 32, non-centrality: eighteen occasions). This is a characteristic which has been uncommon both in most early comics and still is rarely found in many more staid contemporary mainstream comics. Its effect can be unsettling; it is certainly suggestive of movement - either 'camera panning' or characters moving 'out of shot'. Thus it can be said that Carol Swain's strip is unsettling and dramatic not just because of its drawing style but also because of its structure. It is experimental in that it stretches, and comes close to breaking, the rules by which such comics normally operate. It does not allow the viewer to settle into a comfortable reading pattern, but instead demands continual attention and thought to be devoted to the act of comprehending what the strip is trying to say.

This also demonstrates what a complex process can be involved in ascertaining the meaning of any given comic strip. Dividing the different areas crudely it can be said that initially the drawing style and page layout give a series of clues to a reader which will set up a quite definite range of possible areas of meaning. Once the narrative is entered into (and in comics this may be with or without reading text panels, and moving freely from one page to another at the reader's discretion) another, possibly more specific meaning begins to emerge. Finally, and perhaps less obviously, the way in which the comic uses or abuses the rules and grammar of comics bends and shapes the way in which the narrative is followed and understood.

It is impossible to estimate, in the final analysis, how many people read *Ceasefire* and whether it changed anybody's mind about the war. It may have made some of its readers think about the war in new and different ways, and it may have given others a feeling of solidarity and sympathy simply by the appearance of such material in printed form. It is in the nature of such publications that their relatively limited distribution means that they do not reach a wide enough audience. Its publication, both as a protest against the war and an example of the work of women cartoonists was an achievement in itself. The feelings of women cartoonists are probably best expressed by the views of one of the authors discussed above, Jackie Smith, in a statement which refers specifically to women working in comics, but also has wider applications:

> Some women I know are radical in airing their views and the content of their work is also radical.. i.e. lesbian feminist. Other women work away quietly as letterers or colourists. The thing that seems to concern women most is the way they are portrayed by men, and the lack of characters, and therefore interest, that they can identify with in the mainstream comics and in other media. I think there's a lot of rubbish in comics and sexist stuff is so glaringly obvious. But if you read a really good comic book - *Maus*, for instance, it never crosses your mind - you're too absorbed by the story.[25]

Notes

1. *Ceasefire* (1991), published by Tate, Cath and Bennett, Carol, at Knockabout Books, 10 Acklam Road, London, W10 5QZ, ISBN 086166 0943
2. Further details of Knockabout's publishing history, can be found in Huxley, D. (1990), *The Growth and Development of British Underground and Alternative Comics 1966-86*, Ph.D, Loughborough University.
3. Bennett, Carol (1990), What do women want? in *Speakeasy*, no. 115, p. 31, November.
4. *Ibid.*
5. Letter to the author, 24 July 1992.
6. *Ibid.*
7. Kellner, Douglas (1992), *The Persian Gulf T.V. War*, Boulder, Westview Press, p. 250.
8. Women's peace movements, particularly in relation to the first world war, and some of the wider issues involved are discussed in Pierson, Ruth Roach (ed.), (1987), *Women and Peace*, Croom Helm.
9. Kellner, Douglas *op. cit.* p. 74.
10. Brownmiller's wide ranging argument (1975) first appeared in *Against Our Will: Men, Women and Rape*, Simon and Schuster, New York.
11. Eisenstein, Hesler (1984), *Contemporary Feminist Thought*, Counterpoint, p. 31.
12. The Greenham Common Peace Camp and its ramifications are discussed in Jones, Lynne (ed.), (1983), *Keeping the Peace*, The Women's Press.
13. Eco, Umberto (1987), 'A Reading of Steve Canyon' in *Comic Iconoclasm*, ICA, p. 21.
14. This is part of a complicated and wide ranging thesis in Martin Barker's excellent book (1989), *Comics: ideology, power and the critics*, Manchester University Press, Manchester.
15. Evans, Catherine (1991), 'No laughing matter', in *The Guardian*, p. 19, 3 July.
16. Quoted in MacDonald, Heidi (1988), House of Semi-Raging Women in *Amazing Heroes*, no. 141, p. 21, 15 May.
17. Comic Iconoclasm, *op. cit.*
18. It occurs for example in the American mainstream comic book story (1971), '22 Hours to San Francisco' in *Our Army at War* no. 236, DC comics September. This is an anti-Vietnam war story

drawn by John Severin which uses no text panels and no word balloons during the course of a four page story. With the advantage of colour the story is able to flow without interruption between scenes of a return home (in colour) to flashbacks of the war itself (in black and white). A fuller analysis of this and two other Vietnam War stories can be found in my own (1988) 'Naked Aggression: Comic books and the Vietnam War' in *Tell Me Lies About Vietnam*, Louvre, A. & Walsh, J. (eds.), Open University Press, Milton Keynes.

19. Swain, Carol (1992), Letter to the author, 15 July.
20. *Ibid.*
21. Ken Reid was an influential British comic artist whose most famous strips were *'Jonah'* and *'Roger the Dodger'* for the *Beano*. Roy Wilson worked on British humorous comics for over forty years from *Bubbles* (1920) and *Happy Days* to *T.V. Fun* in 1965. George Herriman's *Krazy Kat* (1913-44) is regarded by many critics as the pinnacle of achievement in the field of American Newspaper strips. Hunt Emerson has been one of the most prolific and important artists in British alternative comics since 1972.
22. Huxley, D. (1990), *op. cit.*
23. Will Eisner has been one of the most respected American comic strip artists since the nineteen thirties. His most famous newspaper strip, recently much reprinted, was *The Spirit*. Jim Steranko worked for Marvel Comics in America in the late nineteen sixties, producing elaborate versions of their existing characters such as Nick Fury and Captain America. Victor Moscosco was one of the most surreal of the American underground comic artists of the late nineteen sixties and early seventies whose work appeared in *Zap* comic. Rick Griffin, also an underground poster artist, specialized in 'Surrealist' narratives and forms in his comic strip work.

   Robert Crumb is probably the most famous and most idiosyncratic of all American underground cartoonists. His work appeared in *Zap*, many other of his own comics, and most recently in *Wierdo*. Gilbert Shelton's Furry Freak Brothers are the most lasting creation of American underground comics.
24. They are: 1. Size, 2. Length, 3. Colour/B. & W., 4. Genre, 5. Drawing type, 6. Frame style, 7. Balloon style, 8. Lettering style, 9. Onomatopoeic style, 10. Border style, 11. Reading Path.
25. Smith, Jackie (1992), Letter to the author, 31 July.

12 Monuments and memorials

James Aulich

Some of the inspiration for this essay comes from a photograph of a pro-Iraq demonstration in Amman during the Gulf War (fig.4). The image focuses on a Jordanian child who brandishes a placard. In the centre is the cover of a German magazine featuring a portrait of President George Bush montaged in front of the turret of a battleship. Pasted over a swastika it has the caption 'Kriegs-Kurs' (War Heading). Someone has scribbled on his upper-lip a toothbrush moustache to draw out an uncanny resemblance to Adolf Hitler and underneath are the hand-written words 'Any one could be Hitler...!'[1] Western characterizations of Saddam habitually placed him amongst the most barbaric leaders of the twentieth century, Hitler not least among them. But what this poster implies is that the *de facto* leader of the coalition could also be understood to be a Hitler figure. For sections of the Arab community it was a natural assumption that Bush was guided by the irrationalist principles of national destiny, racial superiority, technological progress and absolute moral rectitude under God, as surely as Saddam.

As we watched the CNN broadcasts live from the heart of the enemy in Baghdad, and as General Schwarzkopf guided the media through a technologically clean battlefield to disarm criticism with the epithets 'friendly fire' and 'collateral damage', it seemed that Jean Baudrillard's concept of 'hyperreality' had come of age. All questions of belief and value had become compromised in the simulacrum of an indiscriminate and undifferentiated Virtual War. Christopher Norris remarked with some scepticism:

> It is a conflict waged - for all that we can know - entirely at this level of strategic simulation, a mode of vicarious spectator-involvement that extends all the way from fictive war-games to saturation coverage of the 'real world' event, and which thus leaves us perfectly incapable of distinguishing the one from the other.[2]

But questions of value could not be avoided. Murmurs of disquiet *were* heard, particularly in relation to civilian casualties. Statements like 'turkey shoots' and the 'luckiest man alive in Iraq today' betrayed an unconscious and callous disregard for human life. Misgiving was compounded by the flimsy arguments surrounding the bombing of the Amiriya shelter in Baghdad as a legitimate target. Indeed, rumours grew that something had not only *occurred* on the road to Basra but what *had* occurred was unjust and un-American. Somebody had been shot in the back. 'The road of death' signified a radical loss of spiritual confidence masked by a grim but curiously unfulfilled sense of purpose not just to 'kick ass' but to depose, if not kill, Saddam Hussein. Not even the defenders of the *Alamo* (1960), led by Jim Bowie (Richard Widmark) and Davy Crockett (John Wayne), had fired on Mexican troops as they withdrew to regroup. Let alone as they fled in headlong retreat. But here lies a duplicity that characterized the whole campaign. Richard Slotkin identified its ideological roots in a rarely recognised, or more accurately, usually concealed contradiction in American myth:

> The antimythologists of the American Age of Reason believed in the imminence of a rational republic of yeoman farmers and enlightened leaders, living amicably in the light of natural law and the Constitution. They were thereby left unprepared when the Jeffersonian republic was overcome by the Jacksonian Democracy of the man-on-the-make, the speculator, and the wildcat banker; when racist irrationalism and a falsely conceived economics prolonged and intensified slavery in the teeth of American democratic idealism; when men like Davy Crockett became national heroes by defining national aspiration in terms of so many bears destroyed, so much land preempted, so many trees hacked down, so many Indians and Mexicans dead in the dust.[3]

In the public realm it is a natural fact that the antimythologists are pre-eminent; yet, history would show them unprepared for the forces of irrationalism. It is the contention of this essay that much of the meaning of the war in the Gulf can be found in the symbolism and the style of public memorials conceived in the years leading up to the outbreak of hostilities both in the United States and in Iraq. The intention is to examine the ideological, iconographical, political and discursive relationships between Saddam Hussein's *Monument* or *Victory Arch* (fig.5) in Baghdad; and in Washington the *Vietnam Veterans Memorial* or *The Wall* and its sculptural additions (fig.6) and (fig.7). In so doing, it is hoped to reveal historical causes for the war in the Gulf and to demonstrate how it is that both Bush and Saddam can be convincingly portrayed as 'Hitler'.

The memorials are different in function. Saddam Hussein's *Monument* (fig.5) is a celebration of the putative victory of the Ba'athist totalitarian state over Iran after a long drawn out war (1980-88). *The Wall* in large part, is a lament for defeat in Vietnam (1964-75) on behalf of a Western democracy. Both are public, ceremonial and symbolic and draw on national and racial myths of superiority, sacrifice, martyrdom and destiny to different degrees. They contribute to the construction of contemporary, if nostalgic, Islamic and Christian national and imperial histories. As Saddam Hussein remarked, 'History has to be made in the image we believe it to be.'

The *Monument* (fig.5) was conceived by Saddam Hussein as head of state in 1985 and was inaugurated in 1989. The original design of a triumphal arch surmounted by ceremonial swords and a flag was modified by the Iraqi sculptor Khalid al-Rashid and completed by Mohammed Ghani under Saddam's close supervision. Given the paucity of literature on Iraq and the enormity of the misunderstandings on both sides of the conflict it is difficult to gauge the effect of the *Monument* on Iraqi consciousness. But some things are relatively clear in the wider context. Saddam Hussein, from the inception of his rule imposed a cult of personality on the Iraqi people. He learned from the examples of Adolf Hitler and, in spite of his anti-Communist credentials, Josef Stalin (Ba'athist dalliance with Nazism in the '30s and '40s, born of anti-British and French feeling, particularly amongst the middle classes and urban intellectual elite is well documented). Saddam's deadly grip simultaneously froze Iraq's secular drive towards modernity and placed him at the centre of Ba'athist quasi-mystical pan-Arabism. Subsequently, the adulation of Saddam Hussein was exaggerated by the needs of the Iran-Iraq war which failed to fulfil its promise of quick victory and flung the Iraqi people into a grinding war of attrition. High octane ideological fuel was needed to sustain the appalling casualty rates. This was achieved in a number of contradictory ways.

The Ba'athist state in typical totalitarian style crushed all opposition and through fear and intimidation promoted Saddam's will. Total identification of the person of Saddam with the state served to ensure his idolization at home, while on a rhetorical level it enabled his international criminalization within the ethics of a liberal, democratic and domestic legal system. A self evidently incongruous system in the field of international law as figured by the behaviour of the United States in Libya, Nicaragua, Grenada, Panama and elsewhere.[4] This disjuncture between the public face and the historical action of the United States' administration stimulated oppositional accusations of bad faith and, as I will demonstrate, is inscribed in the iconography of its dominant aesthetic.

But, for the moment, to return to Iraq. The Islamic faith is egalitarian in essence and would discourage any personality cult, yet there are said to be over sixteen million portraits of Saddam in Iraq (fig.8). As John Simpson observed:

> Not far away a vast cardboard cut-out of Saddam Hussein loomed out of the darkness, ten feet high, on a street corner. He was smiling, but his hand gripped his field marshal's sword, just in case.
>
> Before the Gulf crisis, the stretch of road a 100 yards long beside the Information Ministry had no fewer than forty giant portrait of the President on either side of it. ...so many pictures of Saddam Hussein in bedouin robes, so many of him in army uniform, so many looking relaxed in a white panama hat and sweat-shirt, or in a deer stalker with a hunting rifle.[5]

The effectiveness of Saddam's cult of personality is self-consciously stimulated by calls on history and identification with great figures from the past. Amongst others, Sabiha Knight has pointed out that:

> It is impossible for Muslims to forget that the Islamic empire was the longest lasting that the world has known, that its scientific and mathematical discoveries fired the Renaissance in Europe, that its civilization, for all the contradictions inherent in the nature of imperial power, was the most humane, tolerant and liberal of all empires. Cordoba, Damascus, Cairo and Baghdad are the stuff of dreams and islam has a tradition of saviours - of the Mahdi who arrives to restore justice and prosperity.
>
> This is why Saddam Hussein is a hero to most Arabs and why his ruthlessness and indeed lawbreaking are merely seen as rough and ready Robin Hood corollary - necessary in the circumstances, even forgivable.[6]

At his birthday celebration in 1990 in his home town of Takrit, for example, he identified with Sargon the Great, ruler of Iraq's first great state. Sargon's empire stretched from the Gulf to the Mediterranean and he was deified after his death. Posters often portray Saddam receiving from Hammurabi the heritage of Babylon in the form of a palm tree. Hammurabi was one of the greatest rulers of antiquity and is chiefly remembered for his code of laws, which facilitated his rule of Mesopotamia. Saddam is also referred to as Al Mansour of the Caliphate of Abbasid, 'the one whom god made victorious.' In the 8th Century B.C. the Caliphate stretched from Morocco to Pakistan in an Empire more extensive than that of the Romans.

Not least among the figures celebrated in posters with whom Saddam identifies is Nebuchadnezzar who ruled Assyria between 604-561 B.C. He restored the empire to its former prosperity, practically rebuilt Babylon and was probably responsible for the celebrated Hanging Gardens:

> During one official night-time celebration, diplomats and invited guests were asked to cast their eyes upwards into the black desert sky. There above them hung twin portraits of Saddam and Nebuchadnezzar etched against the night by laser beams. Saddam's features were rendered unusually sharp and hard in order to resemble the ancient carved images of Nebuchadnezzar.[7]

Significantly, Nebuchadnezzar sacked Jerusalem, enslaved the Jewish people and destroyed the temple. During the war the *Monument* (fig.5) was widely interpreted in the Western popular press as the folly of a deluded megalomaniac, 'Saddam thinks he is Nutty King Neb,'[8]: the biblical reference would seem to reinforce the observation, 'Nebuchadnezzar the king made an image of gold, whose height was three-score cubits, and breadth thereof six cubits.' (Daniel 3). A characterization also linked with his attempted and fanciful reconstruction of the ancient city of Babylon. In the West, biblical references were archetypal, if a little fogged. Indeed, Saddam's claimed historical precedents have an apocalyptic edge that was not missed in the Bible belt of America, nor by those who opposed the war, and, not least, by the administration (see below): 'And it shall come to pass, that the nation and the kingdom which will not serve the same Nebuchadnezzar the king of Babylon, that nation will I punish, saith the Lord, with the sword, and with the famine, and with the pestilence, until I have consumed them by his hand.' (Jeremiah 27). Associations such as these generated feelings of disquiet in the Western liberal intellectual community and were aggravated by another of Saddam's claimed antecedents in the figure of

Saladin, protector of Jerusalem as an Islamic shrine. Ironically for Saddam, Saladin was the Kurd who unified the Arabs to drive the Crusaders away.

In general, Saddam's irrationalist claims were easily dismissed as the ramblings of a drug-crazed lunatic, akin to Hitler in the last days of his bunker. In contrast few gave any consideration to the parallel claims made by Bush and Prime Minister John Major for a 'just' and Christian war. Most left-liberal opinion was irritated by the cant, and saw no more in it than a feint to fool the 'masses' and conceal the 'real causes' of the war which were to be found in economic imperatives rather than in questions of 'freedom' and 'democracy' promulgated by the leaders of the coalition.

Artists like the Polish exile Krzysztof Wodyczko, famed for his iconoclastic subversions of national symbols, took this line with an anti-war laser projection. It showed skeletal hands holding an M-16 assault rifle and a petrol pump nozzle juxtaposed with the word in Spanish for 'How Many?', beamed on to Franco's *Arch of Triumph* monument at an entrance to Madrid. This was a general tendency amongst oppositional artists in the United Kingdom, for example. In *The New World Order* (1991) and other apocalyptic images of death, Peter Kennard reproduced Wodyczko's humanitarian impulses in a montage of the globe dominated by a skeleton, an hourglass and a clock. Printed in the national daily newspaper *The Guardian* they represent a visual record of liberal opinion. Other photomontagists, in more marginal outlets pursued similar lines of attack. Cath Tate in *Happily Ever After* (1991) and *Victory to the Motor Car in the Gulf* (1991); and South Atlantic Souvenirs in *Western Roulette* (1991) set the conflagration of war in the Gulf against the folly of rampant consumerism and the good-life in the West. The video installation artist Mike Stubbs set the empty propaganda of the television war against the realities of birth and death in *Bedtime Stories: Highlights from the Gulf War* (1991).[9]

This imagery was complicit with a liberal discourse of dissent, rooted in the present and unable or unwilling to confront the power of the historical stereotypes at work within the rhetoric that carried the coalition to war. It was an intellectual discourse that made use of and subverted technically advanced media in the tradition of the avant-garde to limited effect at a time of cultural and political conservatism. Aesthetic authority, it seemed, rested elsewhere, outside the liberal elite. Nevertheless, its partial success must be registered in the negative fact that when much of this material was exhibited at Manchester City Art Galleries in the summer of 1991[10] it received only one national review.[11] Even the regional events magazine *City Life* panned it for being 'liberal' and 'political'.[12]

In Iraq, by way of contrast, every historical legitimation helped articulate Saddam's pan-Arabism. Each reinforced the belief of millions of Arabs that only a single charismatic leader could overcome the shame of their successive defeats and humiliations suffered at the hands of the Christian West and their Zionist ally, Israel. According to the back of the official invitation to the dedication of the *Monument* (fig.5) the iconography of the crossed swords embodies these desires: 'The ground bursts open and from it springs the arm that represents power and determination, carrying the sword of Qadisayya.' And, as expressed by Saddam himself in his speech of 22 April 1985:

> The worst condition is for a person to pass under a sword which is not his own ... brave Iraqis have recorded the most legendary exploits in defence of their land and holy beliefs ... we have chosen that Iraqis will pass under their fluttering flag protected by their swords which have cut through the necks of the aggressors. And so we have willed it an arch to victory, and a symbol to this Qadisayya...[13]

Saddam had called this war with Iran 'Qadisayyat Saddam', drawing a parallel with the battle of Qadisayyat in 637 AD, when Islamic Arab tribes defeated the Zoroastrian Persian rulers of Mesopotamia to establish the state of Iraq. The swords draw attention to the foundation of Islam in the area and give religious legitimation to Saddam's secular state, conveniently ignoring the fact that he was involved in a war of aggression against a fundamentalist Islamic foe, Iran. In the seventies Saddam had claimed direct descent from Mohammed in a genealogical inheritance that preceded the Sunni/Shi'ite schism, thereby increasing his influence and promoting the cause of national unity at a stroke. The claim was particularly effective in the countryside where genealogy is considered important, but was received with some cynicism amongst the urban middle classes.

Saddam thereby connects himself with a whole past, both pre-Islamic and Islamic. A past run through with memories of Empire to soothe the tensions between nation state and Arab nationality. Under the crossed swords of Qadisayya, *The Monument* (fig.5) commemorates a victory that was never achieved and embodies the contradictions of Saddam's secular Ba'athist one party state with the demands for an Islamic Arab nation and *Jihad* (Holy War) against the United States which had effectively created Israel in 1948.

The *Monument* (fig.5) is part of the wider complex of the symbolic fabric of a Baghdad largely rebuilt over the last twenty years. As a triumphal and processional artifice it is larger than Napoleon's *Arc de Triomphe* in Paris and challenges any of Hitler's dreams for Berlin. It is figurative in style unlike two other related but abstract monuments: the *Shaheed (Martyrs) Monument* (1983), based on the traditional onion dome and *The Unknown Soldier Monument* (1982), based on the traditional Iraqi shield. All three are inhuman in scale and are equally dedicated to the glory of Saddam and the martyrs of the war with Iran. They are conceived in the womb of Saddam's dream of Arab unity and the reality of the Ba'athist state. Like *The Wall*, with one arm pointing to the *Washington Memorial* (an obelisk simultaneously signifying the origins of political life in Egypt and the New Republic); and the other, to the *Lincoln Memorial* (a Greek temple signifying the origins of democratic life), the *Monument* is unquestionably at the heart of a symbolic fabric. A fabric charged with spiritual potency in the truth of lost lives and the historical actions of the state. But if the Mall in Washington uses history to legitimise an ideal of manifest destiny and the Christianizing of the savage wilderness; then the Baghdad complex seeks to legitimise an absolutist Ba'athist state centred on a single personality in the name of the equally powerful myth of a unified Islamic Arab nation.

The *Monument* is run through with contradiction. Its realism is grotesque and fragmentary, but is wholly Western and at odds with Islamic taboos on representational art. Shamir Al-Khalil, an Iraqi exile, liberal intellectual and author of a book on the *Monument* notes:

> It is the arm of the Leader-President, Saddam Hussein himself (God preserve and watch over him) enlarged forty times. It springs out to announce the good news of victory to all Iraqis, and it pulls in its wake a net that has been filled with the helmets of the enemy soldiers, some of them scattering into the wasteland.[14]

He goes on to recount with some distaste the accuracy of the facsimile, recording every blemish and follicle of the president's single, repeated forearm. Saddam's arms, like the sculptural additions to *The Wall*, and the almost contemporaneous sculpture park in Basra, with its eighty realist figures based on the photographs of men killed in action, (who point accusingly towards Iran), are permeated by a realist aesthetic that leaves little room for ambiguity. Literal-minded and apparently transparent, this aesthetic rests on received notions of national identity and purpose and a contradictory faith in scientific objectivity; its limitations are revealed in the illusion of authentic truth. As W. J. T. Mitchell has pointed out in relation to the realist tradition:

> The effect of the invention [perspective] was nothing less than to

convince an entire civilisation that it possessed an infallible method of representation, a system for the automatic and mechanical production of truths about the material and mental worlds. The best index to the hegemony of artificial perspective is the way it denies its own artificiality ... Aided by the political and economic ascendance of Western Europe, artificial perspective conquered the world under the banner of reason, science and objectivity.[15]

In public art, realist styles are invariably associated with the telling of national myth rather than history. In the twentieth century they are primarily, if indiscriminately, identified with societies which are less than democratic. More accurately, realist styles which rely heavily for their effect on the description of authentic detail are used to tell particular histories, especially in America. The painter and sculptor Frederick Remington, for example, immortalised the American West as a national morality play within conventional codes of representation 'to tell it as it was' during the early years of this century. More than film, popular art derives mythic authority from attention to historical detail.

In the *Monument* this aesthetic has a gargantuan expression: at the base of each of the four identical and colossal facsimiles of Saddam's sword-wielding forearm are amassed a total of 10,000 used and captured Iranian helmets as a testament to a warped ideal. The arms ape the giantism of Stalinist art and architecture, and their partial realism proffers faith in Western scientific reason within a corrupted, or, literally, butchered version of modernity that places the individual at the mercy of the state and religion. Significantly, Saddam's vision is repetitive, perhaps neurotic, and dislocated: it reveals the contradictions at the core of the Ba'athist regime. As Edward N. Luttwak has pointed out:

> ... his mentality is that of the Ba'athist (renaissance) movement, neither new nor original to the man - and certainly not an 'Arab' mentality, that creation of Western Arabophiles ... the ideology of Ba'ath was born as an amalgam of now wholly discredited Western ideas - the more unbalanced fragments of Nietzsche, the racism of H S Chamberlain and Alfred Rosenberg, statalist socialism before its downfall, and exclusive nationalism in the rabid style of Eastern Europe. ... it rationalises oppression as justice, tyranny as freedom, and indeed death as the most valid expression of life - given that the highest purpose of life is to advance, by death if necessary, the cause of the Ba'ath: the renaissance of a mighty Arab power, indeed a superpower able to match the United States.[16]

In contrast to the *Monument*, the *Vietnam Veterans Memorial* was not conceived by the state or its rulers but by a private group of citizens under the inspirational guidance of former infantry corporal Jan C Scruggs. The choice of Maya Ling Lin's design was determined by the largest open art competition ever held in America. Completed in 1982 it was immediately controversial. As a result the National Capital Planning Commission, the Commission of Fine Arts and the Department of the Interior only gave approval for the memorial on the addition of Frederick S Hart's *Three Fighting Men* (fig.6) and a flag. It seems that the political right had been unable to accommodate *The Wall's* uncompromising late modernism despite, or, perhaps, because of, its capacity for individual redemption and its claims for universality. The first, achieved through the discovery of inscribed names of the dead and the reflective surfaces of the polished granite; the second, achieved through its colour, black, and in the formal or abstract representation of mourning and death, variously analogous to a 'tombstone', 'wailing wall' or 'scar'.

The conflicting opinions over *The Wall* are well-documented. But to refresh our memories: Tom Carhart, a Washington lawyer, former West Pointer and an early organiser of the Vietnam Veterans' Memorial Fund, 'heard the voices of his dead buddies' objecting to *The Wall*; he called it 'a degrading ditch', 'the most insulting and demeaning memorial to our experience that was possible'. Carhart had originally raised the seed money of $165,000 for the project from Ross Perot.[17] Later Ross Perot came to regard 'the Vietnam Veterans memorial as a sneaky plot to insult veterans, and backed the addition of statues added to the memorial, ... saying it took 'eighteen very unpleasant months' ... to win that battle for the veterans 'who wanted it, and are happy.'[18] For many veterans and the jury *The Wall* made 'no political statement regarding the war or its conduct,' but was a 'symbol of national unity, a focal point for remembering the war's dead, the veterans and the lessons learned through tragic experience.'[19] But for Tom Wolfe and the *Washington Enquirer* it was a 'tribute to Jane Fonda.' The editors of the *National Review* objected that:

> this Orwellian glop does not issue from any philistine objection to new concepts in art. It is based upon the clear political message of this design. The design says that the Vietnam war should be memorialized in black, not in the white marble of Washington. The mode of listing the names makes them individual deaths, not deaths in a cause: they might as well have been traffic accidents. The invisibility of the monument at ground level symbolized the 'unmentionability' of the war - which war ... is not mentioned on the monument itself (sic). Finally, the V-shaped plan of the black

retaining wall immortalizes the antiwar signal, the V protest made with the fingers.[20]

Alan Borg described *The Wall* as traditional in form,[21] which as an 'abstract' memorial it is, echoing the *Washington Memorial*. But such a reading is simplistic. *The Wall* has few iconographical references aside from the simplicity of the gravestone and certainly none of the historical resonance of the obelisk. It has no classical detailing to give it imperial or colonial signification. In some respects, such historical resonance that it does have, is contemporary and ironic. By the end of the seventies the extreme abstraction of Minimal styles had led to an expressive bankruptcy in high art. Abstraction was pursued by an avant-garde eager to outrun the recuperative powers of a corporate system seeking to legitimize its commercial objectives within the military industrial complex through the acquisition of cultural capital. *The Wall*, for all its redemptive and healing capacity, echoes this stylistic hegemony of Mies van der Rohe's late modernism of corporate America and international banking. Its reflective surfaces envelop the individual and the environment of the Mall, while, at the same time, they refuse a glimpse into the deeper structural and institutional meanings of the war. *The Wall* is both an assertion and a denial of the individual.

The original Maya Lin design captures the solemnity and presence of sculptural high art styles associated with artists like Richard Serra, Donald Judd, Robert Morris, Carl Andre and Ronald Bladen. But by means of its social function as a memorial it avoids the dual institutional and ideological traps of corporate patronage and the delusory marginality of outsider status that accrues to avant-garde art. What is more, as a memorial to those who perished in a national defeat it is excluded from dominant orthodoxies. Sunk into the ground, it shares something of the oppositional aura of earthworks like Michael Heizer's *Compression Line* (1968) in the Mojave Desert or Robert Morris' *Observatory* (1971), for example. Their obscure ceremonial and pantheist references are linked with concerns for the environment and the 'Other' in the shape of Native Americans who, in the popular imagination, doubled for the Vietnamese in the 'Indian Country' of South East Asia. It has none of the chauvinist recuperative energies of the later sculptural additions (see below & figs.6 & 7). While its cathartic power is bespoken by the hundreds of objects left at the wall as tributes to the memory of the dead.

Even before the smoke and dust from the bombardment of Baghdad had settled around Saddam Hussein's unscathed *Monument* so, in the United States, as a measure of consolidating ideological shifts, designs were selected for the *Korean War Veterans Memorial*, (to be sited in Ash

Woods on the Mall) and the *Women's Military Memorial*, (to be sited at the entrance to Arlington Cemetery). Even more significantly the decision was reached to complete the *Vietnam Veterans Memorial* with an American flag at *The Wall*'s apex and a further sculpture, commissioned by the Vietnam Women's Memorial Project and executed by Glenna Goodacre, portraying women of the Vietnam era with a wounded soldier (fig.7).

In these monuments Bush's 'New World Order' of American military supremacy and economic vulnerability was symbolised by an aesthetic antagonistic to the dominant post-Vietnam war liberalism implicit in the Minimalism of Maya Lin's memorial. These recent memorials are executed in heroic mould in figurative styles familiar from not only history painting but also memorials to the fallen of the First and Second World Wars. The *Korean War Veterans Memorial*, for example, apes many Soviet memorials to the Great Patriotic War (1941-45) and, controversially, succeeds in re-establishing on an aesthetic level a narrative of war within the fabric of a moral crusade. The designers of the Korean memorial ,[22] for example, filed complaint because:

> Vermont sculptor Frank Gaylors, commissioned last June (1990) to create the 38 pieces (a column of impressionistic soldiers marching towards the American flag), has positioned the infantrymen in realistic poses such as those as might be assumed on the battlefield. Indeed, Kent Cooper, principal of Cooper Lecky (Architects of Washington DC), believes that the figures now afford 'the feeling of what it's like to be under combat, with people dying around you, and the courage that it takes to be in that situation.' While the peace-invoking symbolism and imagery envisioned by the original designers may have been obtuse, a battalion of fighting soldiers is clearly not what they had in mind.[23]

The men depicted in these sculptures, like Frederick Hart's *Three Fighting Men* (1984) (fig.6), emerge dazed but resilient. Unlike the figures in totalitarian art and the sculpture park in Basra, for example, they are neither authoritarian nor idealist, rather they share the sentimentality of the film industry. Their bearing and ethnic mix recall the studied desire of Oliver Stone's *Platoon* (1986) 'to tell it as it was,' and in so doing subconsciously consign the war to national myth rather than history.

These controversies reveal some of the contradictions which lie at the heart of American society. Crucially, *The Wall* failed to respond to national myths of manifest destiny and a providential and expansionist mission under God. Many wanted something more traditional and positive, something more fitting to the triumphalism of a crusade, something in the manner of Felix De Weldon's realist World War Two *Marine Corps War Memorial* (1954) dedicated to the raising of the Stars and Stripes by marines on the summit of Mt. Suribachi on Iwo Jima during the Pacific campaign. The statue had derived its imagery from a widely published photograph taken by Joe Rosenthal during a second flag-raising. As the representation of a representation of a simulation it garnered much of its power from a clear iconographical resonance with religious imagery and *The Raising of the Cross*. The image was inscribed in the popular imagination as the figurative embodiment of American heroism and the triumph of good over evil. The currency of the image was further enhanced in the *Sands of Iwo Jima* (1949) and John Wayne's re-enactment of the scene as a piece of authentic action under fire.

As Soviet influence declined and the Cold War waned so the 'Iwo Jima' memorial became vulnerable to nostalgia. America's world role had dissipated in imaginary conflicts in Central America and combined with domestic instability, caused by the financial profligacy of the eighties, there was a widespread sense of insecurity. 'Iwo Jima' represented a time of undeviating national purpose attested to by George Bush and his appropriation of the monument in 1988 during his campaign to criminalize the desecration of the American flag. Indeed, as if the point needs labouring, in 1984 Frederick Hart's *Three Fighting Men*, 'a Vietnam-era update of the Iwo Jima memorial,'[24] had been added to the *Vietnam Veterans Memorial*. Iconographically it owes much to Paul Manship's sculpture *Buddies* and its association with the Iwo Jima monument harnesses memories of the *Twelve Stations of the Cross*. A religious connotation not missed by Hart himself when he remarked that he would put the 'folds of those (bronze) fatigue jackets and pants up against the folds of any medieval angel you can find.'[25]

Ironically, in the wake of the patriarchal 'Waynism' of Bush's triumph in the Gulf which vanquished national self-doubt, enshrined in the 'Vietnam Syndrome' and represented in the fabric of the original Maya Lin design for *The Wall*, the sacrifice of American women in Vietnam was finally recognized in 1993 with the dedication of Glenna Goodacre's statue (fig.7). Like the Hart statue, it is realist in style and mawkish in execution. It also reaffirms the nobility of fighting for the Lord. In a compositional echo of 'Iwo Jima' two women support a blinded and wounded soldier who falls back like the Dead Christ across the Virgin's lap as a martyr to a cause. In effect, the sculpture is a *Pieta*. Simultaneously, the pose evokes memories of Benjamin West's *The Death of General Wolfe* (1770). The imagery makes an iconographical reassertion of sacrifice and the use of sanctified violence in the cause of a 'just war' at a point of identification between 'Holy War', Christianity, moral rectitude, democracy and the Pax Americana. The issue being, in part, that these sculptures find their strength in popular iconographies and sentiments rarely analysed for their effect on American public and political life. They remain unrecognized because of blind faith in the apparent cognizance of an unflinching pragmatism on behalf of the governments of technologically advanced Western societies.

These iconographies and sentiments are inseparable from the American national myth summoned by Bush as his justification for going to war. In other words his justifications for going to war are cast in bronze just as much as Saddam's and hang on ideology just as much as they do *realpolitik*. Even amongst those who opposed the war, as Martin Walker observed, the dominant rhetoric was irrationalist and religious:

> As the torchlight march for peace trudged down the long hill from the national cathedral to the White House, there was the constant hum of chanting. ... I heard the phrase "The King of Babylon", and edged closer to hear the reading from the Book of Ezekiel. "In Jerusalem he will set up the battering rams and give the command there for slaughter, to sound the battle cry ... O profane and wicked prince of Israel, whose day has come, whose time of punishment has reached its climax.[26]

Edward N Luttwak had noted the President's discomfiture at having to explain his reasons for going to war and maintains that one rational excuse fell after another. On the question of individual freedom and democracy, Congressman Dornan had pointed out 'Americans do not die for princes'; later the argument circled oil prices, but if they should rise, it would do far more damage to the United States' competitors: 'It was indicative that only ever-faithful Britain, not a beneficiary of cheap oil at all, was willing to join the expedition in earnest, fundamentally for reasons neither economic nor geo-economic.'[27] Sure enough the Conservative Party produced a paper justfying the case for a just war in Christian terms. Saddam was utterly and quickly demonized in stereotypical fashion: '... in early August 1990 appeared a new Satan, our staunch ally of the previous week, Saddam Hussein.'[29] Soon he was to become a Herod figure capable of infanticide. As has been shown elsewhere, American public opinion was cleverly manipulated by the Al-Sabah family, the then former rulers of Kuwait. Misled by an 'authentic' story of Iraqi soldiers throwing babies from incubators in Kuwait the Congress voted to catapult the nation into war. This process of demonization was not helped by Saddam's own action of taking hostages: ironically, a traditional Arab device for allowing warring parties to take stock and avoid actual conflict. Regardless, Bush, in his speech of 16 January 1991, could say: 'While the world waited, Saddam Hussein systematically raped, pillaged and plundered a tiny nation, no threat to his own. He subjected the people of Kuwait to unspeakable atrocities, and among those maimed and murdered, innocent children.' A week later in a speech to religious broadcasters Bush emphasized in almost messianic terms the importance of the Gulf as a reaffirmation of America's international destiny in an exact parallel of a Radio Amman broadcast of a sermon by a preacher at the state mosque who said:

> The infidels of the twentieth century, the so-called civilised nations, are killing the children of Baghdad ... the civilisation of the infidels is led by wolves who are destroying Baghdad without shame ... this battle ... the mother of all battles, is the great confrontation between Islam and the infidels who are trying to destroy our civilisation and religion.[30]

Edward Said, in the words of the historian Richard W. Van Alstyne in *The Rising American Empire*, observed:

> One statesman after another arguing in Rheinhold Niebuhr's words that the country was 'God's American Israel,' whose 'mission' was to be 'trustee under God of the civilization of the world.' It is therefore difficult not to hear in the moralistic accents of American leaders today echoes of that same grandiose self-endowment couched in the view that Saddam's wrong against Kuwait is to be righted by the U.S. And as the Iraqi infraction seems actually to grow before our eyes, Saddam has become Hitler, the butcher of Baghdad, the madman (as described by Senator Alan Simpson) who is to be brought low.[31]

By careful news management at home and devastating firepower in Iraq, Saddam was indeed brought low. It was the kind of total war philosophy that had prevented Sir Arthur (Bomber nee Butcher) Harris from being fully honoured by the establishment for his morally ambiguous role in the carpet bombing of German cities in World War Two. Yet within months of the end of full scale hostilities in the Gulf, despite protests from the Mayors of Dresden, Pforzheim and Hamburg, a rather staid, realist sculpture was erected in his honour. The policy had been vindicated in another war of 'just' and 'moral' cause. As Bush had said at the outbreak of war: 'I've told the American people before that this will not be another Vietnam, and I repeat this here tonight. Our troops will have the best possible support in the entire world, and *they will not be asked to fight with one hand tied behind their back.*' (my italics).

This was a holy war fought within a theological framework. It was a Crusade, a war of ideologies whose histories found concrete expressions in the symbolic fabric of the capital cities and monuments of the warring nations. Or as Martin Walker expressed it: 'Saddam Hussein claims the mantle of Allah and the Prophet, but George Bush has Billy Graham, who gave the service at the Fort Myer military base on the first day of the war and preached a call for a "Christian century'.[32]

In ending this essay it is hard not to think of W. J. T. Mitchell's Warburgian identification of a struggle in the image between iconoclasm and idolatry, suspended somewhere between disdain and awe:

> the image ... (is) a site of special power that must be contained or exploited; the image, in short, as an idol or fetish. ...(it is) an assurance that images are powerless, mute, inferior kinds of signs; the fear stems from the recognition that these signs, and 'others' who believe in them, may be in the process of taking power, appropriating a voice.[33]

Notes

1. *The Guardian*, 15 September 1990.
2. Norris, Christopher (1992), *Uncritical Theory, Postmodernism, Intellectuals and the Gulf War*, Lawrence & Wishart, London, p. 15.
3. Slotkin, Richard (1973), *Regeneration through Violence, The Mythology of the American Frontier, 1600-1860*, Wesleyan University Press, Middleton, Connecticut, pp. 4-5.
4. see Gowan, Peter (1991), 'The Gulf War, Iraq and Western Liberalism', *New Left Review*, 187, May/June.
5. Simpson, John (1990), 'The Night Watchman' *Weekend Guardian*, 15-16 September. He notes that following the Gulf crisis Ba'athist apparatchiks soon realised Western antipathy to personality cults and, for example, confiscated such film footage with the excuse that it was 'bad'.
6. Knight, Sabiha (1990), 'Washington prepares its jihad' *The Independent*, 24 August.
7. Miller, Judith & Mylroie, Laurie (1991), 'The Nebuchadnezzar delusion', *The Sunday Times*, 27 January.
8. *Daily Star*, 4 September 1990, pp. 18-19.
9. Installation, Manchester City Art Gallery, 7 September - 13 October 1991.
10. 'Photomontage Now' 13 July - 15 September 1991.
11. Fox, Genevieve (1991), *Art Monthly*, September.
12. Noon, Mike (1991), *City Life*, 17 July.
13. quoted in al-Khalil, Samir (1991), *The Monument, Art, Vulgarity and Responsibility in Iraq*, Andre Deutch, pp. 2-3.
14. ibid p. 2.
15. Mitchell, W. J. T. (1986), *Iconology: Image, Text Ideology*, Chicago, p. 37.
16. (1991), 'Saddam and the agencies of disorder', *TLS*, pp. 3-4, 18 January.
17. see Howett, Catherine M (1985), 'The Vietnam Veterans Memorial: Public Art and Politics' *Landscape*, Vol. 28, No. 2, pp. 1-9.
18. Wills, Gary (1992), 'The Rescuer' *The New York Review of Books*, p. 34, 25 June.
19. quoted in Clay, Grady (1982), 'Vietnam's Aftermath: Sniping at the Memorial' *Landscape Architecture*, Vol. 72, pp. 54-58, March.
20. quoted in Howett.
21. Borg, Alan (1991), *War Memorials from Antiquity to the Present*, Leo Cooper, London.

22. Burns, Lucas, Leon, Lucas Architects of State College, Pennsylvania against Cooper Lecky Architects, the Army corps of Engineers, the Korean War Veterans Memorial Advisory Board and the Battle Monuments Commission.
23. 'Architects File Suit over Changes in Korean War Memorial Design' (1991), *Architecture*, February. 'Cooper Lecky has experience in the execution of controversial memorials; the firm oversaw the construction of several heroic figures near Maya Lin's Vietnam Memorial, which ultimately caused Lin to disassociate herself from the scheme.'
24. quoted in Marling, Karal Ann and Watenhall, John (1991), *Iwo Jima: Monuments, Memories, and the American Hero*, Harvard University Press, Cambridge, Mass. & London, p. 205.
25. Hart, Frederick (1987), quoted in Marling, Karal Ann & Silberman, Robert, 'The Statue near the Wall. The Vietnam Veterans Memorial and the Art of Remembering' *Smithsonian Studies in American Art*, New York, Part 1, p. 15.
26. 'American Diary: The beginning of the End', (1991), *The Guardian*, 26 January, p. 23.
27. 'Saddam and the agencies of disorder', (1991), *Times Literary Supplement*, pp. 3-4, 18 January.
28. *Politics Today: The Gulf War*, (1991), CPC Bookshop, 32 Smith Square, London.
29. Boal, Iain A (1992), 'The Clerisy of Power: US Intellectuals and the Gulf War' in Peters, Nancy J. (ed,) *War After War. City Lights Review Number Five*, City Lights Books, San Francisco, p. 17.
30. Darwish, Adel (1991), 'Arab Media Watch: Iraq sees silver lining in Storm cloud', *The Independent*, 26 January.
31. 'Empire of Sand', *Weekend Guardian*, (1991), pp. 4-7, 12-13 January.
32. 'Washington war diary', *The Guardian*, (1991), p. 2, 19 January.
33. ibid. p.151.

13 Who's responsible? Bobbie Ann Mason's *In Country,* popular culture and the Gulf War

W.D. Ehrhart

If you look at the copyright page of Bobbie Ann Mason's *In Country,* you will find the following sentence: 'Special thanks to W.D. Ehrhart for helpful advice.' That acknowledgement came about in the following manner.

In the winter of 1984, I got a telephone call from Mason. She explained that she had heard of me through a colleague of her husband's at Rodale Press, where I had worked the previous year. Her husband had told his colleague that she was working on a novel about the Vietnam war, and the colleague told him about me and suggested she read my book, *Vietnam-Perkasie*. She told me she had indeed read the book, along with a great many other books about the Vietnam war, but that she was still fearful of getting the story wrong.

She of course had not been in Vietnam or in the military, and the war and its attendant domestic repercussions had largely passed her by. Now she worried that she might embarrass herself, introduce military terminology or hardware that was not appropriate to Vietnam, or create scenes or situations that were not possible in reality. The bottom line was a polite, almost timid request that I read her manuscript with an eye toward technical accuracy.

I had never heard of Bobbie Ann Mason before this phone call came out of the blue, and I was a little sceptical, in those days, of a non-Vietnam veteran expropriating the experience of Vietnam and making it her own. But I was flattered that she thought well enough of my own book to ask me for help, and having been the recipient over the years of a lot of help from others acting under no obligation but generosity, I told her I'd do it. And I did.

For the most part, I liked the story very much, and I was deeply impressed by the obvious fact that Mason had done her homework. I don't recall the specific errors I brought to her attention - small things like the wrong kind of rifle here, the misuse of a term there - but they were very few and very far between. I remember that Mason had been especially concerned about the voracity of the white birds Emmett remembers so wistfully, but she needn't have been. She had given me, it turned out, a very easy and enjoyable task as well as a bit of an honour: I don't suppose there are all that many people who can claim to have read a bestseller before it has ever been published.

Being an opinionated fellow, however, I could not resist the temptation to exceed the parameters of my charge and offer her some advice concerning the shape and substance of the story itself. Two elements of the narrative did bother me, and I told her so.

The first is the absence of any significant Vietnam veteran who has not been, in one way or another, visibly and permanently damaged by his collision with Vietnam. Emmett Smith can't hold a job or open himself to the attractive and nurturing Anita Stevens. Tom Hudson is sexually impotent. Earl, who is not given a last name, is belligerent and confrontational. Pete Simms fires his shotgun at nothing and wallows in the delusion that some nebulous 'they' wouldn't let 'us' win. The one man who appears to have his life together, Jim Holly, subsequently discovers that his wife has left him.

Vietnam veterans, as a group, *have* had a tough time. The statistics on suicide, incarceration, divorce, unemployment and other indicators of trouble have been widely broadcast in the years since the war ended. You can look them up easily enough. Vietnam was a very peculiar war in many ways, and some of the burdens Vietnam veterans have had to cope with are rare in the American experience. But the truth is that, in many significant ways, we have had it no tougher than veterans of any war, a historical fact that has been lost amid the popular mythology that has risen up since the early 1970s. Read McKinley Cantor's *Glory for Me,* or Paul Fussell's *Wartime,* if you don't believe me. War is a brutish and vile business. It does things to the lives of those who survive it, and to their souls.

It is also true, as a corollary, that most Vietnam veterans, whatever specific baggage we may be lugging around, have come to a workable accommodation with our experience and got on with our lives. We may be scarred, but the overwhelming majority of us are functional and productive. I can no longer count the number of Vietnam veterans who serve in the halls of Congress (though one might argue that such is neither functional nor productive!). Two Vietnam veterans have already won the National Book Award - three if you count Gloria Emerson - and one ought to. A Vietnam veteran founded Federal Express.

As for myself, not a day passes of which Vietnam is not a part, if only in thought, yet I have been happily married for eleven years, I own my own home, I have consistently plied my trade as a writer for over two decades, my students are convinced that I give too much homework, and my daughter thinks I'm usually a pretty nice guy. Pity the poor Vietnam veteran, a refrain much in evidence during the recent assault of the yellow ribbons in Desert Storm, is largely a misplaced sentiment.

If you read *In Country* carefully, you will notice that Mason tacitly acknowledges what I am saying. Along with Emmett and Tom and Pete, there is Allen Wilkins, owner of a menswear store and Little League coach, and Larry Joiner's acquaintance 'who's got a good job in public relations,' and Dawn Goodwin's cousin who 'was in Vietnam, but you'd never know it.' But Allen makes only a few cameo appearances, Larry's acquaintance is worth only a paragraph, and Dawn's cousin gets three brief sentences; we never meet these last two men, who are not even given names.

Thus I suggested to Mason that she include at least one 'healthy' Vietnam veteran among her more important characters. Mason didn't go as far as I would have liked, but in the novel you read, there is at least the suggestion that Jim and his wife might yet work things out. The manuscript version offered no such hope. Whether Mason made this change on my recommendation or not, she has never told me and I have never asked. So long as I don't know, I can always claim, in my secret heart, credit for Jim and Sue Ann's possible future happiness together.

The other element of the narrative that bothers me is the ending: the scene at the Vietnam Veterans Memorial, which almost immediately after its creation became known as 'the Wall.' And the Wall has become an awful cliche. Photographs of the Wall adorn the jackets of dozens of books about Vietnam. Mention of that sombre recitation of names, both visual and verbal, has come to substitute for substance and fact, as if the Wall says it all when in truth it tells us only what each of us chooses to hear. It precludes discussion or critique or wisdom, as though its dark polished face is all we will ever need to know, or ought to know, about the Vietnam war.

This is very convenient for those in whose interest it is not to raise such questions as: What was accomplished for the price of so much blood? How was it permitted to go on for so long? Where are the names of the three million dead of Indochina? Be moved by the terrible beauty of your own reflection in the silent, smooth granite. Consider the wonder of so many young men, and women too, willing to give everything for their country. Notice the little offerings - the flowers, the handwritten notes, the high school yearbook photos - left in the cracks of the Wall by parents and children, lovers and friends still grieving after all these years.

That the Wall has become such an intoxicating and misleading artifice is no fault of Mason's. At the time she was writing *In Country,* the lawn surrounding the Wall was still mostly mud. Her use of the Wall as a literary and cultural symbol was, as far as I know, an original and even prescient choice. It is others who are the copycats.

But it was apparent to me, even then, that the Wall was going to become what it has in fact become: a moving and inarticulate substitute for accountability. And indeed, at the end of *In Country,* as Sam ponders the mystery of that other Sam A. Hughes chiselled onto the wall and Emmett's face 'bursts into a smile like flames,' we can't help feeling like everything is going to come out okay after all. We like stories that end that way. We like wars that end that way.

But real stories seldom end so neatly, and wars never do. Not even Desert Storm. Ask the Kurds. Thus, I strongly urged Mason to find another venue for her conclusion. Having read the book, you know how persuasive I was. I console myself with the knowledge that had I been playing baseball instead of offering literary criticism, I'd still be batting better than Ted Williams.

My criticisms not withstanding, however, I retain a healthy respect for *In Country* and teach the book regularly in courses of my own. Mason does a number of things very well, and I would like to examine some of them.

To begin with, Mason doesn't try to think like a veteran. The story is told not through Emmett's eyes, but through Sam's. This is a coming-of-age story, finally. Whatever else is going on, Sam is a child, a teenager, trying to find the right way to be a woman, an adult. She is intelligent, funny, endearing. She thinks going to the mall in Paducah is big league excitement, but in the end we know she is going to college in Lexington, and it's not hard to imagine she'll grow beyond Hopewell one day. Much of what we see in Sam is us, what we are or used to be when we were younger: awkward and spiky, confident, fiercely naive. It's fun to watch her growing up. We like Sam.

Another thing I like is the way in which Mason turns the entire narrative into one long exercise in American popular culture. She captures effectively the homogenization of America, a depressing evolution for those of us who grew up in a nation where regional and local differences still abounded, but the way things are, like it or not. While we know that Hopewell is a small town in rural Kentucky because we are told as much, there is little to set Hopewell apart from the mass culture that has absorbed it: Dorritos and Pepsi and Music Television, *Pac-Man,* Home Box Office, McDonald's, Bruce Springsteen and 7-Eleven. It is culture reduced to the lowest common denominator, which is what our culture has come to. I happen not to like that fact, but it's Sam's world nevertheless, and I like the way Mason handles it. Sam could be any kid in Anytown, USA.

Into this universal story, Vietnam is introduced as naturally as if it came with the territory, which it does. There is nothing contrived about Sam's curiosity about her father and the war that denied him to her, about her attraction to a handsome older man, or even the trip to the Wall. Since 1965, Vietnam has become a constant companion to millions of Americans. Millions more, the young who remember nothing, wonder what strange power this word 'Vietnam' has on those who remember. And indeed, like the fictional Sam, there are real children, now adults themselves, who do not know their fathers because of the American war in Vietnam.

Vietnam, in fact, is the quintessential American experience of the second half of the twentieth century, the stamp of a generation, equalled only by the civil rights movement. To write about the United States in the second half of the twentieth century is to write about Vietnam. It can be avoided only with effort.

But there are a lot of books about Vietnam. David A. Willson, the librarian at Green River Community College in Auburn, Washington, and author of the wonderful Vietnam novel *REMF Diary,* has a collection of several hundred pornographic novels using Vietnam as the backdrop. Danielle Steele has written a Vietnam novel. The use of Vietnam in literature, as in most other facets of our culture, is frequently contrived. It's all in how one handles it.

Mason handles it very well. Emmett, for all that he is clearly a very troubled man, is also a nice guy, a caring man. He's fond of Moon Pie, he loves his niece, and he is touchingly solicitous of Mamaw Hughes. There isn't a mean bone in his body. He isn't crazy. None of Mason's vets is. They may be floundering, but they're not dead weight. Mason's portrayal of veterans is sympathetic without being lurid or romantic.

Her depictions of the war itself, and the anti-war movement it spawned, are also well handled. Dwayne Hughes's letters to his young wife are credible. And Mason offers a gentle view of the hippies and protesters, some of them, like Emmett, former soldiers themselves. In an age in which the war has been hideously transformed into a noble cause lost, at least in part, because of an anti-war movement frequently portrayed as an irresponsible exercise in immaturity, it is worth noticing that Emmett and most of the other vets have nothing good to say about the war. Those that do, like Pete, are otherwise discredited by their own subsequent words and actions. Emmett may not have flown any Viet Cong flags from the top of the courthouse lately, but he never even hints at any remorse for having done so. And Irene still remembers her hippy boyfriend fondly. Like Sam Hughes, we see only fleeting and frustratingly incomplete glimpses of those times, but what we see is neither gloss nor fantasy.

It is Sam who has the fantasies. She thinks the Sixties were a lot of fun; going home with Tom is like walking point. Her efforts to understand what Vietnam was really like are almost comical, and here what I said earlier about pop culture becomes especially cogent, for Sam has no point of reference to use as a touchstone except *Born in the USA, Apocalypse Now,* and re-runs of *M*A*S*H*. Even after she realises, on one level at least, that 'whenever she [has] tried to imagine Vietnam she [has] had her facts all wrong', she still urges Emmett, with absolute sincerity, to 'do the way Hawkeye Pierce did when he told about that baby on the bus.' For her, the Watergate scandal that resulted in the resignation of a sitting president for the first time in US history was only 'a TV series one summer,' and she thinks C-47s with Gatling Guns - devastating killing machines, I can tell you from experience - are 'wonderful' aircraft.

In this, Sam is much like virtually every student and young person I've spoken to within the last fifteen years. I can't tell you how many times I've been asked, 'Was it really like *Platoon* [or *The Deer Hunter,* or *Full Metal Jacket,* or whatever]?' Not long ago, a thirteen year old boy asked me, 'Did you really go on patrols and do stuff like in *Tour of Duty?*' It was clear from his voice, his posture, his saucer eyes, that he thought it must have been wonderful. Real was what he had seen on television.

But the young cannot know unless someone teaches them, and the entertainment industry is not in the business of education. The poem I read to that boy and his junior high school classmates, Bryan Alec Floyd's unrelentingly graphic and horrifying 'Sgt. Brandon Just, U.S.M.C.', got those kids thinking hard, at least for a while.

Dwayne's description in his diary of his friend Darrel, dying with 'blood shooting out of his mouth and his back,' gets Sam thinking hard. And Irene challenges Sam's romanticized notions of the Sixties: 'it wasn't a happy time, Sam. Don't go making out like it was.' However imperfectly, by the end of the story, Sam is beginning to replace her fantasies with something approaching understanding.

I like other things in this story, too: Mamaw Hughes, who says that her son died 'fighting for a cause,' though she makes no attempt to explain what that cause might have been, no doubt because she doesn't have an explanation; she has only her memories and her grief. Lonnie Malone, poor Lonnie, who 'fished from a pontoon boat and roasted weinies at a campfire' while Sam's father had eaten 'ham and beans from a can and slept in a hole in the ground,' and who hasn't got a chance in hell of competing with Tom Hudson in Sam's imagination. Mason relentlessly excoriates the US government in general, and the Veterans Administration in particular (now called the Department of Veterans Affairs), for poisoning its own soldiers with dioxin and then refusing to accept even the slightest responsibility, a fact which remains largely true to this day.

But I want now to turn to a few more general thoughts. I made passing reference earlier to the fact that Vietnam veterans are not unique in the burdens they have had to bear. Yes, we lost our war, which is a rare burden indeed in the American experience, but it is not unique; we lost the war in 1812, too, our capital taken and burned to the ground, the only battle we won taking place after the treaty to end the war had already been signed, facts that may not have been fully emphasized in high school history classes. And of course, half the United States, more or less, lost the Civil War.

And yes, we veterans were often treated in less than kindly fashion after we came home, though you might stop to consider that World War One veterans who came to Washington at the height of the Great Depression to demand better treatment were chased out of town with machineguns and cavalry.

And yes, a great many people opposed the war openly and vehemently, but the Mexican War was none too popular either; Henry David Thoreau went to jail, for instance, rather than pay taxes to support the war, and his essay on civil disobedience has become a model for war resisters from Mahatma Gandhi to Martin Luther King, Jr.

Neither the particular political or military circumstances surrounding the Vietnam War, nor the way in which US soldiers were treated when they came home, can account for the behaviour of the veterans the reader finds in *In Country*. The veterans in Mason's novel, most of them, to a greater or lesser degree, like many actual veterans of the Vietnam war, are suffering from what is now called Post Traumatic Stress Disorder. PTSD for short.

During the recent lunacy in the Persian Gulf, we were urged over and over again to get behind the government and support the troops, not to let the Desert Storm soldiers suffer the same fate as Vietnam veterans, as if Vietnam veterans suffer from PTSD because they were not supported and appreciated enough. Somebody made a hell of a fortune in the USA manufacturing and selling yellow ribbons during the Gulf war, but the fact is that PTSD does not result from lack of appreciation or support; it results from being subjected to the almost unbearable terrors of the modern battlefield.

PTSD comes from being eighteen or nineteen or twenty years old and finding yourself in an environment where every blade of grass and chirping bird is potentially deadly. It comes from living in abject fear day in and day out for months on end, never knowing if the next breath you draw may be your last, if the next step you take may dismember you. It comes from seeing the boy who was your friend a moment ago lying on the ground at your feet with half a head and no arms and his belly split open like a butchered pig. It comes from inflicting that sort of punishment on other human beings.

Moreover, PTSD is not a phenomenon limited to Vietnam veterans or unpopular wars. In the American Civil War, the first truly modern battlefield in the military sense where weapons of mass destruction obliterated the old virtues of skill at arms, courage and honour, bringing death down equally and at random upon the brave and the fearful, the skilled and the inept, PTSD was mistaken for cowardice or 'nerves'. In World War One, it was called shell shock. In World War Two and Korea, it was known as combat fatigue.

What the medical community finally began to realize in the last stages of the Vietnam war, though they did not put it all together until nearly a decade later, and then largely due to the refusal of Vietnam veterans to slink away in silence, is that in the face of the lethal pressures of the battlefield, apparently aberrant behaviour is a perfectly normal response, even years after the fact. Not that the behaviour is normal, of course, but that it is predictable and to be expected under the circumstances. PTSD is how normal people react to abnormal stress.

All wars have produced men like Emmett Hughes and Tom Hudson and Pete Simms. The only way to prevent PTSD is to keep young men, and women too, away from battlefields. (I am less concerned about old men. They are usually the ones who start the wars in the first place; then they send the young ones off to die.) And if the soldiers who fought in the Persian Gulf don't end up with the kinds of problems Vietnam veterans have had, it will only be because, in the words of Captain LeAnn Robinson, a Persian Gulf veteran, 'This sure as hell wasn't much of a war.'

Another thought *In Country* brings to mind is how Sam's yardstick for judging the past has become our yardstick for judging the present. What I mean is this: when Sam thinks of Vietnam, she does so in terms of movies, television and music. She can conjure her own history, for the most part, only through popular culture - and the results are hardly satisfactory. We can see this because we are outside the book looking in. We know that Emmett and his friends are not Eddie and the Cruisers. We know that Cawood's Pond is not Dak To. And if Sam eventually comes to know it, too, or begins to, it is because Emmett and Irene and her own dogged determination to understand force her to get beyond her illusions.

Now consider the recent Gulf war. George Bush boasted of 'kicking butt' as though he were a high school coach. Others explicitly likened it to the Super Bowl. For months on end, we read in the newspapers and heard on the radio and saw on television only what the government wanted us to read and hear and see. We watched those nifty videos of Smart Bombs dropping down chimneys and tank shells obliterating enemy targets that looked like blips on an Atari screen. Many of the pilots and gunners explicitly likened what they were doing to playing video games. Meanwhile, the troops - all but the very few who actually saw any combat - wiled away the hours playing handheld video games. Shall I say 'real' video games, as opposed to the fake video games that only killed people instead of blips on a screen? And now the Pentagon is making, for free distribution to all Desert Storm soldiers and their families, an actual video of the Persian Gulf war, complete with a rock-and-roll soundtrack. Maybe we'll all get to see it on MTV.

What we didn't get to see, and most of us never will see, are the stinking, broken bodies of anywhere from 100,000 to 200,000 dead human beings - no one knows for sure, or at least no one is telling. What we didn't get to see is what happened to the Kurds and Iraqi Shi'ites George Bush publicly incited to rebellion, only to stand idly on the sidelines insisting it was not our responsibility while Saddam Hussein butchered them. We didn't even get to see the flag-draped coffins of our own dead soldiers, let alone their mangled, lifeless remains.

And we didn't get to see where all those Dumb Bombs landed. Oh yes, there were a lot of stupid bombs dropped on Iraq and Kuwait. Nobody mentioned this at the time because they didn't want anyone to think we might actually bomb, even by accident, civilian shelters or baby formula plants, but over ninety per cent of the bombs dropped during Desert Storm were dumber than stumps, the same old iron clunkers that were dropped on Vietnam and Korea and Germany and Japan. More than seventy per cent of them missed their targets. Even the Smart ones missed, as often as not.

But we didn't get to see any of those things. And most of us never even considered what we might not be seeing or reading or hearing. It never even occurred to us to wonder. We just sat there glued to our television sets, transfixed by all those wonderful bombs miraculously dropping down those impossibly narrow chimneys and thinking, 'Golly damn, that's amazing.' And then we were told that we'd won, and there were a lot of parades and celebrations, and everybody got to feel good about America.

Like Watergate for Sam, the Gulf War was just a series we saw on TV. Who is outside our book looking in? Who will be our Emmett and Irene? Who will teach us the difference between imagination and fact, illusion and reality?

There is one more thought I would like to share with you. Did it sink in just how young Dwayne and Emmett and the others were when they went to war? Mason tells us that Dwayne was nineteen. Emmett couldn't have been much older. The average age of American soldiers in Vietnam was nineteen and a half and that average includes all those generals and crusty old sergeant majors. I was seventeen when I enlisted in the Marines. I went to Vietnam when I was eighteen. I had three stripes, a Purple Heart and a ticket home before I turned nineteen and a half. Like Emmett, I didn't know beans when I went. Like Dwayne, I discovered that Vietnam was not what I had imagined it would be. I have been paying ever since, and will continue to pay until the day I die, for having been so ignorant.

Of those Americans who supported the USA in the Persian Gulf few had ever heard of the al-Sabah family before August 1990. Even fewer could write a paragraph or two describing the system of laws and institutions governing Saudi Arabia? Not many could find Kurdistan on a map or detail the interactions between the United States and Iraq between 1980 and 1990. Doubtless few of the young men and women who were deployed to the Persian Gulf understood exactly why they were sent there, yet they went, most of them willingly, some of them eagerly. They were mostly naive but they went because they loved their country and they trusted those who were sending them. So did I when I went to Vietnam.

Most of them were lucky. If we build a Gulf War Veterans Memorial, it won't be much bigger than an expensive headstone. But will we be so lucky the next time, or the time after that? If anyone thinks the Vietnam war was a fluke, he or she ought to read more history. Emmett tells Sam that the study of history teaches only that you can't learn from history. I don't happen to believe that. I'm not convinced that Emmett does either.

The Vietnam war didn't just happen. It didn't gather cosmic dust somewhere out in the universe until it gained enough mass to come crashing down on Planet Earth like some sort of random bad luck. United States involvement in Vietnam, what we call the Vietnam war, happened because distinct individuals made distinct choices over a period of time. Virtually all of those decisions was wrong.

If you actually study the history of the Vietnam war, what you will learn is a valuable lesson in the way the US government and the various individuals who constitute that government at any given time actually work. You will learn that our government is capable of profound arrogance, willful self-deception, and deliberate lying. You will learn that what is done in the name of liberty, freedom and democracy is often none of those things.

The study of history, of course, can be boring. As Sam discovers, all the names run together. Ngo Dinh Diem. Bao Dai. Dien Bien Phu. Ho Chi Minh. You get bogged down in manifestos and State Department documents. It's more entertaining to read a book like *In Country*. And *In Country* is a wonderful story to read.

But it's not the whole story. Not by a long shot. The poet John Balaban, in his book *Remembering Heaven's Face,* tells of a saying he learned from Vietnamese peasants in the Mekong Delta: 'Go out one day, and come back with a basket full of wisdom.' Unless you are willing to open your minds and set aside the things you believe only because you have heard them all your lives, unless you are willing to acquire knowledge, you will be forever at the mercy of those who depend upon your ignorance. You will be Emmetts and Sams and Irenes, just waiting to happen.

(Note: This chapter is based upon a discussion of Bobbie Ann Mason's *In Country,* originally given as a talk to the Freshman Forum at La Salle University, Philadelphia, Pennsylvania, October 15, 1991.)